Quotes

"Ger Graus is a black belt storyteller."
Mark Sylvester, Executive Producer,

"Education is not just about acquiring knowledge, but about empowering individuals, building communities, and creating a more just and equitable world. This book, *Through a Different Lens*, offers us a unique and invaluable perspective on the critical role that education plays in our society. Through his personal experiences, the author has shown us that we must use education as a tool for creating positive change, empowering children to write their own narrative of the possible. Ger Graus stands for me along with Antoine de Saint-Exupéry and Gianni Rodari as the best broadcasters of the children's voice."
Professor Sergey Kosaretsky, *Director, Pinsky Centre of General and Extracurricular Education, National Research University – Higher School of Economics, Moscow, Russia*

"Ger Graus – he hasn't changed! This book is a must-read for everyone who loves teaching and being a teacher, who thinks differently, and who, first and foremost, loves children."
James Neill, *(favourite) former pupil and International Director, GL Education, United Kingdom*

"A menu of educational deliciousness! This book is where knowledge meets experience, wisdom meets creativity, and where inspiration and optimism meet all of us."
Miriam Uono, *Former Director General, KidZania São Paolo, Brazil*

"To those who believe in reimagining education for the benefit of the children, who believe in the benefit of hindsight and in the power of storytelling I say, if you read one book this year, read this one."
Thandeka Tutu-Gxashe, *CEO, Desmond Tutu Tutudesk Campaign, Republic of South Africa*

"Drawing on experiences both personal and professional, this book paints a vivid picture of the joys and challenges, successes, and failures, which make up the fabric of a meaningful and fulfilling career in education. Through his own stories, Ger offers valuable perspectives on what it truly means to be an educator, and how we can all come to appreciate the power of education to shape, inform, and transform lives."

Anjum Malik, *Founder, Global Impact Initiative, India*

"He trobat el Johan Cruijff de l'educació [I have found education's Johan Cruijff]."

Andreu Gual Falcó, *Co-Founder, Nexgen Careers, Spain (Barcelona!)*

"An education. This book is unputdownable!"

Professor Amal Fatani, *Former Cultural Attaché to the United Kingdom, Kingdom of Saudi Arabia*

"I can thoroughly recommend this book. Read it critically; use it to reflect on the lessons of your own experience, and never lose sight of three central truths. One that Ger Graus has borrowed from Desmond Tutu: "Whatever the question, education is always the answer;" a second which his career has taught him, "One size doesn't fit all;" and the third he first learnt at the primary school which set him on the road to Wythenshawe, KidZania and beyond, the Pius X RC Lagere School, and on walks with his grandfather: happiness is important."

John Cosgrove, *Retired Headteacher and Author, United Kingdom*

Through a Different Lens

In *Through a Different Lens*, Ger Graus, a global authority on education, especially in the areas of experience-based learning and human potential, gives us a unique and invaluable perspective on education, children, and schooling. His personal and professional reflections and thoughts remind us that we all need stories and personal narratives to help us understand and navigate today's world, and that education can be a powerful force for change – "Whatever the question, education is always the answer".

Through his own experiences, Ger Graus shows us that we must use education as a tool for bringing about this positive change. He implores the reader to feel empowered to share their own stories and experiences, with an understanding that "everybody is an educator". In this professional autobiography he includes:

- The importance of early childhood, children's contexts and social mobility
- The multi-dimensionality of childhood: one size never fits all
- The value of experience-based learning and the importance of heroes and sheroes
- Zero to 99: lifelong learning
- Innovation, purpose and measuring what we value
- The future of education and schooling

Throughout the narrative the author skilfully leaves us with his personal stories and lessons learned, anecdotes – sometimes sad, sometimes funny, including tales about his grandad, Bob Geldof and the Band Aid Trust, Archbishop Desmond Tutu, Marcus Rashford and KidZania, to name a few, and most importantly, stories and observations about magical teachers, inspirational leaders, wonderful children and families, over forty-plus years and across forty-plus countries. This important book is an inspiring read for all those who teach, for parents and carers, for policy advisors and for anyone who cares deeply about the education of the world's children.

Ger Graus is a globally recognised figure in the field of education, once described as "Jean-Jacques Rousseau meets Willy Wonka". Driven by his famous mantra that "Children can only aspire to what they know exists" he champions the causes of equity and social mobility, purpose and experience, creativity, and awe and wonder in children's learning, so that each child becomes empowered to write their own narrative of the possible.

Contents

Foreword by Carla Rinaldi — x
Introduction — xiii

1 The benefit of hindsight and lessons learned — 1

2 Children can only aspire to what they know exists — 13

3 Thoughts about schooling and education — 45

4 "Technology, bloody hell!" — 86

5 The role we play — 107

6 More than a school – measuring what we value — 141

   And finally — 177

Afterword by Andreas Schleicher — 188
Acknowledgements — 192
Biography — 194

Foreword

In a world where education stands as one of the cornerstones of continuous progress for good, we find ourselves in a unique position. Every day, we face the harsh realities of a society that is increasingly becoming governed by those who seem to lack the understanding and empathy for our daily struggles – the reality gap is real. This, in turn, has made it all the more crucial that we tell stories, share personal and professional narratives, and perspectives, that allow us to navigate our lives, our communities, and the world at large.

Ger Graus is someone who has dedicated his life to education. In his many years of experience, he has come to understand that our lives are inextricably linked with our educational experiences, and he sees clearly the role our schools play in this. Through his work as a teacher, researcher, thought leader, and advocate, he has come to believe that the most effective way to create positive change is by looking at things through a different lens. He is also a very special, personal friend, and one of the most incredible dreamers, visionaries, educational journeymen, and utopians I have ever known – with, at the same time, both his feet firmly on the ground.

In this book, Ger invites us into his world, sharing with us his educational journeys, his observations, and his insights from a lifetime spent working in the field of education. Through his personal and professional experiences, he offers us new perspectives on the critical role that education plays in our society, how good schooling leads to a better education, and how we can use this as a tool for creating positive change. Every word comes from a true and deep experience, and this makes this book rare and special.

Ger's journey in education began as a young boy growing up in the Netherlands. His passion for learning and his love of teaching led him down a path that would, via the United Kingdom, eventually take him around the world. Over the years, he has worked as an educator in over 40 countries as far apart as the United States of America, the United Arab Emirates, Qatar, India, Pakistan, Chile, Brazil and Mexico, Australia, Malaysia, the Republic of South Africa, China, Kazakhstan, Russia, his native Netherlands, and fortunately for me, my home country, Italy.

Through his travels, Ger came to realise from experience that education is not a one-size-fits-all approach; rather, he recognised that each society's cultural, social, economic, and historical realities must be taken into account when designing effective educational and schooling systems. He also saw how societal values play a significant role in shaping the educational landscapes.

Ger's experiences have taught him that education is not just about acquiring knowledge; it is about empowering people, building communities, and creating a more just and equitable world. He believes that education should be a lifelong process, a journey that starts at birth and continues throughout our lives. He continually argues that education should be accessible to all, regardless of their socio-economic status, race, nationality, gender, or other contexts.

In these pages, we are invited to consider the ways in which we are currently approaching education and to envision new possibilities for the future. He challenges us to look at education more experientially, with purpose, and holistically, considering factors such as emotional and mental well-being, social and personal responsibility, and the cultivation of creativity and critical thinking.

Ger's book is not just a reflection on his life's work; it is also a call to action. He sees education as a tool for social change, and he believes that we must use it to create a better world. He advocates for a more humanistic approach to education, one that emphasises the development of the whole person, through answering why questions, rather than merely the acquisition of knowledge.

Through these pages, Ger Graus, in conversation with us, has given us his unique and valuable perspective on the world of education. He also reminds us that, in a society increasingly governed by those who seem to lack a connection with reality, understanding, and empathy, we need stories and personal narratives that can help guide us in navigating the world. Through his work, he has shown us that education can be a powerful force for good, if we approach it with an open mind and a willingness to see things through a different lens.

Through his personal experiences, he has shown us that we must use education as a tool for creating positive change. He lives Archbishop Desmond Tutu's message to him: "Whatever the question, education is always the answer."

Carla Rinaldi
President, Fondazione Reggio Children
Reggio Emilia
Italy

Introduction

> It is a human need to be told stories. The more we are governed by idiots and have no control over our destinies, the more we need to tell stories to each other about who we are, why we are, where we come from, and what might be possible.
>
> Alan Rickman
> *Actor and Director*

"Tell me what happened" – a phrase used by every parent, carer, and teacher across the globe, sometimes as an expression of concern, sometimes as one of nosiness. From our children's story, we want to find out what has occurred and how. Once we know this, we will work out what to do next.

"Tell me a bedtime story" is another example of a story-based interaction; this time, we, as adults, tend to be the storyteller, while the children are the listeners and the learners, hopefully reassured and then ready to fall asleep.

Stories play such an important part in our lives from a very early age. Told stories, read stories, heard stories, seen stories, social media stories, experienced stories, fictional stories, stories passed on through generations, and stories based on fact. We use stories for pleasure, awe, and wonder, to reassure ourselves, to feed our curiosity, to learn, to make a case or score a point. Our need for stories is literally never-ending. So too, I believe, are the need and desire to share stories. By reflecting on and sharing our stories, we can learn from each other and build a deeper sense of connection and understanding so that tomorrow can be better than today. I have always been aware of the importance of storytelling, per se, but had never really understood its democratic, societal, and political importance. That was until the day I read an interview in 2008 with the actor and director Alan Rickman for the American *Independent Film Channel*, or *IFC*. In the interview, he follows that now-famous quote about the human need to tell stories with: "We are agents of change. A film, a piece of theatre, a piece of music, or a book can make a difference. It can change the world."

Whatever the story – its format, or its motivation – all stories are based on the journeys of experience, even the fictional ones. In storytelling terms, *experience is everything*. Experience is typically the foundation upon which storytelling is built. As humans, we use storytelling as a way to share experiences, both our own and those of others, with different audiences. At its core, storytelling is about making connections with other people by sharing common experiences and emotions. When we tell stories, we tap into the fundamental human desire to be understood and to understand others. By sharing experiences, we can help others understand our perspectives and connect with us on a deeper level. The story as an explanation – the words "for example" at their educational best. In this way, storytelling can be a powerful tool for building understanding, empathy, and community.

Stories are, of course, also a contextual, local, or national representation, in that they have their own values. On my very first visit to the KidZania headquarters in Mexico City in 2014, I came across the calavera. In Mexico, the calavera has become one of the most recognisable cultural and artistic elements of the Día de los Muertos, or Day of the Dead. The skeletons and skulls, *calaveras* in Spanish, are not meant to be scary. On the contrary, calaveras are a way in which several cultures throughout Mexico celebrate life through death. The story behind this is that when we accept our mortality, we are able to feel more alive. An everyday part of Mexican culture and storytelling, the calavera were greeted very differently by my then 9-year-old daughter, Imogen, and her English friends upon my return. Fear and horror! The same, but in reverse, might of course be said about the brothers Grimm and their tales in other parts of the world, had it not for the softening up of the stories by Disney. Here, globalisation transformed local, at-times-terrifying stories into family cartoon films, their original meaning almost entirely lost.

Experiences, memories, reflections, hindsight, and storytelling are all, of course, deeply interconnected. They are also universal and of equal value – everyone has them, from the very young to the very old. They are all valid, although they do not all have the same value; sometimes, experiences become more valuable with age. Experiences shape our memories, and memories become a powerful tool for reflecting on the past and understanding how they have influenced our present. To coin a phrase, this interconnectivity empowers us to look "back to the future." Through reflection, we can gain insights and understanding, which in turn shape our perceptions of events and help us make better decisions going forward.

Experiencing in itself is, of course, also contextualised, locally and nationally. In children and young people, the exposure to experiences influences the rate and pace of growing up, for example. Comparing children and young people across KidZanias globally, from Mexico to Mumbai and Moscow, and from Dubai to Tokyo and London, we all reached a similar conclusion that, for example, mentally, emotionally, and experientially, a Mexican 14-year-old is probably the equivalent in growing-up terms of a London 11-year-old. Context, experiences, differing influences of technology and social media in various cultures no doubt play a very significant part in this.

I like the words "child" and "children." I am a child of the 1950s, someone who has been very influenced by that particular period. Being a child, and childhood, is the one thing we all have in common. It also sounds less clunky than "young person" and "young personhood." Everyone is or has been a child. Everyone is somebody's child, for better or for worse. I will always be my grandfather's grandchild. My children, whatever their age, will always be just that. We get hung up on semantics: pupil, student, toddler, teen, tween, Gen A to Z, job descriptions, person specifications, or just jars to put children and people in general into, with the lids firmly closed. This is where semantics become hype over substance, and we, too, often expend our energies on trivia. We must also be careful that classifications don't become self-fulfilling prophecies. The young people I had taught throughout my life were always somebody's child, and in school, they were our children: in loco parentis. Parents evening. To me, *child* and *children* signify something personal, precious, there to nurture, someone I know, and not a number on roll.

Hindsight, the act of looking back on past journeys and events with the benefit of knowledge and experience, is particularly enhanced by storytelling. The benefit of hindsight allows us to look back with a more searching eye, evaluating our actions and decisions. We can identify patterns, extract lessons, and discover hidden meanings that may have eluded us in the moment. This powerful tool allows us to navigate the labyrinth of our memories and reinterpret them in light of our present understanding, enabling us to extract wisdom and insights that may have otherwise remained concealed. "With the benefit of hindsight" is often seen as a negative. I believe, however, that if we can see learning from experiences, good and bad, as a good thing, the benefit of hindsight, in turn, becomes a positive.

Telling stories to me is like being in a conversation, both involving a back-and-forth exchange of experiences, ideas, and information. When we tell a story, we aim to engage our conversation partners by capturing their attention and conveying a narrative that they can, at least in part, relate to or learn from. At the same time, we are receptive to their reactions, whether they be verbal or nonverbal, and we adjust our storytelling accordingly. In this way, telling stories is a collaborative act that requires both a skilled storyteller and an attentive and skilled conversation partner.

I love stories – always have and always will. My list of stories is as long as anyone else's, and as meaningful. From my grandfather's memories and recollections via the stories of my first headteacher at Taverham High School, to my first proper full-time teaching job, to those of the charities Voice of Slum in Mumbai, India, and the Instituto Ayrton Senna in the favellas of São Paulo, Brazil, to the reminiscences of Emeritus Archbishop Desmond Tutu over a shared vanilla ice cream on his 86th birthday in Cape Town, South Africa. In between are the stories of wonderful teachers, children, and families, work colleagues, and friends across at least 40 countries globally where I have plied my trade: Bob Geldof and the Band Aid Trust, the Children's University, KidZania, Wythenshawe, and a tiny bit of Marcus Rashford, my wife, my three children, and my two little dogs, to name but a few.

What all my storytellers have in common is that they have left me with something to put in my back pocket, ready if needed, in reserve, prepared, available for use whenever it might be advantageous. Perhaps that should be a part of the definition of a good story.

It is often said not to mix the professional with the personal. I have always found this to be as good as impossible. What influenced me to become a teacher, and then the teacher I became, were personal experiences from my childhood. What influenced me to then work with certain groups of children in certain communities where there were certain types of schools was part of my personal development as much as the professional one. The same applies to what I do now. Somehow, communities, and especially their children, who are "up against it," will, for me, always come first. Perhaps mixing personal experiences and professional vision is particularly pertinent in what used to be known as the "caring professions," with teaching and education in its widest sense absolutely at the centre of this.

Introduction

In the today of technology, speed, and haste, there sometimes seems less time for stories, certainly amongst grown-ups. Adults seem to have redefined the concept of expertise in favour of knowledge that has been acquired purely as a result of qualifications, as opposed to understanding as a result of experience. Books on leadership are now very often written by managers; education policies are devised by those who wouldn't recognise a child if it shook their hand. Children, on the other hand, thankfully still tell and listen to stories, albeit in many more, speedier, and different formats – they are authors and readers, viewers, and listeners on TikTok, Instagram, Snapchat, BeReal, or whatever else is around the next corner.

When we hear stories, we can place ourselves in the shoes of others and gain a deeper understanding of their struggles and triumphs. When we engage in experiences, we are actively involved in the learning process and can retain the information often better than if we simply read about it in a book. In addition to this, storytelling and experiences can foster empathy, creativity, and critical thinking skills – all essential qualities that will serve everyone well throughout their lives.

Stories are personal, human, and full of emotions; they make us laugh and cry; they test our inquisitiveness and our empathy. Stories about education and schooling affect everyone who likes and loves children. This collection of my stories and thoughts is for all those, in the hope that they will tell their stories and listen to and learn from those of others. It is for the experts of experience, who are never too old to learn or to make a difference, for those who see education as a collaborative process and journey of experiencing, and especially for all those who are part of Antoine de Saint-Exupéry's "few": "All grown-ups were once children, but only few of them remember it."[1]

If there is one thing I would like you to take away from my thoughts and stories, it is the notion that "everybody is an educator." Whether you have spent the past 30 years steadfastly dedicated to teaching or you haven't set foot in a school since the age of 16, this book is aimed at you appreciating your influence and power as an educator, a change maker, a role model, and as a storyteller.

At the point of writing this book, I am 67 years young. I have spent 63 of those years in and around schools, and all of them in education. As, over the years, my menu of experiences, and with this my stories, grew fuller and richer, the sentence "You should write a book" appeared more and more often. It has taken a while, but here it is. My aim has been for my book to be like a conversation, a dialogue,

Introduction

a collaborative exercise, a journey, thoughts and hindsights wrapped in a series of stories, both personal and professional, that are based on my life experiences, my subsequent priorities, and those of the many others I have met along the way. At heart I am a constructivist, I suppose. I believe in actively establishing understanding through experiences, rather than just passively accepting information. As we, as individuals, sample the world and reflect upon our experiences, we can build on our learning and add new details into our pre-existing knowledge. Connect. Extend. Challenge. I hope that this book plays its part, however small, in this constructivist agenda, and that you enjoy reading it as much as I have enjoyed looking at my life in education, with the benefit of hindsight and through my own very personal lens.

Ger Graus
23 June 2024

Note

1 Antoine de Saint-Exupéry, *The Little Prince*.

CHAPTER 1

The benefit of hindsight and lessons learned

When I was a little boy, my grandad would often talk to me about the importance of happiness. These conversations would mostly take place on our way to or back from "et kruuts," the holy cross in the field, with his little dog, Fan. Time after time, my grandad would cement the importance of happiness by answering many a question or statement from me with, "Es doe mer gelökkig bös." *As long as you are happy.*

When I was older, towards the end of my primary schooling, my teacher, Meester Vincken, once asked me what I wanted to be when I grew up. I remember thinking about my grandad and proudly answering: "gelökkig." *Happy.* Meester Vincken smiled and told me I didn't understand the question.

With hindsight, I wonder . . . Hindsight, as the saying goes, is a wonderful thing.

Hindsight is the understanding or knowledge that comes after an event has occurred. It allows us to see what we did well, as well as the mistakes we made, or the things we could have done differently. It allows us to be proud and humble at the same time. Hindsight is gained through the journey of experience, and experience is everything. Experience helps us gain wisdom, which we can then apply to future situations. When we have experience, we are better able to recognise patterns and make better decisions. The benefit of hindsight is only possible because of the experience we have gained.

The benefit of hindsight, based on experiences and intermingled with memories and reflections, implies that we now have knowledge about how events turned out, and that we can use that knowledge to gain a deeper understanding of what happened, often resulting in new and valuable insights. It also implies that, at times at least, we can, and should, learn lessons from the past. "Before I make a mistake, I don't make that mistake," so said the most famous Dutchman of the 20th century, footballer par excellence, manager of dream teams, life philosopher sine pari, Hendrik Johannes (Johan) Cruijff. Ultimately, the benefits of hindsight come down to one thing: learning. Whether we are looking back at our personal lives or our professional endeavours, the ability to learn and to make better choices moving forward is an invaluable asset. Hindsight can help us gain a deeper understanding of ourselves and the world around us in all its detail and paves the way towards a brighter future.

Most importantly, we can reap the benefits of hindsight if we can better understand who we have become, and why. We need to see this before we can benefit from it. Perhaps only then can the benefit of hindsight really be a "wonderful thing."

"I was born in a place called Hope" is one of the opening sentences in Bill Clinton's autobiography. I have always loved that line. In my case, I was born in a place called "Real," or *Echt* in Dutch.

Echt, in those days, was a small, reasonably affluent town, depending mainly on three industries: First and foremost, there was the coal mining industry in the Netherlands' most southern province, Limburg, and I can see now, looking back, that a great deal of the town's life was connected with this. Secondly, and in almost complete contrast, there was "the future," Phillips Electronics, in the nearby and commutable towns of Sittard, Roermond, and even Phillips' hometown, Eindhoven. Thirdly, in Echt itself, there was also still De Valk, once upon a time Europe's largest roof tile factory. Of course, there was also farming, but in relative terms, this was small fry. White asparagus, fruit, vegetables, wheat, as well as dairy, egg, and pig farming – the latter two in those days, more often than not, very ethical, although there were exceptions to that rule.

Echt is at the narrowest point of the country, six miles from the Belgian border and seven miles from the German border, foreign travel a mere 20-minute bike ride away, including different languages, different cultures, and in those days, even different currencies. It was only much later in life that I realised what an important impact this trans-country freedom had on me. These were the days long before Schengen, when passport controls were still present between the borders of the Netherlands, West Germany, and Belgium, unless, of course, you cycled through the woods when earning some pocket money whilst buying cigars and cigarettes in Belgium or schnapps in Germany for your nearest and dearest.

The province itself speaks its own dialect, Limburgs: a mishmash of German, French, Dutch, and its significant own input. Many argue that Limburgs is a language in its own right – I certainly did in my thesis at the Mollerinstituut many years later. Anyone from outside Limburg had no idea what we were on about most of the time. Years later, on my way back from university, we travelled on what was, by fellow students from the north of the Netherlands, mockingly called the "Limland Express." In my childhood, "posh people" brought up their children speaking Dutch and not "the coal miner's language," Limburgs.

The community in Echt was tightly knit, not least around the Church. Limburg was a strict, very Roman Catholic province. As if pre-designed for you, everyone went to the Roman Catholic Church, read Roman Catholic newspapers, watched Roman Catholic television, listened to the Roman Catholic radio station, went to Roman Catholic schools and, in some cases, even Roman Catholic universities. I daresay that the first qualification achieved by many of my generation, born in Roman Catholic Echt 12 years after the end of the Second World War, was the equivalent of an A level in "Guilt," the trademark of a Roman Catholic upbringing – nothing was ever good enough, and following confession, punishment followed.

It was only years later that some of what I now perceive to be horrors related to the Roman Catholic Church in my hometown came to light. From appalling child abuse to my mother's very own personal story. My parents had been married for four years before I was born, which, apparently, in the eyes of the Roman Catholic Church, was too long. My mother once told me the story that the local priest would come knocking on the door at regular intervals, enquiring as to when the offspring might be expected. If a woman in those days had sex without the intention of creating life, they were obliged to go to confession, to confess her sins and seek forgiveness. The control of, and the lack of respect for, individual people is beyond my comprehension. I no longer go to church and haven't done so for many years, and I disconnect myself from religious institutions – although there is no doubt that my A-level Guilt certificate occasionally still makes an appearance, even after all those years. I very much respect people who believe but cannot respect the institutions. Religion should also be divorced from education and schooling. That kind of influence and control is simply wrong.

Otherwise, the community that was Echt, like many others, resembled the great number of coal mining communities in other countries, including the United Kingdom. Brass bands, pigeon racing, working men's clubs (Roman Catholic, of course), almost entirely White- and male-dominated. It all appeared happy, but parochial.

Few young people left, let alone went to university. The coal mines, Phillips, and De Valk provided supposed job security for life. Except, of course, they didn't. In the mid-sixties, enormous gas reserves were discovered in the north of the Netherlands, and plans for the closure of the coal mines in Limburg were developed and implemented relatively quickly – and badly. Like in many other parts of the world where industries were, and still are, being closed down, the impact on the communities and their self-worth was, and is, devastating. The coal miners of Limburg and their families had been told for years that the country's post-war redevelopment was based on their hard work. They were all owed eternal gratitude. Then, almost overnight, all this was taken away, along with any existing pride and self-worth. Suddenly, and without warning, white laboratory-style coats and warehouses replaced the heroics of going underground. It reminds me of the story of his youth in the 1950s in Glasgow told by the Scottish comedian Billy Connolly. In full-time education until the age of 14, when the school gates opened for the last time and, simultaneously, the gates to the shipyards on the river Clyde also opened to full employment. The flow from one to the other was automatic – it was the "done" thing. A sense of security no doubt played a big part here too; everybody had their place. Things in those days didn't work out that well for young Connolly, however: "I joined the wrong queue and became a welder," he quipped. Not long after, he found a very different place, of course. Like the coal mines in Limburg, the shipyards on the Clyde didn't last; the final one closed down in 1971. Like in Limburg, in Glasgow, too, pride and self-worth rapidly disappeared down the drain. What was left were stories.

All this was going on as I, on a daily basis, walked to and from the Pius X RC Lagere School, my primary school, past some houses that still had bullet holes in the walls as souvenirs from the Second World War – the house of the Fokkema family on the Kerkveldsweg, not far from my parents' house, particularly sticks in the memory.

Within this context, my parents were, relatively speaking, middle class. My father was a finance manager, and my mother a housewife. They had scrimped and saved and managed to build their own house: Oranjestraat 100. The house was near the railway line, along which, 24 hours a day, the coal trains travelled for the early years of my childhood. Across that railway line, a five-minute walk away, lived my favourite person: my grandad, or "Opa" in Dutch – Opa van Peij. Peij was the village the other side of that railway line, where my grandad's house was.

My early education, as opposed to my schooling, consisted of, without knowing it, learning through play, and learning through experiences. Much of this learning in the wild came in the company of my grandad. From walking through the fields to watch the farmers harvest to learning about gardening and listening to his stories, as well as, at a very young age, watching a pig being slaughtered and, as a result, peeing my pants.

My grandad was born in 1891, on the 7th of July. He remembered the first car in the village, and how this was accompanied by a man waving a red flag so that people and animals wouldn't be scared. Through two world wars, the recession of the late 1920s and early 1930s, radio, and then television, he died, not long after the first man landed on the moon. Even to this day, that life journey seems to me both magical and scary, as well as incomprehensible. His wife, my grandmother, was German. As a teenager, she worked as a maid on farms across the border in the Netherlands, as did her younger sister. When, in the 1920s, her parents' house in Germany burnt down, uninsured, it was the two young women's wages, paid in the hard Dutch currency the guilder, that funded the reconstruction of the parental house across the border in Germany. At that point in time, the German mark, along with its economy, had collapsed, and the inflation had reached stratospheric heights. Years later, when she was married to my grandfather, and with children, her German relatives, now turned German soldiers, were part of the invasion of the Netherlands on 10th May 1940 and came for her Dutch husband (my grandad) and their eldest son, who both, subsequently, had to hide out underground in order not to be captured, taken, and deployed in ammunition factories in Germany.

My other grandparents, Oma and Opa van de Bosch, lived what seemed an enormous distance away – a 45-minute or so bus ride – in the village of Koningsbosch, very close to the German border. Because of the distance, or rather the time it took the local bus service to cover that distance, I didn't see them as much as I would have liked. My parents didn't have a car, so transport was by bike, by bus, or for longer journeys, by train.

Playing and experiencing in the small town where I grew up felt very safe. Everybody knew each other, and everybody looked out for each other. In that sense, I can't ever remember being scared. In fact, playing outside, being out there in the wild, was joyous. Those experiences, and that kind of play, felt like something from a television programme (including, inadvertently, setting fire to the railway line whilst playing Cowboys and Indians). The only downside of playing and experiencing with such freedom was the dread of having to go home.

My grandfather's love was the opposite to the abuse I experienced at home. Opa was the epitome of fun, happiness, safety, and warmth, juxtaposed with the coldness of my parents. This was demonstrated abstractly through our feelings towards each other, but also through a literal divide. The railway line that separated us became a symbol of that gulf – the happiness, safety, and warmth plainly draining out of me as I crossed the steel lines back to Oranjestraat 100. My mother was a very "hands-on" parent, literally – the wooden spoon was her favourite tool. My father was an all-rounder: Wooden clothes hangers and belts were his tools, but he was also guilty of emotional abuse. I was never good enough and never as good as he was. I could never understand why it was this way – it must be my fault, I thought. So I became a pleaser, hoping to shake off this guilt and to become loved. It didn't work, and never has since, but being a pleaser as a coping mechanism remained – and does to this day. As does going quiet. I still disappear into my shell, shut up shop, stop speaking. Anything is better than confrontation. I also became an observer, a listener, a judge of moments and circumstances, and a calculated risk-taker. A survivor. By the time I got to secondary school, the need to rebel had developed, to sometimes kick and scream. Nothing made sense to me, which brought about a toxic narrative: "Nobody cares, so why should I?" "Don't become like your parents." "You are in danger of becoming just like your father." Advice turned insult, somehow supposedly well-meant but felt like bullying – take your pick. These are phrases that have been used throughout my life. At best, they are ill-qualified and based on no firsthand knowledge. They have always been hurtful, even when they were meant well. In all cases, they were ill-informed. As an individual, you learn to cope. Each, no doubt, in their own way. Sometimes, those with supposedly the highest qualifications cause the greatest hurt, no doubt more often than not unintentionally. Top-down approaches from the book mostly don't work. Theory over practice. A bit like the worst of schooling, really. Empathy rules – the concept of standing in others' shoes.

My grandad died on 25th October 1969 at 11:20 a.m. The intercity train from Amsterdam to Maastricht was too fast for him at the unmanned crossing near his home. He always used to say when crossing the road without regard for the traffic, "They've got more time than me." He was wrong, and he left me a metaphorical orphan. I miss him still, and I speak to him every day.

My early schooling was, to a very significant degree, joyous. The Pius X RC Lagere School was a small primary school where everybody knew each other and was just a short walk away from my house. I loved my teachers and had a feeling that many of them loved me too. This mattered more to me than words can say. The Pius X RC Lagere School was more than a school. My primary school became a place of happiness away from home. Meester Jutten and Meester Vincken in particular were two teachers I wanted to learn from, and with. I was able, clever, and keen but, according to my parents, never quite good enough. My father used to frequently compare my report cards with his, pointing out my shortcomings. In many ways, I believe that my primary school was the way primary schools should be – a home away from home, filled with kindness and with teachers who, through sharing their passion, their brilliance, and their love of children, brought the best out of these children. My teachers were my role models. Meester Jutten was also brilliant at football, despite his shiny black winklepickers.

My early teenage question, "Nobody cares, so why should I?" was answered when I came to know my secondary school German teacher, Meester Beurskens, at the Bisschoppelijk College Echt. Four years into secondary school, and for the first time since primary school, a teacher was seeing me as an individual, and as someone who had the potential to do great things. He reinforced to me the power a good teacher has to shape the future of a child – not referring to the qualifications they have but the quality of their attitudes towards you and their want for you to succeed.

I was very good at German. I was also rebellious at school – and bored. Perhaps I didn't fit the mould, or maybe the mould didn't fit me. However, Meester Beurskens was the person who changed that, the person who got to me; he was the one teacher at secondary school, above any others, who, in a sense, got to know me, trusted me, and gave me responsibility. He also gave me a book to read: *Wanderer kommst Du nach Spa* by Heinrich Böll. Before him, my German teaching had been dull, to the middle, making no allowances for aptitude or motivation. After my very first lesson with Meneer Beurskens, he said,

"You are really good, you should read." I was 15 at that time. I did, and then went back the next day, like Oliver Twist, asking, "Can I have some more, please?" I still have that book, *Wanderer kommst Du nach Spa*. Heinrich Böll was followed by Wolfgang Borchert's *Draußen vor der Tür*, Bertolt Brecht's *Mutter Courage*, Anna Seghers's *Das siebte Kreuz*, and many more. To this day, I remember the joy and the pride. Because of him, I became a German teacher. Meester Beurskens persuaded my parents that I should go into higher education to study German. At the age of 16, I left home for good; at 18, I went to the Mollerinstituut Tilburg to become a German teacher. I was the flea that jumped out of the jar . . .

I refer here to the famous "fleas in a jar" experiment, a scientific investigation which has been used as a prompt in many motivational speeches. The experiment starts with several fleas in a glass jar. To begin with, they jump extremely high, right out of the jar, in fact. A clear lid is then placed on the jar, and after a while, the fleas begin jumping slightly below the lid to avoid hitting it. After a few days, when the lid is removed, the fleas will not jump any higher, even though there is a whole new world out there, waiting for them. What is more, when they have offspring, they, too, will not jump beyond the lid. They have been conditioned to believe that they have no business beyond the jar, that they don't belong there.

Growing up in communities like Echt also put a lid on aspirations. There was an unspoken message that you should be happy with your lot, and that the boat did not need to be rocked. Everything was far away, and all things new were dangerous. But I jumped.

I want to bring in a story here about a place in northern England called Wythenshawe – a sinking boat that needed to be rocked. I was at that time, in 1999, the senior schools inspector for the Salford City Council. We had a relatively new government in the United Kingdom, the Blair government, wed to the mantra "Education, Education, Education." This government had clearly thought about and planned its education strategy, as well as its approach to schooling, and where to invest in the most disadvantaged parts of England. Wythenshawe was one of those 50 identified places which were then given the status of "Education Action Zones," just one of the projects that was put in place to bring about change for good.

Wythenshawe was a council estate built in the 1930s to alleviate the slums of the city of Manchester and had a population of around 80,000. As industries, including the mills, disappeared, the area became more and more disadvantaged. It had, at that time, 29 schools and was for a while known as being the largest council estate in Europe, and one of the most disadvantaged areas in England.

However, what set Wythenshawe apart from those other disadvantaged parts of the country was its neighbour. Sat next to the council estate was Manchester Airport – a place of growth, excitement, and opportunity, as, at that time, it was one of the fastest-growing businesses outside of London. Manchester Airport importantly wanted to invest and recruit locally – but when *locally* meant Wythenshawe, this wasn't always possible. The Education Action Zones status meant that this was about to change, and Manchester Airport became more than an airport.

When I was approached to be the founding education director of the Wythenshawe Education Action Zones, I jumped at the opportunity. I had worked in the area before, as adviser for modern foreign languages, introducing French, German, Italian, and Spanish into all primary schools and establishing partner schools in Clermont-Ferrand, Chemnitz, Bologna, and Madrid, with significant support from those countries' consulates as well as the European Union. I had enjoyed good relationships with the headteachers and the schools and felt that I knew the community. The opportunity to work with Manchester Airport, and particularly its inspirational Group Chief Executive Geoff Muirhead as chair of the board of directors, was a dream come true. This new way of working was an opportunity for Wythenshawe and its children to jump outside the jar. Because of the size of the area and the complexity of its problems, Wythenshawe was awarded additional funding to effectively create two Education Action Zones in order to address better the challenges ahead and make the most of the opportunities available. The Wythenshawe Education Action Zones were the only two Education Action Zones in the country led by one director in partnership with the private sector, Manchester Airport Group Plc, raising aspirations and standards of achievement across all their 29 schools and the entire community.

The recruitment question was key to Manchester Airport's involvement in the project. The question was: "Why are we not recruiting people from our own doorstep?" Very early on we agreed that this was not something to talk to 25-year-olds about but to children of primary age and their families.

When children grow older, stereotypes, expectations, and aspirations begin to set, and change is much more difficult to achieve. This would become a central part, many years later, of my global research for KidZania, which I will talk more about later.

To change hearts and minds, we wanted to find out what educational obstacles existed in the Wythenshawe community around our children. What constituted their jar and their lid? A large number of meetings were organised, arranged with 5-, 6-, and 7-year-olds as well as their parents. My key questions were: "Tell me the things you can do at Manchester Airport? Tell me about the jobs that exist there?"

It became apparent very quickly that the answers I got were the things they could see. At a rough calculation, you can only see about 45 per cent of the jobs at an airport. The other 55 per cent are invisible, behind walls and screens, in offices, and in all sorts of places, sometimes even off-site. Instantly, those children, however young or old, can only aspire to approximately 45 per cent of the jobs at Manchester Airport because that is all that is visible. The same incidentally applied to their parents and carers.

After asking the children my first two questions, I concluded, "There is a job you haven't mentioned but that you can see. What about the planes themselves? What about the pilots?" The response I invariably got was, "People from Wythenshawe don't fly planes." Two things were happening: The aspirations of the children were restricted because of a lack of exposure and education, because of things they could not see, and the system, the community, all of us, had put a lid on how high the children's aspirations could go. We, as adults in some shape or form, put the children of Wythenshawe in a jar and then put on the lid. My mantra, "Children can only aspire to what they know exists," was born there and then.

Manchester Airport, with the benefit of hindsight, learned its lessons and acted accordingly. In partnership with the schools, it opened its doors and entered into projects where its employees would visit schools to become the children's mentors – reading mentors, maths mentors, careers mentors, aspiration mentors. Prior to 9/11, it also built classrooms inside the airport's Terminal 2, and we even took children onto the runway – safely, of course. Relationships with the community improved. It also adapted its success criteria and started to look at returns on involvement as opposed to merely focus on returns on investment. In other words, the organisation started to measure what it valued. Manchester Airport became "More Than an Airport," a slogan, I am proud to say, that is still visible around the airport to this day.

One child who jumped so far past the lid that you couldn't see the jar anymore was Marcus Rashford. I know Marcus Rashford not as the

England and Manchester United footballer but as the little boy who went to Button Lane Primary School who, as a young adult during the global pandemic of 2020, eloquently expressed his views that "no child should go hungry," constantly linking this narrative back to his own Wythenshawe childhood experiences. What made him who he is – kind, thoughtful, clever, self-evaluative, not resentful, and determined to do the right thing, all despite the challenges he experienced during his upbringing? It was his experiences, personified by his mother and the role she played, and the benefit of his hindsight.

The reason for painting this picture is that, in the end, we are who we have become. "Children can only aspire to what they know exists."

When we look at our experiences and how we have lived these, we must consider our context. Who are we? And how have we become who we are? The answer is hindsight and the benefits we have been able to reap from it. The ability to positively learn from our experiences becomes what defines us. Hindsight can help us appreciate the progress we have made, as we have the chance to see how far we have come and how much we have learned. This, in turn, can boost our confidence and encourage us to keep moving forward despite any obstacles we may encounter. Ultimately, hindsight can be a valuable source of wisdom that can help us make better decisions and live more fulfilling lives. The benefit of hindsight, I feel, is not a solution – it is a way of life. In that sense, to a greater or lesser degree, I will always remain a pleaser, and Marcus will always have his mum. The difference for me is that I am now fine with this; I can't speak for Marcus Rashford, but I am certain he always has been happy to have his mum. On this I am with Harry Potter's Professor Albus Dumbledore: "It is not our abilities that show what we truly are. It is our choices."

A memory that will stay with me always is that of a sunny day with my coal miner, short-of-breath, arthritic grandad, sitting on his knee by the front door. I was 9. It is one of those memories that, when you close your eyes, are just there: black corduroy trousers, grey work jacket, cap, swollen and painful hands, blue kitchen chair, brown front door, sun on my face. He turned to me and said, "Promise me you will always do your best at school." I did what 9-year-olds are programmed to do and asked him why. His answer was, "Because I don't want you to have hands like mine."

Looking back now, I understand what he meant. It wasn't about my schooling, what job I would later go on to do, or how much I would be paid to do it. It was about progress and ensuring tomorrow is better than today – his definition of *social mobility*.

So after years of experience, and still fully comprehending the question, if I would be asked by Meester Vincken again, "What would you like to be when you grow up?" I would repeat my original answer: "Happy."

CHAPTER

2

Children can only aspire to what they know exists

> If you have strong purpose in life, you don't have to be pushed. Your passion will drive you there.
>
> Roy T. Bennet
> *Author*

The inception of the Children's University, initially at a national level in the United Kingdom, in April 2007 marked a significant milestone, although its origins as a local idea can be traced back to Birmingham many years earlier, into the mind of the late professor Sir Tim Brighouse. This national initiative was not just about mere task completion; it revolved around travel of the mind, purpose, and connection. It delved into the fundamental question: *Why do we attend school and acquire knowledge in specific subjects?* These why questions have always struck me deeply, both in my personal and professional life.

Growing up in the most southern province of the Netherlands, close to the borders of Germany and Belgium, I had the privilege of experiencing a multicultural and multilingual environment, which the bureaucrats called an "Euregio." I would watch German, Dutch, Belgian, and English television programmes, often with subtitles in various languages – if you watched an English-language programme on Belgium television, you were served with Flemish, or Dutch, and Walloon, or French, subtitles. Being exposed to multiple languages seemed natural to me. Whether it was for everyday activities like shopping or cycling through the woods on a Saturday, crossing borders, and earning my pocket money by buying cigars in Maaseik for one grandad, schnapps in Breberen for the other, or even jewellery at Küppers in Waldfeucht with an aunt. These experiences were an integral part of my normal life and nothing particularly special to me. If I include Limburgs, it is fair to say that I, and many of my local contemporaries, grew up at least quadrilingual, not by design, but by *experience*. I was, in those days, a big *Coronation Street* fan – with subtitles, of course – and was once, not long after I moved to Norwich, accused of sounding like Hilda Ogden. I was good at accents too.

Years later, when I was a German teacher in the United Kingdom, the question of why English-speaking individuals should learn another language often raised its head. This bewildered me, because my own experiences had never left me. Each time someone posed the question, they inadvertently revealed their own reasons not to: *Because everyone speaks English, anyway*. This always struck me as a very rude and ignorant statement, stuck in the mentality of an empire that was no longer relevant. The notion is, of course, nonsensical, and far from accurate. It also represents a very narrow view of the purpose of schooling. Little did I know at that time that as we entered the second decennium of the 21st century, these views would become more extreme and, sadly, commonplace. This thinking dismisses the significance of diverse cultures, behaviours, and respect that define us as human beings. It turns us into the sort of neighbours nobody wants in their street.

The question did, however, highlight to me again the importance of why answers, not from a textbook or, heaven forbid, a tabloid newspaper, but through experiences. It would also change my view of who a teacher is. No longer just the purveyor of knowledge but, at least in equal measure, the facilitator of learning, of experiences, and the advocate of "free-range learning" in environments where not all classrooms have four walls. In those environments, they were also, of course, the safety lollipop ladies and men. In my mind, experience-based learning had arrived. Why would anyone learn a language without experiencing the country and its people, the culture, and the customs, the good and the bad, the awe and wonder? I am, incidentally, envious of the language teachers of the 21st century. The technology available can make staggering contributions to the experiences the learners have. From Facebook to FaceTime, from TikTok to Instagram, from emails to WhatsApp, from the internet to artificial intelligence, everything is easy and natural and, most importantly, fast and of its time. Technology adds relevance, reality, and makes the why answers even better.

I also learned that I wasn't alone in my thinking. The English department at Taverham High School, for example, would very carefully research which Shakespeare plays to read. If at all possible, only those plays that could be seen locally, or further afield in a theatre, would be studied. *Julius Caesar* was also a favourite. All the young people at Taverham High School learned either Latin or classical studies, taught by Mrs Daines, the headteacher. Exploring and exploiting the links between subjects was a no-brainer. Alternatively, children could often also take part in their own productions. I will never forget Jason Carter as Sykes in *Oliver*. In some shape or form, these principles applied across this extraordinary school in its early days – geography, religious studies, history, the sciences, the arts, technology, home economics. Everyone was, in their own way, involved. I am, incidentally, convinced that Shakespeare would be continually turning in his grave if he knew what, in the 21st century, we are doing to his plays in our schools: reading, rote learning, not experiencing. Shakespeare would have supported what we were doing all those years ago.

The "Connect. Extend. Challenge"[1] thinking routine helps learners connect new phenomenon and their current knowledge. When children link classroom learning to their personal experiences, they begin to think critically about new ideas and build bridges across their knowledge gaps. The learners are also taking ownership of their own learning process, which increases engagement levels. This learner-centred thinking routine encourages learners to ask questions and use what they already know about the world around them in the classroom. By extending their current knowledge to new concepts, learners can answer complex questions themselves. When they collaborate on activities that put theory into action, they practice the important skills they will use throughout their education and career. In 1983, I had no idea about Harvard University, Project Zero, Howard Gardner, the Reggio Emilia approach, or indeed, who Carla Rinaldi was. How funny and wonderful that nearly 30 years later, Carla and I became colleagues and friends for life.

It became clear to me that we didn't necessarily need different answers; we just needed better answers – contextualised answers, to answer the question about language learning and purpose. So I extended the fledgling school partnership between Taverham High School and the Städtisches Gymnasium Am Turmhof, Mechernich, in the then West German geographical triangle between the then capital of Bonn, Cologne, and Aachen.

Penfriend arrangements, as they had to be in those days, were established carefully based on detailed knowledge of the children involved and, of course, their own and their parents' contributions.

Communication between penfriends in those days resembled more the television programme *The Flintstones* than it did the 21st century. Letters, postcards, birthday cards, and Christmas cards were written and posted, received at least one week later in Mechernich, then replied to, arriving back at Taverham High School weeks after they were originally sent, where many senders had probably forgotten the original content of their writing. No threads in 1983.

Annual exchange visits became the norm, and the numbers grew. Mechernich became used to having Taverham High Schoolers around, and vice versa. In February 1988, my last year at Taverham High School, some 75 11- to 16-year-olds made the journey to Mechernich, which was well in excess of 15 per cent of the school population. We always travelled to Germany in February or early March, at carnival time, to experience the snow, the festival, the German songs, and the fun.

For those who were courageous, confident, and ambitious enough, we developed six-week to three-month stays, which we called "Trimester Aufenthalte" (trimester stays), where 14- to 16-year-olds would travel to Mechernich on work experience during the summer holidays to live the language. Their slightly older German counterparts would return to Norwich for a whole school term. Purpose was not invented; it was experienced.

Apart from purpose, confidence, linguistic ability, cultural appreciation, and friendship, the one other bonus this experience brought was aspiration. We found ourselves with young people writing their own narrative of the possible. *In German.*

Purpose was also not just experienced by our "exchangers." It went further. Into families and neighbourhoods. Into communities. On both sides. They all became "exchangers" too. Families became involved – emotionally and educationally. Parents, carers, grandparents, brothers, sisters, uncles, aunts, nieces, and nephews were looking forward to the next visit, to letters, postcards, birthday and Christmas cards. Families became friends with families. Neighbours and friends organised get-togethers and parties. Communities literally displayed "Welcome" banners. To me, the Sistigs, Henneckes, Wahlens, and "Frenkie" Cremers in Mechernich became like the Lords, Uptons, Paramours, and Neills in Taverham. Of those there, at carnival time in Mechernich, who will ever forget the piano-playing of Father Vossell – *Kreuzberger Nächte sind lang*?[2] Now, many years later, I recognise all this again through my youngest daughter's friends Eva and Leyre from Madrid and Palm de Majorca, respectively. Their families have become ours.

When in 1988 I moved from the comfort and relative affluence of Taverham High School and Norwich to the challenges and disadvantage at Winifred Holtby School in Kingston upon Hull, we established similar programmes in Germany, France, and Spain. The socio-economic and socio-cultural contexts meant that this was more difficult, more challenging, harder, but the benefits were equally significant, if not more so. In the greater scheme of things, the young people at Winifred Holtby School needed these experiences more than those at Taverham High School did, as their everyday lives afforded them fewer opportunities and often lower aspirations. It was a lesson I took with me in 1991 when I became adviser for modern foreign languages at Manchester City Council. There I introduced modern languages into all primary schools across the City of Manchester, training teachers in France, Germany, France, Italy, and Spain and establishing school links for every primary school, thanks to funding support from a post–Maastricht Treaty European Union.

The experiences at two very different schools in very different circumstances served me well; there was plenty to put into my back pocket for later. The children and teachers at both schools fill me with awe and wonder to this day. They taught me that our accountability lies with them, the children, and that their teachers are their allies of empowerment.

The greatest challenge we face every day is to do the right thing for every child. It is the lottery of inequality from birth that it is so hard to apply fairness to, especially in education systems that appear obsessed with maintaining the status quo, mass approaches, and where there is little room for knowing the individual and what makes them tick.

"Children can only aspire to what they know exists." It is our collective duty to open curtains, windows, and doors and widen horizons to a better possible future for each and every child. We need to build scaffolding around every child so that they can each climb as high as they can and want to. For that, we need to know them better, and on the journey to achieving that, we will see that experience and purpose go hand in hand. One size does not fit all. To quote the author Haruki Murakami: "If you only read the books that everyone else is reading, you can only think what everyone else is thinking."

One notable achievement for me was the project I initiated in partnership with the northern Italian city of Bologna, building on the education partnership between the two cities I had established in 1992. With the support of the Consolato d'Italia and the European Union, a significant number of schools in Manchester began teaching

Italian to primary school children. Although this programme was implemented citywide, its main focal point was the south Manchester area of Wythenshawe, where I found myself in 1999 as director of the two Education Action Zones.

The reason for introducing French, German, Italian, and Spanish into the primary phase to me was blatantly obvious. Why not? There was plenty of national and international research, supported by organisations like the Association for Language Learning and the Central Bureau for Educational Visits and Exchanges, which indicated very clearly the advantages of starting language learning early. The European Union was also supportive in many ways. I also had, of course, my own personal experiences as a child growing up in a multilingual environment. The aim was for every participating school to have a partner school in either France, Germany, Italy, or Spain, for every teacher to have a partner teacher in their partner school, and for every child to have a friend in a school in another country with whom they would be regularly in touch. We needed to create learning contexts and environments in which the children and their teachers could find purpose and through which they could answer why questions. From here I established links with Clermont-Ferrand, Bologna, and Alcalá de Henares in Madrid and re-established the links with Chemnitz, formerly Karl Marx Stadt in the former German Democratic Republic.

Every school where Italian was taught had a partner school in Bologna, and teacher visits and exchanges were in full flow. Primary-aged children from Wythenshawe annually visited Bologna and from there made excursions to Venice and Florence. The links between the schools in Bologna and Wythenshawe continue to this day. A number of curriculum projects had already been executed between the schools, mainly focusing on the arts, music, and sports, supported by external organisations such as the Consololato d'Italia, the Bologna-based Teatro Testoni, the British Council, and the arts group CAPE UK. During my time as senior inspector in the city of Salford in the late 1990s, I had also instigated projects between schools at secondary level. One of these projects included a partnership between Bologna and Manchester City football clubs, whilst another focused on the works of L. S. Lowry and the Bolognese painter Antonio Saliola, culminating in an opera performed at the Conservatorio de Musica Laura Bassi in Bologna and at the Lowry Centre in Salford. Its title: *Tutti abbiamo avuto dieci anni ma molti se lo dementicano*, or *All grown-ups were once children although few of them remember it*, from Antoine de Saint-Exupéry's *The Little Prince*, of course.

But in terms of Wythenshawe and Italian, nothing big had happened, nothing really eye-catching. Manchester Airport and the Wythenshawe Education Action Zones would change that.

We all have certain memories that are as clear as a bell and seem as if they happened only yesterday. I vividly recall in November 2002 my journey on the way back from meeting Adriano Monti, the then Italian consul to Manchester, to Tatton Park in Knutsford when I got stuck in traffic at the lights at Bucklow Hill. As I sat there, pondering my meeting with the consul about language learning and role-play, a question came into my mind: *How many of Shakespeare's plays are set in Italy?* In my eagerness to find an answer, I phoned my friend Julian Chenery, the founder of *Shakespeare 4 Kidz*. He informed me that there are 14 such plays but cautioned that two of them were too macabre for the primary-age range, so we should focus on the other 12. This led to my next question: Could we condense each play into a ten-minute performance à la *the Reduced Shakespeare Company*? Julian's response was an affirmative "yes." And then I posed another question: Can we then divide the plays into five minutes of Italian and five minutes of English? Once again, the answer was an enthusiastic "yes." With this idea in mind, I collaborated with my colleagues at the Education Action Zones and our friends at Manchester Airport, and together, we presented the concept to various potential funding partners. *Shakespeare per i Ragazzi* was born.

Then, seemingly out of nowhere, a truly remarkable project materialised. We invited all Wythenshawe children aged 7–14 who were learning Italian and were interested in the project to come and audition one weekend in early 2003, and from there, we narrowed down the selection to 40 talented budding actors. To add a touch of celebrity to the project, we had the privilege of the company of the actor Neil Morrissey as the chair of the judging panel, deciding who would progress and who wouldn't. Neil, with his own personal background as a foster child, clearly understood and signed up to the project's essence, its principles, and its values. With his involvement, the project gained even greater momentum. "Kids behaving Bardly for Neil" was the headline in the Manchester Evening News.

Over the next 12 months, these chosen Wythenshawe thespians would dedicate their Saturday mornings to rehearsals and Italian lessons. Commitment was crucial, and attendance was key. It was a joint responsibility between the children, their parents and carers, the schools, and the Education Action Zones to ensure their active participation.

And then, 12 months later, the moment arrived. We boarded a plane at Manchester Airport courtesy of British Airways, accompanying 40 talented Wythenshawe children, and embarked on a journey to Italy, to showcase their skills and talents in the city of Bologna, home of Europe's oldest university.

On 26th May 2004, 40 children from Wythenshawe primary, secondary, and special schools performed 12 Shakespeare plays set in Italy, part in Italian and part in English. Each play lasted no more than ten minutes. The two-hour evening performance, with a matinee rehearsal thrown in for good measure, was performed in the Piazza Santa Stefano and shown on Italian television. In the 700-plus-strong audience were the United Kingdom ambassador to Italy, Sir Ivor Roberts, and his wife, Lady Sarah; British Council and Bolognese dignitaries; teachers and headteachers, including those from Wythenshawe; and most importantly, parents, grandparents, uncles and aunties, brothers, sisters, and friends of the families who had made the journey from Wythenshawe of their own accord, by train, plane, and automobile. You could taste the pride in the air. That the project won the Association of Language Learning Award in that year came as no surprise to anyone.

Years later, I managed to convince a Wythenshawe film producer to transform the footage we had captured in Bologna into a film. Four years after the actual event, we proudly premiered the film in the Wythenshawe Forum, complete with an Allied Carpets red carpet. The parents and their actor-children were there, of course.

As part of the film, we conducted interviews with the young people, now four years older, and the overwhelming sense of pride was still palpable; it was still all there. Among the many heartfelt quotes, one in particular remains etched in my memory. It came from Sammy, the girl who played Juliet: "For me, the most important thing was that I proved to my parents that I can do things." The sentiment echoed a profound truth and reminded me of the story where the quote "Children can only aspire to what they know exists" originated: back to that moment where children candidly told me they couldn't become a pilot because people from Wythenshawe don't fly planes. Unearthing this new truth, this purpose, was the very essence of our undertaking. The spark? In that meeting with the then consul Adriano Monti and some of my Wythenshawe headteacher friends in November 2002, when discussing possible big-scale projects between Bolognese and Wythenshawe schools, someone sitting in a corner said, "You can't do this with these kids."

I would love to see those remarkable 40 individuals again, now some 20 years later.

It was within this framework of the Education Action Zones that I found increasing conviction in the idea that if we wished for young people to be at school, to arrive at school prepared and punctually, motivated, and ready to engage, to stay behind for more, we needed to cultivate an environment that imbued them with a sense of purpose, a sense of discovery, and a sense of positivity. Consequently, my mindset shifted even further away from a rigid focus on teaching, testing, and booster classes, towards learning styles and experiences that encapsulated this philosophy and served the learning needs of individual children.

Roy T. Bennet is an American author, observer, optimist, and thought leader I greatly admire. I see his thoughts as tapas of positivity which, as I get older, I increasingly like the taste of. Roy's famous quote from his 2016 book *The Light in the Heart* indicates that if you possess a strong sense of purpose in life, you won't require constant prodding; your passion will propel you forward. I believe this applies not only to academia or professional pursuits but also to all aspects of our existence. It seems to be an innately human characteristic. The focus needs to be on instilling purpose, not through dry textbook explanations, but through discovery, by creating environments and scenarios that lead to experiences which then naturally reveal that purpose.

To be frank, my mind, heart, and soul have never been in the teach-test-and-boost culture. It was fake news, even then. It is also disrespectful towards the children and their contexts, and of course towards the teaching professions, demonstrating the biggest issue in our schooling systems over the last 40 or so years – a lack of professional trust by government in those who teach and those who are being taught. Whatever next? Lining up silently in corridors and not being allowed to the toilet during lessons in secondary schools? All as part of preparation for their futures? No, thank you. And surely, if and when there are genuine, evidenced concerns about standards of achievement and quality of provision, you engage with all those who hold shares in our children's futures, first and foremost the teaching professions. You don't create a culture of political bullying and disrespect. No wonder we experience teacher shortages.

However, when you find yourselves in areas of significant disadvantage, where everybody is up against it, including the schools, you will find that the pressure from on high is disproportionately unfair and unnecessary. Schools that, in order to serve their children and communities, need to know their children better and develop alternative, individual strategies and pathways in order for them to be successful are constantly under the cosh of government, education departments, and inspectorates. There seems to be a belief that pressure equals a drive for improvement and at one-size-fits-all is the solution. How can schools from totally different contexts, for example, the most affluent borough in England, Kensington, and Chelsea, on the one hand, and Jaywick, the most deprived ward near Clacton-on-Sea, on the other, be generally seen and judged as the same or similar? In any case, to quote journalist, founder of the American Newspaper Guild, and member of the Algonquin Roundtable Heywood Broun: "No essence can be measured by a yardstick."

Another initiative the Education Action Zones in Wythenshawe developed was a work experience project called the Royal Bank of Scotland Diploma. This involved collaborating with groups of academically gifted but purpose-disconnected teenagers aged 14, 15, and 16. The design was that a group of around 25 young people spent three days per week at school, engaging in key subjects such as English, mathematics, foreign languages, computer science, and sport. Additionally, they dedicated one day per week to life skills at one of Manchester's further education colleges. Most significantly, they embarked on a work placement or junior apprenticeship at the Royal Bank of Scotland at Spinningfields in the heart of Manchester. If, after two years, they met the established criteria – passing examinations and assessments, maintaining good attendance, exhibiting appropriate behaviour, and demonstrating high motivation – they were offered apprenticeships, offered jobs, or in rare cases, funded further study by the bank. Out of the initial group of 25 young people, only 3 dropped out. This echoed the experience we had with the Wythenshawe Shakespeare project, where out of the 40 initial participants, none withdrew. It became evident that when the purpose is recognisable and owned, there is a journey to be discovered, and when the environment is conducive, the desired outcomes naturally follow. It certainly required hard work but, equally, thinking differently about learning, teaching, and relationships, including roles and responsibilities. The results spoke for themselves. They were Wythenshawe results that could not just be copied and transplanted elsewhere. The results were about contexts, knowing our young people, and trust. Just like the Children's University. Education is the key to unlocking the world. Schooling is the passport and the visas to a better education.

When the opportunity arose in 2007 to become the founding chief executive officer of the national, and in time, the international, Children's University, I felt like it was the logical next step – a chance to delve deeper into the exploration of purpose and its transformative impact. Connect. Extend. Challenge – Part Two.

Amidst its undoubted pitfalls, one thing became abundantly clear to me very early on: Everyone seemed to recognise the importance of out-of-school learning experiences, but no one had tangible evidence to support their beliefs. It felt like wishful thinking and hearsay. Recognising the need for solid proof, independently arrived-at evidence, the Children's University engaged in a partnership with the University of Cambridge. The aim was to produce evaluations that would either confirm or debunk the impact of these experience-based activities. In the realm of education, guesswork was simply not acceptable. While innovation and calculated risks were encouraged, we needed sound foundations and could not afford to walk on quicksand.

Even the government had invested in out-of-hours learning, albeit with a tight agenda around improving numeracy and literacy standards in disadvantaged areas – booster activities with knobs on. Playing for Success, involving sports clubs all over the country, from the Premier League to canoeing clubs, led by the inimitable, late Rex Hall, was the prime example. The Children's University wanted more, however.

We turned to the University of Cambridge not for simple demonstrations of improved maths or English results but for something deeper. We sought evidence that children who voluntarily participated in validated, quality-assured, out-of-school activities became better, more confident learners. We also wanted proof that these experiences instilled purpose in their lives. The evaluations were critical in addressing these questions. The journey of self-confidence is generally undervalued. Confident learners put themselves in charge of their journey and write their own narratives of the possible. When you have been told for years that you can't fly planes, because of where you're from, self-confidence is very likely to be in short supply. The Children's University evaluations by the University of Cambridge, and later the global research at KidZania, would prove this point. As a child, the more disadvantaged your context, the less confident you are likely to be. In its own way, research by the Sutton Trust[3] concluded in 2023 that there is a very strong connection between the earnings of children and the earnings of their parents – in social mobility terms, this paints an uncomfortable picture. Everybody seems to still be in the jar, and the lid appears to be firmly on. The journey to academic improvement via the confidence route takes time, and certainly longer than the lifetime of a parliament. But equally, we also wanted children to enjoy the Children's University, to be proud of their achievements, and to rediscover curiosity and, à la Roy T. Bennet, purpose, and passion. Curiosity, purpose, and a love of learning were there when they were very little, but like creativity, as the late Sir Ken Robinson said, "we teach these out of them."

As for how it all worked at this Children's University, simplicity had to be key. If a 5-year-old could not understand what we were doing, then there was no point. From an educational perspective, it was clear to me that the Children's University needed to be built around the contextualised main principles of the Reggio Emilia approach. Enter Carla Rinaldi and the start of our friendship.

The Reggio Emilia approach is an educational philosophy and pedagogy which is mainly focused on preschool and primary education, but with clear implications for lifelong learning, 0 to 99. This approach is a child-centred and constructivist self-guided curriculum that uses self-initiated, self-directed, self-sustained, experiential learning in relationship-driven environments. Connect. Extend. Challenge. The programme is based on the principles of respect, responsibility, and community through exploration, discovery, and play.

At the core of this philosophy is an assumption that children form their own personality during the early years of development and that they are endowed with "a hundred languages," through which they can express their ideas. The aim of the Reggio Emilia approach is to teach children how to use these symbolic languages, for example, painting, sculpting, and drama, in everyday life. This approach was developed after World War II by pedagogist Loris Malaguzzi and parents in the villages around Reggio Emilia, Italy; the approach derives its name from the northern Italian city.

During the post–World War II era in Italy, the country was overcome with a "desire to bring change and create anew," brought on by significant economic and social development, including in education. An account described how a 1976 opposition to the primary education policy of the municipality of Reggio Emilia opened up the preschools to public scrutiny. This resulted in the introduction of the Reggio approach to early education, which was supported by parents and the community. The approach itself was based on Malaguzzi's method, which became known to and appreciated by many educators thanks to a touring exhibition titled "A Child has 100 Languages. On

Creative Pedagogy at Public Kindergartens in Reggio Emilia, Italy," which opened in 1981 at the Modern Museet in Stockholm, Sweden. As a result, the National Group for Work and Study on Infant Toddler Centres was formed in Reggio Emilia. By 1991, Newsweek reported that the early years provision in Reggio Emilia was among the top education systems in the world.

On 24th May 1994, shortly after his death, the non-profit organisation Friends of Reggio Children International Association was founded to honour and promote the work of Loris Malaguzzi and to organise professional development and cultural events around the approach.

In 2003, the municipality of Reggio Emilia chose to manage the system and the network of school services and toddler centres by forming the Istituzione Scuole e Nidi d'Infanzia. This enabled municipal schools and preschools to have independent Reggio-inspired programmes and activities with support from the Italian government. In February 2006, the Loris Malaguzzi International Centre was established in Reggio Emilia as a meeting place for professional development and a research hub for the Reggio philosophy. On 29th September 2011, the non-profit Reggio Children-Loris Malaguzzi Centre Foundation was established at the Loris Malaguzzi International Centre to foster "education and research to improve the lives of people and communities, in Reggio Emilia and in the world."[4] The Reggio Emilia methodology now has schools on every continent, except Antarctica, and is the world's fastest-growing preschool teaching approach.

Carlina Rinaldi started working in Reggio Emilia in 1970, first as a "Pedagogista," then as the pedagogical director of municipal early childhood services. President of Reggio Children since 2007, in 2011 she was appointed as president of Fondazione Reggio Children–Centro Loris Malaguzzi. Since 1999, she has been working as an adjunct professor of pedagogy at the University of Modena and Reggio Emilia. She was one of the international consultants to the *Thinkers in Residence* project at the Department of the Premier and Cabinet, Government of South Australia. In 2015, she was awarded the LEGO Prize. The LEGO Prize is presented to individuals or organisations that have made an outstanding contribution to the lives of children while championing the importance of play. Carla Rinaldi was awarded the prize for her ability to effectively communicate the importance of child-centred early learning over several decades.

It took a very considerable amount of time, researching, thinking, consulting, collaborating, and planning, and hours and hours of train journeys, meetings, calls, and emails, before the franchise-type framework of the Children's University took shape. It took even longer to understand and get to know who would be our children and what makes them tick.

The original brief was short and simple: Children aged 7–14 from disadvantaged parts of England would be given the opportunity to have experiences out of school hours, which would translate into credits of some sort. This, in turn, would lead to a form of certification to be awarded at junior graduation ceremonies in actual universities in the presence of their parents, carers, and wider family. The aim was for most of the young people to have learning encounters they would possibly not have otherwise, and to experience a sense of achievement in fields that were unfamiliar to them. The graduation was the culmination in the form of a celebration of pride – and all of it was meant to be fun. Again, we should remind ourselves that children can only aspire to what they know exists.

This original brief served us well, although very soon both boundaries and rules would be stretched. Research had shown us that whatever operational framework we developed needed to be simple, understood, and owned by all. And the inspiration came from a very unlikely source.

The Campaign for Real Ale (CAMRA) is a simple and brilliant, originally English, concept. Beer lovers visit as many different bars or pubs across the United Kingdom as they can or want to. Each of these pubs is mentioned in a guide, *The Good Beer Guide*. All the CAMRA member pubs also have a sticker, or seal of approval, prominently displayed on the window, and most are nowadays also accessible on the CAMRA website. This seal of approval means that someone who was authorised to do so has, on behalf of the Campaign for Real Ale, visited all the pubs that merit a mention, tried and tested their beers, and according to a range of criteria, has judged these beers to be of a good quality – good enough to be mentioned in the aforementioned Good Beer Guide. When visiting the CAMRA pubs, the beer lovers collect stamps in their Campaign for Real Ale passports, for their own records, but also to be able to show and tell their achievements to others. Important also is that when you enter a pub endorsed by CAMRA, you personally may not always love the taste of the beer, but you can trust that it is of a good-enough quality, because it has been tried, tested, tasted, and given the Campaign for Real Ale seal of approval. The concept is brilliant. It is voluntary; it encourages curiosity, a sense of independence, adventure, teamwork, and enjoyment; it is purposeful and full of passion; and it is, of course, also quality-assured. In the development of the Children's University, this concept or, better maybe, framework became key. We sometimes need to look in the unlikeliest places for answers and go beyond the boundaries of the ordinary, of what is expected.

And now, in the context of the Children's University, imagine replacing the pub with a museum, gallery, library, zoo, or sports club – essentially, any place children choose to participate in high-quality, voluntary, out-of-school activities, including, for example, Mumtaz, the fabulous Indian restaurant in Bradford which supplies its spices to Harrods London. Then, envision a process where someone has already tried, tested, and tasted, or otherwise evaluated and validated, the quality of the learning experience within these venues. We called the places and venues *Learning Destinations*, which were advertised on our local and national websites. With the University of Cambridge, we developed an assessment-and-evaluation framework, called *Planning for Learning*, and trained countless local Children's University managers and others to ensure the validation process was rigorous, consistent, and of a high standard. We wanted *Learning Destinations* to think of themselves differently, as welcoming places of education for all as opposed to at times elitist venues, almost in the style of the American collector and patron of the arts Peggy Guggenheim, who, in 1949, turned her Italian Venetian home, the Palazzo Venier dei Leoni, into what later became known as the Peggy Guggenheim Museum: "I dedicated myself to my collection. A collection means hard work. It was what I wanted to do, and I made it my life's work. I am not an art collector. I am a museum."

Locality played a vital role in the Children's University. Its initial target audience were children aged 7–14, primarily those from disadvantaged contexts and locations. It was essential that these children could easily, safely, and affordably access their *Learning Destinations*. It was also key that local Children's University managers and teachers knew the children and understood them. This more personalised approach ensured that scaffolding could be built around the children in order to empower them to individually climb as high as they could and wanted to. Each local Children's University paid a membership to the national organisation, depending on the number of children they took under their wing. The children's, and their families', membership contribution was the cost of their *Passport to Learning*. These contributions were important; if you get something for nothing, it almost naturally is perceived to have a lesser value. In the Children's University, everyone was a shareholder. In 2010, having learned from the Reggio Emilia approach, the starting age was lowered to 5.

In a manner similar to the Campaign for Real Ale, the children were issued their *Passports to Learning*, becoming adventurers on a quest for knowledge. As they visited different *Learning Destinations* and participated in activities, they collected stamps in their passports. Once they accumulated a certain number of hours, they would receive an invitation to a graduation ceremony, where they would be presented with a well-earned certificate. Bronze, silver, or gold awards and certificates, diplomas, and degrees – the more stamps, the higher the recognition. After a few years, we had to differentiate between undergraduate and postgraduate recognition as the demand was so great. The graduation ceremonies were no ordinary affairs; they took place at universities, which served as important partners in our endeavour. The inclusion of parents and carers in these ceremonies was intentional, as it served multiple purposes. It not only encouraged parental involvement but also allowed parents, many of whom had never set foot in a higher education institution, to experience the transformative potential of such spaces. Caps, gowns, speeches, proud adults, even prouder children, tissues, and not a dry eye in the house. The overarching goal was to promote social mobility from an early age and show children that these universities were places where they, too, could belong, should they choose to. People from Wythenshawe do fly planes!

This franchise-style model worked. It recognised the importance of locality to the children, to the families, to the *Learning Destinations*, and also to the universities involved. The overall framework could best be likened to a colouring-in book for children. The (inter)national picture has been drawn, but the colouring in itself needs to happen at the local level, depending on the context and the needs of the children, their families, and the communities, as well as their schools. This is something, as I discovered years later, that is much harder to achieve in a commercial franchise than in a social, charitable one.

True differences are made at local levels, where the children are, be that in schools, KidZanias, or local Children's Universities. Head offices have a purpose, of course, in management and finance, for example, through economies of scale, and can be important in leadership, but in terms of direct impact on children, they play second fiddle. The closer we are to the children, the more important we are. This goes for, for example, KidZania, Children's University, but also local government and school groupings, such as multi-academy trusts in England. National governments play third fiddle – they are even further removed. School groupings only work if they have common values and principles and elements of true friendship, where schools help each other out, share ideas, and innovate together. I would like to think that the Wythenshawe Education Action Zones, for a good deal of the time, were exactly that. Bottom-up collaboration in the interest of the children. I can't help thinking that the more challenging the circumstances are, the better this should work.

The Children's University experiences were meant to be catalysts, inspiring children to explore further. Each achievement was an opportunity to encourage them to consider new possibilities and embark on different adventures. Voluntary participation played a crucial role in this journey, as it required commitment, courage, curiosity, and a sense of joy and fun from the children and the adults supporting them.

Often, amongst ourselves and with children and parents, but also during speeches at the graduation ceremonies, we mentioned two aspects: firstly, learning outside the box and, secondly, venturing outside one's comfort zone. The emphasis was also often on the fact that these are not the prerogative of youth, but that they happened to us all, at all stages of life.

I regularly share the story of my first black-tie dinner with young people and their parents, exemplifying and emphasising the importance of stepping outside one's comfort zone and embracing new experiences and, with hindsight, maintaining a sense of humour. My upbringing, in many ways, had been very sheltered, and I had certainly never been exposed, until then, to something I might have called "posh." I had never attended a black-tie dinner in my then 44 years, until Geoff Muirhead, the Group Chief Executive at Manchester Airport, and my Wythenshawe Education Action Zones' chairman, extended an invitation to such an event at the prestigious Midland Hotel in Manchester, where, so legend has it, many moons ago Mr Rolls met Mr Royce. My initial reaction was a mix of uncertainty and intrigue. However, the prospect of attending this unfamiliar affair left me flummoxed. This was uncharted territory, and I had no clue what I was supposed to do. In my mind I came up with every excuse under the sun not to attend. However, I gave in, of course, and with some trepidation, I decided to rent a suit and a dicky bow, determined to embrace the occasion. Upon my arrival, I was directed to my assigned table, where my name was carefully displayed in front of my seat. As I surveyed the scene, I was taken aback by the sheer number of knives and forks adorning this table – never before had I witnessed such a display. Feeling anxious, I just watched those around me, determined not to make a fool of myself. Despite my nerves (I can't recall fully enjoying the food), I managed to navigate the evening by mimicking others, feeling mightily relieved when it was all over. A few months later, I received another invitation, this time for an event at the Radisson Hotel near Manchester Airport. Surprisingly, I felt less apprehensive, and with each subsequent dinner, my confidence grew. By the third invitation, approximately a year after my first experience, I found myself quietly looking forward to it. By the fourth occasion in December, I approached the event with a newfound sense of self-assuredness, even bordering on cockiness. Yet just when I thought I had mastered it all, at the fifth dinner, lobster was served . . . and I was back to square one again!

This story speaks of a journey – an odyssey, however big or small, that each of us embarks on at some point in life. It is important for children to understand that they are not alone in facing new experiences that can knot their tummies with nervous anticipation. It is normal, and it is okay. It is also okay to get it wrong – as long as we have the will and the honesty to learn and try better. The Children's University sought to impart this wisdom. It aimed to instil in children the knowledge that stepping into uncharted territory, whether joining a new club, meeting new people in new places, or attending an after-school activity, may evoke a mix of emotions. However, it is precisely in these moments of discomfort that personal growth takes place. The graduation ceremonies celebrated that more than anything: the lifting of the lid, then the cracking of the jar.

The University of Adelaide, Australia. November 2013, blossoming jacaranda trees outside the Bonython Hall. The first graduation of the Australian Children's University, in the presence of the vice chancellor, the pro-chancellor, assembled dignitaries, mums and dads, and of course, the children, the young graduates. It was my last formal engagement as founding chief executive of the Children's University.

Cyndi Johnson, mother of First Nation twins: "I was crying, and I don't cry. I started crying. I am very proud of them." The highlight of my seven years – there were many, but this was it. My message:

> We need to come to the point where we understand that, in life, learning matters. Children can only aspire to what you know exists. And it is our job to twitch curtains, to open windows, and eventually, to open doors. If we do that together, we will achieve together,

and the world will be a slightly better place. Learning is a satellite navigation system to better places in life.

By then this could have been anywhere. Essex, Manchester, Bradford, London, Edinburgh, Cardiff, Douglas, Belfast, Rotterdam, Singapore, Kuala Lumpur, anywhere and everywhere there are disadvantaged communities – the focus of the Children's University. The Children's University had grown exponentially and turned international too.

The pride was there, amongst the children, of course, but also their parents and carers, their teachers. The pride was made visible through the local centres, the passports, the *Learning Destinations*, the certificates, the presence at a university, the pomp and circumstance of the graduation itself. Pride, like social mobility, is often a family affair, and beyond. It takes a community to raise a child.

That particular sense of pride in children and their families is also infectious. Anybody who experienced these graduation ceremonies became hooked, especially when they understood the simplicity of it all and saw the impact for good they themselves could have on the lives and experiences of the young people. As an example, Jackie Cooper, Edelman's global chief brand officer and senior adviser; Joel Cadbury, founder and chair of Longshot Ltd; Michael Norton, founder of the Centre for Innovation in Voluntary Action (CIVA); and James Bradburne, architect, designer, and museologist, then director general at Florence's Palazzo Strozzi, thus became founding members of the then Friends of the Children's University, and my friends for life.

Joel Cadbury was also the founder of KidZania London. He and a group of friends and investors had secured the rights for the United Kingdom and Ireland in 2012 – and there was much to be done.

KidZania is a Mexican privately held international chain of indoor family entertainment centres currently operating in some 25 locations worldwide, allowing children to role-play adult jobs and earn currency. It receives around 9 million visitors per year. That is the official Wikipedia blurb. It is, of course, much more than that.

KidZanias are child-sized cities designed to empower and inspire children: "from inspiration to aspiration." They offer fun, real-life career awareness and role-play-based experiential learning for children aged 4–14. Realistically, the ideal age range is 7 to 12, with exceptions like Careers Weeks, where the young people also get to meet real pilots, surgeons, newsreaders, actors, etc.; here, the KidZania potential touches older age groups too. The first KidZania opened in Mexico City in 1999 as *La Ciudad de los Niños – The City of the Children*.

Children can choose to role-play any number of careers, globally, including working in a bank, performing onstage, landing an airplane or serving food and drinks, presenting the news, performing a liver transplant, YouTubing, flying to the moon, working in a supermarket or hotel, cleaning windows, or being a courier. For their efforts, the children get paid in KidZania's own currency, KidZos, after which they can open a KidZania bank account, save, and spend. Experience, again, is everything. Another key factor is that the accompanying grown-ups are there to be seen and not heard. No helicoptering at KidZania. The motto? "Get Ready for a Better World."

It was in late 2012 that Joel Cadbury got in touch with the message: "Can you come and help?" He was a friend, so of course I could.

One of the main challenges was that KidZania had not really defined what exactly it was. For marketing purposes, it was hidden behind the terminology "edutainment" but was very slow in qualifying what that meant. In terms of visitors, weekends and school holidays were targeted at families, whereas during the academic year, weekdays were for schools. So did that mean that at the weekend it was more "-tainment" than "edu-," and that during the school week, the focus was more on the "edu-" and less so on the "-tainment"? I also never understood the question whether KidZania is educational or fun. To this day, I cannot get my head around the fact that people perceive that it cannot be both at the same time. As KidZania London developed, it was clear that the messaging was confused. To make matters worse, communication, public relations, and marketing were, by the franchisor, deemed of secondary importance. You have a story but are not really committed to telling it.

The other key challenge was that KidZania is a business, there to make profit. This made "Get Ready for a Better World" for all children that little bit harder.

Credibility, and particularly educational credibility, was an issue. How serious were we? Working with teachers and schools, parent groups, home educators, charities, community groups, local and national government, and others, we set about defining our approach, and in the end, we focused on seven key jigsaw pieces that would each contribute to the bigger picture.

First and foremost, *Education KidZania London* would focus on all children, however financially difficult that sometimes might be. We annually handed in excess of 7,000 tickets to local schools in disadvantaged circumstances and found ways whereby similar schools from elsewhere could be with us at much reduced rates, at times when it would normally be less busy. In a way, peak- and prime-time visitors subsidised those who might otherwise not have been able to afford the KidZania experience. KidZania London had turned Robin Hood – and proudly so.

Later, when I was global education director for KidZania, we adapted these principles and values to national and local contexts. One size does not fit all. At KidZania Delhi, we worked differently with a number of industry partners, outside the box, in a big way. Instead of paying their annual sponsorship fee, those industry partners bought at reduced rates tens of thousands of tickets from KidZania and then, in turn, donated these to a local charity, Voice of Slum. This different way of thinking meant that more constituents were served better. KidZania Delhi still got its funding, the sponsors still contributed, and the charity got its donation, and tens of thousands of children were able to access the KidZania experience and concern themselves with a better narrative for their futures. In India, too, children can only aspire to what they know exists.

Secondly, learning has to be the focus, not teaching, or even being taught. KidZania learning had to be self-initiated, self-directed, and self-sustained, as well as experience-based and independent, in the mould of the Reggio Emilia approach. Connect. Extend. Challenge. Many conversations with Carla Rinaldi and the Fondazione Reggio Children were had and enjoyed.

Thirdly, engagement with parents, carers, families, support organisations, and schools was, and is, very important. Communication, the development, mutual support, and ultimately, joint ownership are key. As an example, we partnered with Swiss Cottage School's Development and Research Centre in London to make KidZania more and better aware of special educational needs and disability issues in children and education in general. No price can be put on these aspects of partnership working.

Fourthly, we established that industry partners are learning partners. One of the three pillars of the business model for KidZania consisted of sponsorship, or industry partnerships, as they were known. The other two were, of course, family visits and school visits. Industry partners would sponsor an activity that was close to their essence. The jobs children would undertake in those activities effectively reflected the sponsoring organisations. In London in 2015, British Airways had its name on the aeroplane and paid for the privilege. Others included, for example, Renault, Global Radio, Al Jazeera Television, the Dorsett Hotel, Alder Hey Children's Hospital. Mostly, the financial contributions would come out of the industry partners' marketing budgets and, in some cases, out of corporate and social responsibility: Alder Hey Children's Hospital got in for free. What we discovered over the years, from conversations with children, parents and carers, teachers, and others, was that the contribution of the sponsors amounted to far more than the financial aspect. During an evaluation project with Arbourthorne Community Primary School in Sheffield, we posed the question: "What are your favourite activities?" Somewhat to our surprise, the answer was, "The branded ones." When asked why, the children answered that they made the activity real. After all, the *KidZania Gazette* didn't really exist, did it? But the *Metro* newspaper did. We were also determined to address social values and social conscience issues through content. After all, there is more to a job than just work. A wonderful example of this was my work with the charity Team Margot, which aims to help save and improve lives by educating, inspiring, and motivating people, especially from ethnically diverse communities, to register as blood, organ, stem cell, and bone marrow donors and to provide a range of support to families caring for child cancer patients. Margot was a beautiful little girl, daughter of Vicki and Yaser Martini, who died of a rare form of leukaemia on 27th October 2014. Team Margot is made up of the family and friends of the toddler. As a friend, I am a member and the education spokesperson of the United Kingdom's All-Party Parliamentary Group: Ethnicity Transplantation and Transfusion. For Margot. The KidZania London courier activity was swiftly adapted to include collecting donor bags from the airplane and delivering them to the hospital, where the transplant operation could then take place. Awareness-raising matters, as does supporting friends.

An education advisory group, or "KidZania Think-Tank," was established, with the aim to become better at thinking. It consisted of friends from all walks of life, including headteachers and teachers, former schools minister and secretary of state for education Lord Jim Knight and Baroness Nicky Morgan, former children's commissioner for England Professor Maggie Atkinson, Mumsnet co-founder Carrie Longton, representatives from the world of business and the charity sector, and parents. Thinking with children was done in other forums, through schools, clubs, charities, and parenting groups. Years later, an equivalent group would be set up globally and included, amongst others, Andreas Schleicher, director for the Directorate of Education and Skills at Organisation for Economic Co-operation and Development (OECD).

Parenting and carer groups are really important and, by and large, not taken seriously enough. They are often seen as a must-have, sometimes even as a nuisance. Parents and carers are rarely recognised as co-educators, and in turn, they often don't see themselves as co-responsible for schooling and education, for the learning and the outcomes of their children. Over the years, that relationship has begun to mirror that of a provider-and-client interaction. Wrong! The education and schooling of our children need to be an ongoing dialogue focused on the young people, not a series of definitions of roles and responsibilities. If we get this wrong, our interactions about our children become disjointed, wrong even. The consequences are always to the detriment of the child, often to the detriment of the parent or carer, and never a good look for the school or other educational organisation. In all cases, there are lessons to be learned. The lesson always is to talk more and better, to recognise all stakeholders for who and what they are and could be, and to put the child in the middle. Occasionally, this lack of joint-upness can also lead to surprising, funny, if also awkward, stories. Matthew was 13 or 14 years old at that time. His mum, Debbie, a friend and former colleague, had been informed by the secondary school that sex and relationship education was going to happen that week, in fact, during a certain hour on a certain day during that week. Like the usual tickbox way of thinking and operating. Debbie had spent time with Matthew, talking things through, beforehand, especially the relationship part. When Matthew returned home late on that particular day, Debbie was already there. After a little while, she asked him how his day had been and, in particular, how the sex and relationship lesson had panned out. Matthew, apparently, didn't seem too bothered. He understood almost everything and seemed quite okay with what he had been told. There was something puzzling him, however. Being Matthew, he asked a question of his mother without flinching, directly: "Why are condoms flavoured?" Debbie, by all accounts, all of a sudden was in a real rush to put out the bins, ready for the next morning. When the context is forgotten and, like a tickbox exercise, only the content matters, things go wrong. Schooling, then, is just schooling, and education matters less. It takes a village to educate a child. But if we don't talk to each other, communicate around and with the child, it all feels a little bit pointless and muddled. Although, in this particular case, with hindsight and its benefit, it is also very funny.

In our KidZania London, development, research, evaluation, and quality assurance were crucial from the start, or even from *before* the start, and the inclusion of all stakeholders, especially parents and carers, was key. We needed to know what was working or what was not, and why or why not. A whole network was developed that allowed us to conduct this work, starting with my acquaintances of old at the University of Cambridge. In fact, to evidence and proof our educational intentions, and thereby our credibility, we commissioned the University of Cambridge to conduct a piece of research about KidZania London before its opening. Were our aims, values, and principles, and our educational approach, reflected in the cold realities of business plans, budgets, appointments, job descriptions, board and shareholder meetings, and their minutes? The answer, I am proud to say, was affirmative. We were, at that time, already walking the talk.

And finally, it was very important to us that whatever we did, other KidZanias should be able to contextualise and adapt. There lies a tension within the franchise world that is about central control and local context. The same applied to KidZania – a "push-me, pull-me" of doing the right thing. From an educational perspective, it was crystal clear how much national, regional, and local contexts matter. In simple terms, the context of Wythenshawe bears little comparison with that of Kensington and Chelsea; the same principle applies between Mexico City and London, Istanbul, Moscow, Dubai, Santiago, Dallas, et al. The wonderful David Winner describes this beautifully in his book *Brilliant Orange* about Dutch football and Dutchness:

> Every country and every culture has its own way of seeing. Ask any Dutch person to draw the horizon and they will draw a straight line. To make sense of the vast flatness of their land, the Dutch developed a way of calibrating distances from the horizon, paying meticulous attention to every object within this space. This is the Dutch way of seeing, the Dutch approach to space, instinctively and naturally: selective detail. You see it in their paintings, their architecture and in their football too.

And then there is the English way, the Turkish, Russian, Emirati, Chilean, Texan, etc. We are who we are.

Two years later, the call from KidZania headquarters in Mexico City came. They asked if I would take the London role worldwide, as KidZania's first global director of education. In so very many ways, the answer was, of course, "Yes, please."

When I assumed my position as global education director at KidZania, my old-school atlas took on a whole new meaning. It became more than just a collection of marks on a map; I had started highlighting places I thought I, in future, might want to visit as an 11-year-old in 1968 – a result of a school trip to Rotterdam. Now, my atlas became new, curious, wonderful, at times slightly mad experiences and people who, in turn, became friends. As I travelled the world doing my job, I found myself ticking off the places I had marked as a child, fulfilling my childhood dreams. Although there are still a few boxes left to tick, I feel that I am not too far from reaching the 100 per cent mark. It is an extraordinary realisation – how a childhood aspiration stays with us and can unexpectedly become a reality through the world of work much later in life. For me, it is a deeply personal achievement that adds a touch of magic to my professional life. I just wish I could now show my atlas to my grandad, born 12 years before the Americans Wilbur and Orville Wright first flew the Wright Flyer at Kitty Hawk, North Carolina, on 17th December 1903, with Orville at the controls.

The children at KidZanias all over the world were embarking on their own personal journeys too. When children arrive at KidZania, they are given a special bracelet, a symbol of their independence in a way. The bracelet serves multiple purposes. Firstly, it empowers the children to safely go off into their world of work, on their own, independently. It also allows KidZania to track their whereabouts in case of emergencies, or just if they need to be contacted. Additionally, the electronic bracelet enables KidZania to monitor the choices children make throughout their visit. Each time a child participates in an activity, they log in using their bracelet, providing KidZania with valuable data.

Curiosity led me to inquire about and investigate the potential of this data. I contacted the data experts at our head office in Mexico and asked what we were doing with this wealth of information. Initially, the data was used to provide feedback to industry partners, letting them know how many children had visited their endorsed and paid-for activities – a return-on-investment exercise. But I wanted to delve deeper. I posed the question, "Can we determine a child's first choice on their first KidZania visit with a school?" The learning during school visits was more independent than during family visits – in that aspect there was still some de-helicoptering to be done. The answer was a resounding "yes." Not stopping there, I ambitiously requested as much data as possible, spanning multiple countries. Over time, we accumulated a dataset of nearly 600,000 children across six countries – a sample size that left no room for doubt or scepticism.

The significance of this extensive dataset became apparent as time went by. It held the potential to reveal insights about children that traditional teach-and-test school settings don't have. It bridged the gap between out-of-school experiences and in-school learning. I wanted to uncover valuable information about children's interests, abilities, aptitudes, and loves outside of the classroom, knowledge that could enhance their educational and schooling journeys. I also wanted to understand those insights better and answer the why questions.

Once the children's first choices were listed, from London to Mexico City, Guadalajara, and Monterrey, from Moscow to Istanbul, Dubai, Delhi, and Mumbai, the next step was to discover from the anonymised data who these children were. Their age, their gender, their ethnicity, their socio-economic status, their urban or rural background, and the country they resided in – all these factors hold significance. It led me to collaborate with a whole range of data analysts and specialists globally from organisations as diverse as Havas; Edelman; the Instituto Tecnológico y de Estudios Superiores de Monterrey, also known as Tecnológico de Monterrey; the National Research University – Higher School of Economics, Moscow, where I consequently was awarded a visiting professorship; the University of Oxford; and much later, the United Kingdom–based market researchers the Insights Family.

The importance of the findings became the content of keynote speeches, interviews, and articles worldwide. It received media coverage in many countries, from CNN Chile and ABS-CBN in the Philippines to *Forbes* in both Russia and the USA, and was featured three times in the *Financial Times* alone. It allowed me to travel even more, to share the story, and it also meant that I was invited to join many advisory boards and think-tanks, including the Dubai Future Council for Education, BETT's Global Education Council, the Advisory Board for Junior Achievement Worldwide, the Beaconhouse Advisory Council in Pakistan, and DIDAC's Advisory Board in India. It also led me to work with organisations as diverse as my university in Moscow; Tata Consultancy Services; the Fondazione Reggio Children, Italy, and YGA, Turkey; the Children's Media Conference in the United Kingdom; teacher training organisations, such as the University of Cumbria, where I am a professor of practice, as well as advise a number of start-ups globally.

The research's main findings were staggering. They were also obvious, with the benefit of hindsight.

Stereotypes, it appeared, were set by the age of 4, if not earlier, although statistical evidence for earlier age groups was yet to be fully established. From the age of 4! Activities within KidZania showcased distinct gender biases, with cabin crew positions overwhelmingly filled by girls and pilots dominated by boys. The automotive experiences were almost entirely the domain of boys, whereas girls took charge of the hotel reception desks and the supermarket tills. Similarly, the maternity unit attracted predominantly girls, while the role of surgeon saw a vast majority of boys. Intriguingly, in London, boys of Indian heritage displayed the strongest inclination towards the surgeon activity, further reinforcing established stereotypes.

Another significant finding emerged – the choices made by children exhibited minimal change between the ages of 4 and 14. The implications of this trend raised thought-provoking questions about the persistence of gender biases in STEM (science, technology, engineering, and maths) fields and girls' career aspirations. While girls may outperform boys academically in the sciences, for example, their career choices all too often hark back to societal stereotypes. How can a young Black girl aspire to be a female pilot if she has never witnessed such representation? The importance of KidZania as a window of opportunity became evident – a catalyst for dispelling limitations and expanding horizons.

Troublingly, irrespective of their backgrounds, girls globally tended to choose activities below their age range, while boys leaned towards age-appropriate or slightly higher activities. This discrepancy speaks volumes about self-confidence, self-esteem, and societal expectations. It echoed the anecdotal observations of adults cautioning little girls at a playground to be careful while cheering boys on with expectations of swift progress and climbing to the top. The implications are profound – the narratives we weave and the expectations we place on children mould their perceptions, subtly influencing their self-worth and aspirations. As a father of two girls, I also found this a parental eye-opener. All these insights, but I think particularly this one, demonstrate how what may be seen as external factors should impact on day-to-day teaching and learning. Once, as a teacher, I am aware of the fact that 9-year-old girls choose 7-year-olds' activities, and that this is a significant discrepancy in comparison to the behaviour of boys, I need to be aware that if I do not take this into consideration, I might be considered to be professionally negligent. This particular complex issue reaches far beyond the simplistic notions of pink and blue. It calls for a deliberate examination of how we, as adults, more often than not, subconsciously shape and portray gender roles and expectations. It urges us to transcend narrow confines and embrace a more inclusive perspective, where every child is empowered to explore and discover their own potential. KidZania's role as a facilitator of self-discovery and confidence-building took on a new dimension – a profound reminder that the environment we create plays a pivotal role in shaping the future of our children.

We must elevate our approach and give our young ones the credit they deserve. This leads me to an additional finding and a confirmation that "children can only aspire to what they know exists." When children from disadvantaged contexts visit KidZanias worldwide, their initial choices rarely include pilot, surgeon, newsreader, actor, or radio presenter. Instead, they gravitate towards jobs like window cleaning, supermarket work, hotel bed-making, or being a courier. These are the jobs they are familiar with and have seen in their own families and communities. This is the jar, with the lid on. However, as they return to KidZania multiple times, something remarkable happens – they venture into the airplane cockpit and the operating theatre. For some children, confidence-building just takes longer. There is an undeniable correlation between investing in experiences and the courage it instils in young minds. As an 11-year-old, the more limited your life experiences, the more investment is needed to expand your horizons. We must acknowledge this when allocating funding for schools – there needs to be investment in inverse proportion to where many children find themselves, at the bottom of the socio-economic and social mobility ladder. And investment does not just mean cash; it also means time, teaching, resources, and non-teaching staff allocations, and of course the flexibility to make the curriculum appropriate to the individual learner, so that with the right scaffolding in place, they can climb out of the jar. Many of these young people, just like those in the Children's University, come from socio-economically disadvantaged areas, where traveling to a country's capital city and attending a theatre show, or visiting the country's parliament, is simply unaffordable and probably not on the aspirational horizon, anyway. If our intention is genuinely to level the playing field and uplift those who need it, we must extend our gaze beyond the confines of the traditional classroom. The notion that "not all classrooms have four walls" should become our rallying cry, prompting us to invest where it truly matters. The KidZania research echoed the findings by the University of Cambridge in a number of evaluations of the Children's University several years earlier. More of that later.

So the KidZania research brought us face-to-face with a pressing question. If stereotypes are firmly established by the age of 4, why in most education systems do we wait until the age of 14 to engage with our children's future pathways? We allow these stereotypes to solidify over ten long years, mistakenly believing that we can make a significant difference from the age of 14 onwards. Why aren't we engaging our children in exploring future pathways from a younger age? It is not about pressuring a 7-year-old to decide on a career; it is about nurturing their imagination and encouraging them to dream of endless possibilities. It is, in the end, about what became the title of my column in the children's magazine *The Week Junior*: "Becoming Me."

As educators, if we know that girls tend to choose activities below their age range, it should reshape our approach in the classroom. We need to plan and design our teaching and connected experiences differently, being mindful of these insights and ensuring equity for all. Additionally, we must address the needs of children from disadvantaged backgrounds by actively incorporating out-of-school experiences, trips, visits to restaurants and theatres, capital cities, airports, and ports, parks, and farms into our educational planning. It raises the question whether we, as a society and communities, should establish a shared understanding and consensus of the experiences we want our children to have by certain ages.

The final key finding took us by surprise. It revealed that the differences in choices made by children across the various KidZanias globally were statistically insignificant. In some shape or form, this says something about the globalisation of growing up. While globalisation undoubtedly has its merits, fostering better global connections and understanding, we must not disregard the value of preserving local culture and identity. It is concerning to witness the influence of globalised media, like *Peppa Pig*, in 40 languages, or the ubiquity of social media platforms like TikTok, YouTube, and Instagram. Even shopping malls, with their uniform brands like H&M, Zara, and Nike, contribute to a sense of sameness that can be disorientating and disheartening.

We should not halt globalisation but, rather, be aware of its side effects by actively creating opportunities that counterbalance its homogenising effect. Our young people should have the chance to celebrate and embrace their local, regional, and national identities. It saddens me to read that, in the Netherlands' southernmost province, where I grew up, the Limburgs dialect, spoken by 70 per cent of the adult population, is being spoken by only around 50 per cent of young people. This decline signifies not only the loss of a dialect but also a potential erosion of local identity in the face of globalisation. The annual carnival in Limburg three days before Ash Wednesday is, in my view, still best celebrated as "Vasteloavend."

It is crucial for us to strike a balance, cherishing our diverse local cultures – I, for example, couldn't even count the number of diverse festivals we proudly celebrate in my local Sheffield – while appreciating the positive aspects of globalisation. We must foster an environment where our young people can navigate the world confidently while maintaining their roots and heritage. It is through this harmony that we can create a generation capable of embracing global perspectives while still proudly preserving their local identities and cultures. For as much as I have travelled, seen, and experienced, and have lived in the United Kingdom for the last 40 or so years – the majority of my life – at least twice every year I long to be back in Limburg, and especially Maastricht: at carnival time, in either February or March, and during the white asparagus season, in May and June. And in my football book, when England play the Netherlands, the future is bright and orange. After all this time? Always!

A fundamental outcome of my involvement with KidZania and especially engaging in the research is the realisation that our views on and discussions around equality, inclusion, and equity often tend to oversimplify the individual. Whether it is in research papers or the news, we, too, often categorise children and people in general as if they possess only one dimension. We divide them by gender (boys or girls), by location (city or country), by socio-economic status (rich or poor), and by ethnicity (Black or White). However, the truth is far more complex and nuanced.

Imagine a young girl, for instance, who happens to be both Black and socio-economically disadvantaged. She lives in Blackpool, a coastal town in the northwest of England and an area that has faced long-standing deprivation and been labelled as one of the most disadvantaged places in the country. This girl's experience is not singular but multidimensional, layered with various forms of disadvantage. She exists at the intersection of gender, ethnicity, poverty, and regional marginalisation, forming a quadruple disadvantage that shapes her life. What chances of becoming a pilot? Four jars, four lids, one girl.

Recognising the multidimensionality of our young people is crucial. Failing to do so will lead us to provide only one-dimensional solutions that miss the true complexities of their experiences. By embracing their multifaceted identities, we can gain a deeper understanding of their needs and develop more comprehensive strategies to address inequalities. It is a vital shift in perspective that challenges us to see beyond simplistic categorisations and instead strive for holistic approaches to promote genuine equality and inclusivity.

I have worked in over 40 countries globally, mainly due to my roles at KidZania and the Children's University, in my work as a modern foreign languages adviser, and more recently, in my capacity as an adviser and consultant. Wherever I travel, I try to meet with children and young people, and whenever I meet them, I ask them the same question: "Why do you go to school?"

I realise that this is anecdotal, not scientific, but I would say that in around 80 per cent of all cases, the reply is along the lines of "Because I have to." This is a bad, and more so a sad, answer. It is an answer that contains a lack of understanding of what schooling and education are for, and it shows a lack of purpose. There are too few why answers. Education is a journey, not a destination.

In the teach-and-test regimes that we witness the world over, schooling has become an end in itself. It no longer serves to educate the learner and put them on the pathway to a better life. We have systemised schooling into a pass-the-parcel culture from primary to secondary and from there to further and higher education, then, somehow, into the world of work. Everything is in straight lines. It has made us marginalise the arts and humanities – the subjects that allow us to explore who we have become – and teach creativity, and often joy, out of the children. The accountability is to the system. There is a risk that our children will become well-schooled yet ill-educated. Or is that perhaps the intention? Let's hope not! Trump, Johnson, Brexit, hardening attitudes towards migration, and a new nationalism make me worry.

If we want change for good, then we need to aim for children, their parents, carers, families, and communities to understand and own that learning is a satellite navigation system to better places in life. And that it is not a selfish act.

For our children to connect with the purpose of schooling and education, we need to, of course, provide knowledge and understanding. But how? And why? We need to utilise what is available to us – in terms of technology, for example, but also in terms of all that says not all classrooms have four walls. We are all the facilitators enabling children to join the dots and recognise that experiences are the appliance of the science, the theory into practice, the why answers, and often, the awe and wonder, the removed lid, and the shattered jar. We need to empower children to make sense of the world as agents of their own change, and to guide them to discovering their own inspirations and aspirations. We all need to introduce into education and schooling early opportunities to be aware of the world around us and the futures it may hold – let us, for now, call it "futures awareness." Then we need to support them in finding their roadmaps and help them get there, from an early age. These roadmaps are not merely about economics; they are about society. They are about who we want to be and why, much more than merely what.

Children need to be able to write their own narrative of the possible. For this to be achieved, we need to be our children's allies of empowerment. We need to make experience-based learning and partnership our modus operandi, *purpose* our watchword, high standards and a sense of achievement our aim, and our children's well-being and preparedness for tomorrow our promise.

We are all teachers: the businesswoman, the bricklayer, the beekeeper, the baseball player, and Meneer Beurskens. Meneer Beurskens was my teacher, and it is because of him, professionally, that I am who I am and do what I do today. And of course, because of my grandfather. "Es doe mer gelökkig bös." *As long as you are happy.*

Perhaps in the future we should not just simply ask children what they want to be when they grow up but, rather, who they want to be like. Purpose with values and principles.

"Competencies to shape the future: It is about acting rather than to be acted upon, shaping rather than to be shaped and choosing rather than to accept choices decided by others."[5]

Notes

1 This thinking routine was developed as part of the Visible Thinking project at Project Zero, Harvard Graduate School of Education, in partnership with the Reggio Emilia Approach.

2 Gebrüder Blattschuß, 1978.

3 The Sutton Trust is an educational charity in the United Kingdom which aims to improve social mobility and address educational disadvantage. The charity was set up by educational philanthropist Sir Peter Lampl in 1997.

4 *The Italian Tribune* – The Premier Italian American Newspaper.

5 Organisation for Economic Co-operation and Development (OECD) Education 2030 Strategy: *The Future We Want.*

CHAPTER

3

Thoughts about schooling and education

leren [ˈlerə(n)][1]
[verb]

learn [verb] to gain knowledge or skill (in)
teach [verb] to give knowledge, skill, or wisdom to a person; to instruct or train (a person)

I have said it before, and I will say it again: The greatest challenge we face every day is to do the right thing for every child. It is this lottery of inequality from birth that it is so hard to apply fairness to, especially in education systems that appear obsessed with maintaining the status quo, mass approaches, and where there is little room for knowing the individual and what makes them tick. Differentiation and personalisation, more often than not, are well-intended tokenisms. The truth is that it is not just the responsibility of education systems to ensure every child has the best start in life and has the ability to write their own narrative of the possible. Remember, "every child is everyone's responsibility,"[2] a quote which will be visited again and again.

The Dutch word *leren* at the top of this page sets the tone for the conversation I would like to have in this chapter. There is something almost educationally romantic about having the same word for learning and teaching, in a wishful-thinking kind of way. However, in our real world, learning, being taught, and teaching, alongside education and schooling, are, in fact, very different things, albeit they are, of course, connected. What connects them more than anything is the learner.

There is an interesting debate to be had on the distinction and connection between education and schooling. While some might perceive them as synonymous, a glance at the dictionary reveals that no two words truly share the exact same meaning. *Education* and *schooling* are further apart than the letters *E* and *S* in the dictionary. It is essential to keep reminding ourselves that schooling serves as a tool to facilitate and empower a better (self-)education. They are not one and the same thing. Schooling serves the greater good: education.

So *education* and *schooling*, though often used interchangeably, are not synonymous – they are not one and the same thing. *Schooling* refers to the formal instruction and learning that takes place within an institution, in classrooms, for example, with structured curricula and trained teachers. It provides a foundational framework for acquiring mostly knowledge and also skills in various subjects. On the other hand, *education* extends beyond the confines of schooling and encompasses a lifelong process of learning, growth, and development. It involves acquiring knowledge, understanding, and wisdom through diverse experiences, interactions, and self-directed exploration. While schooling plays a crucial role in providing a structured environment and key knowledge, education continues throughout our lives, extending beyond the confines of traditional institutions, and allows for continuous personal and intellectual growth. It is through education, rather than just schooling, that individuals can become truly well-educated, possessing a deep understanding and the ability to apply knowledge in various real-life contexts, 0 to 99.

How, then, do you gauge whether someone is educated or not? As we know, in many parts of the world, the answer relates to the level of formal qualifications people achieve through schooling when they are young. Did they get top grades at school or college? Private or state? Do they have a university degree? From which university? In what subject, and at what level? This appeals to the sense that education is something earned and to the belief that schools and universities have the authority to say who is (and who is not) educated, for better or for worse. It is also how economists and social scientists define someone's education level and link that to what their social and economic outcomes might be later in life.

We know, however, that people can work on their educational status throughout life, and that much of the work of being educated is only indirectly tied to the schooling experience. Policymakers miss this point. They assume that formal qualifications attained through schooling are the best measure of educational status. They do not recognise the difference or the relationship between education and schooling. "Being educated" is not just about the credentials you have; it is much more about how these are applied and used continually, further developed, and adapted, and how others credential you. At times, so-called self-made people who have become very successful (this often equals *wealthy* in this instance) are seen to be in this category – Sir Richard Branson, to name but one example. Often, they live by statements such as "School did nothing for me," which is, of course, wrong. They applied and used the credentials they had differently.

My eldest daughter, Anna, is now a senior account director at the global public relations consultancy firm Edelman. Including internships, this is her 14th different job across eight companies in the PR world – all her choice, all her making, over a period of some ten years. She has enjoyed, learned her lessons, changed her mind, applied everything she has experienced, become wiser, and she finds herself on a path towards where her head and her heart want her to be. That path, by the way, has shown her that there are no straight lines. Anna was well-schooled and "well-universitied," but it has been, amongst other contributory factors, her appliance of the science of being schooled that has made her into the well-educated person she has become. "Education is not preparation for life; education is life itself," so the American philosopher, psychologist, and educational reformer John Dewey said. Anna is one small example that proves Dewey's point.

I am often asked what I want for my own children from the schooling and education process. Remembering my grandad, I am certain happiness is, of course, the first answer. Naturally, as their parent, you want them to be successful – *successful* in the meaning that they manage to make their dreams come true, reach their aspirations, and fulfil their ambitions. That in itself, of course, is more than just academic. Again, my grandfather's affinity with happiness springs to mind. Kindness, naturally, makes an entrance here too. "Today you could be standing next to someone who is trying their best not to fall apart. Whatever you do today, do it with kindness in your heart," so said a placard outside Starbucks somewhere in the world during the pandemic of the early 2020s. I also want them to achieve what they deserve. All three of my children have been, and are, incredibly hard workers. Talent in itself is never enough, whether you are Johan Cruijff, Richard Burton, Ruby Turner, Shah Rukh Khan, Jacinda Arden, or Anna, Imogen, and Tom Graus. I have always given all three their "congratulations" and "well done" presents before their tests and examinations: There was nothing more I could have asked of them or they could have asked of themselves. Above all, however, I want my three children to be able to manage the unexpected items that appear in the bagging area of life – not in a reactive, negative way, but proactively and optimistically, knowing that they can do and also understanding that this is not always easy and, sometimes, not always possible. "I tried and failed. I tried again and again and succeeded."[3] And I want them to remain optimistic: "I believe in the sun, even when it rains."[4]

Schooling, in some shape or form, takes place over a defined period of time, in a defined space, according to defined agendas. Broadly speaking, approximately six hours per day, five days per week, 39 weeks per year, over some 12 years, if you are lucky. After that, you can go to college or university – big schools – or enter the world of work in some shape or form.

Worldwide, many governments have determined what it is that school-goers should be taught. This is often called something like a national curriculum. Governments have determined not only what should be taught but also when, where, how, and by whom. They seem to be increasingly less clear about the why. The accountability framework is mainly developed around the what, the when, the where, the how, and the by whom. National tests and examinations are put in place, attendance and exclusion targets introduced, inspection authorities and frameworks established, the teaching professions sidelined in the decision-making processes, and politicians put in charge who have no expertise and often little interest in children, their learning, and their futures. In England alone, for example, there have been ten secretaries of state for education between 2010 and 2023, none of them from an education background, and one even boasting that his wife is a teacher, as if that is a qualification in itself. One of my friends is a heart transplant surgeon; this does not qualify me in any shape or form to don a surgical gown or be let loose in a hospital with a scalpel. As far as the what and the how are concerned, I also remember well the introduction of the literacy hour in the late 1990s. It was so prescriptive that the end of each such hour had to be a plenary where primary school children would sit on the floor, facing forward. I had, and still have, images in my head of some 3.6 million primary-aged children in England being "plenaried" every morning at around ten o'clock – an exercise in North Korean–style diktat. Control of schooling is increasingly being centralised, marginalising the importance of context. It is also worth noting that in England, and elsewhere, almost none of this applies to independent schools. Clearly, socio-economically advantaged children are different and merit different treatment, according to the politics, anyway. In England, perhaps this is, in some way, related to the fact that the United Kingdom spends more financing inequality in favour of the rich than the rest of Europe, according to the Organisation for Economic Co-operation and Development's *Cost of Inequality 2023* report. Some 5.9 per cent of children in the United Kingdom go to private school, yet 48 per cent of all members of parliament and in excess of 65 per cent of the Sunak cabinet were privately educated. Just a thought.

In all this, trust plays a very important part. Trust between national and local government and teachers. Trust between children and teachers. Trust between teachers and parents and carers. Trust between and within the professions. An erosion in professional trust plays its part here too. Teachers have merely become the means by which a national curriculum is delivered. We measure the outcomes of their efforts in grades, not in the passion, for example, they generate in the learners. Meneer Beurskens, my favourite teacher, would now be measured only by my German grades, not by the fact that he changed my life.

"Trust the children as much as they trust us" is the leitmotif of my dear friend Carla Rinaldi, president of the Fondazione Reggio Children, primus inter pares in the global early years education community.

We have a confusing relationship with our children, in our families and beyond. We "love them to bits" but, at the same time, express views that "children are there to be seen and not heard." We speak of a "children's voice" but, more often than not, treat this as no more than tokenism. In the world of commerce and business, children are both a potentially lucrative consumer and difficult to reach. At the same time, elsewhere in the world, 16-year-olds have the right, and the responsibility, to vote in elections.

Perhaps we should look at our children and young people differently, through a different lens. Should we not see them as holders of rights, as competent citizens from the earliest of ages? The child is not a citizen of the future, as we so often see it, but a citizen from the very first moment of life, beginning to write her or his narrative of the possible. The family unit, in its widest sense, is the soil in which the seedling grows and flourishes; society's responsibility is to ensure both protection and nourishment where these might not be in ample supply.

Childhood, we know, is a cultural interpretation and construct. Every society, and every historical period, defines its own childhood. Is it not time to re-imagine childhood for our time, our world? Do we not need to make children visible deliberately and purposefully in our societies, and globally, as an active force for good? And not merely see them as junior apprentices or as merely a mini consumer to be reached? Should we not strive to see the child as an equal member of both family and society, an influencer often being their voice and their conscience?

In our ever-developing relationship with our children, nothing is more important than our interpretation, construct, and joint ownership of trust.

To be truthful, schooling in the United Kingdom, and in other countries too, has not been effective for everyone for a very long time, if ever; in England specifically, this can be observed clearly since the 1944 Education Act. That is a stark reality, despite all the political rhetoric. It is also true that politicians with various affiliations have often chosen to defend their policies or interventions without ever pausing to ask, "Why isn't this working?" At the same time, there has been a growing divide between politicians, so-called special advisers and civil servants on one side, and experts and professionals on the other. The political modus operandi has also been affected by a lack of trust: Local delivery through democratically elected local authorities has been systematically dismantled and replaced by a centrally controlled approach through quangos; this is politics, not education.

As far as I am aware, during my four decades or so of work, in England, there has been only one secretary of state for education who had substantial teaching experience. Estelle Morris, now Baroness Morris of Yardley, stands out as the secretary of state who had been a teacher – a telling indicator. This raises the question: Should a secretary of state possess that kind of first-hand knowledge? In my view, the answer is a resounding "yes." This principle applies not only to education but also to healthcare and other critically important domains. To lead, as opposed to just manage, effectively, one must understand the essence of the field, have walked in the shoes of those involved, and truly grasp the intricacies involved. How about a secretary of state who was a student, is a parent and a teacher, a headteacher even? Preferably even with a broad contextual baseline, including socio-economically? How about a secretary of state for education who actually wants the job, as opposed to seeing the job as a stepping stone to something bigger? As if there is anything more important than the future of our young people. And if none can be found? Appoint a respected specialist, an expert, who can act on the government's behalf. Trust if you dare.

At some point in the 1980s, it became painfully clear that our education system was increasingly not up to par. The world was rapidly changing, yet there was an old, multi-tiered, messy system that was increasingly not serving all our children effectively. That conclusion, with the benefit of hindsight, was spot on. There were also too many schools not achieving the results they should have, even when considering their unique contexts. Blaming it all on resource limitations would not be accurate. Neither was it all the teachers' fault, or the local authorities', or the government's, for that matter. Something deeper was amiss. Instead of pointing fingers, the focus should have been on finding solutions by consensus to serve the children. What we ended up with turned out to be very different.

In response, the government of prime minister Margaret Thatcher determined that it needed more control over schools and what was going on inside them. Local authorities were often labelled as the primary culprits, followed closely by the teaching profession itself. If truth be told, of course everyone bore a responsibility to varying degrees. The government introduced, through the Education Reform Act of 1988, a national curriculum, with the aim of standardising what every child should be taught. Not only were the same subjects mandatory for all but also the content within those subjects. Uniformity increasingly ruled: the curriculum, the programmes of study, the schemes of work, and inevitably, to a degree, the lesson plans. National tests, league tables, and a national inspection framework would follow later, to complete the set. In 1986, the government had already replaced the General Certificate of Education "O" Level and Certificate of Secondary Education with a single General Certificate of Secondary Education (GCSE).

Like many in the late 1980s, I thought the introduction of a national curriculum with a more standardised approach made sense. The subjects that were already being taught mostly ended up as part of the national curriculum, and the content of those subjects itself was developed through a number of working groups. These, in turn, consisted of a broad representation of experts, from university vice-chancellors and Her Majesty's inspectors to examination board representatives, primary curriculum area leads, and heads of department of secondary schools, who made what were, in essence, age-appropriate content recommendations. Mostly, these were accepted and could be found back in the actual published programmes of study and subsequent schemes of work.

While still at Taverham High School in Norwich, I had also started teaching Dutch classes at undergraduate level at the University of East Anglia. One thing led to another, and before I knew it, I was the Southern Examining Group's chief examiner for Dutch IGCSE, which I continued after I had moved to my new school in Hull. To this day, I have no real idea how all this happened, and I can only conclude that there must have been a national shortage of suitable, qualified Dutch-speaking candidates. It came as an even greater surprise to me when I was approached to join the National Curriculum Working Group on Modern Foreign Languages as the representative for Dutch. There were, at that time, 19 modern foreign languages on the statutory orders and each language as such was represented – these included Arabic, Bengali, Chinese, Danish, French, German, modern Greek, Gujarati, modern Hebrew, Hindi, Italian, Japanese, Panjabi, Portuguese, Russian, Spanish, Turkish, Urdu, and of course, Dutch.

What was taught in modern foreign languages before the national curriculum, in essence, was the subject's examination syllabus in the final two years of secondary school and a coursebook, which was followed in the first three years. In my case, this was Deutsch Heute – eins, zwei, and drei. The focus was entirely on the content and, as such, covered the what and the by and for who; the when and where were determined by the timetable of the school. Knowledge before understanding. The why did not really come into question. That was left to the teachers. Luck of the draw as far as the children were concerned. I remember, years later, speaking at a National Union of Teachers conference at Stoke Rochford Hall near Grantham, where I touched on the pre–national curriculum era of my working life. One member of the audience offered, "Those were the good old days." But they weren't. What the children experienced was far too often too hit and miss, too inconsistent, too varied in standards, too loose, and too much of a lottery.

The new national curriculum, its standardisation, programmes of study, schemes of work, and subsequent lesson plans, initially turned out to be more than helpful. In fact, for modern languages teachers, it turned out to be a blessing. In 1988, with the introduction of the national curriculum, the government of the day also made it mandatory for all secondary-aged children to learn a modern foreign language. This was something completely new and unexpected from a Conservative government that appeared much better at picking fights with neighbouring countries than encouraging the acquisition of their languages. It was absolutely the right thing to do. In an age of Europeanisation and, indeed, globalisation, the move was of its time and important. Amongst modern foreign languages teachers, there was a real enthusiasm for this policy, and almost all of us supported it.

The modern-foreign-languages-for-all policy added weight to the why answer. The what, when, where, and who were already set. This time it was the how that caused the headaches. It turned out, there was not just the how, as in "how to teach." There was another how. It was the how to teach children we have never taught before. Traditionally, modern foreign languages was a subject that was studied by the top 25 per cent or so of children in secondary schools, whatever that "top" meant. It was an elitist subject, studied on the basis of no prior experience, achievement, or attainment, but on a judgement about a child's overall ability – being in the top set in maths often meant that a child was judged to be capable of studying German, French, or Spanish. Now this was all about to change. From one day to the next, as teachers of modern foreign languages, we were confronted with the reality of teaching children (1) we had never engaged with before, (2) who had never engaged with the subject and with us, and (3) who all too often did not want to be there, no doubt in great measure because of the former two reasons. The answer to this particular how question did not lie in the national curriculum, in the programmes of study, in the schemes of work, or indeed, in the lesson plans, but instead with my colleagues in other subject areas. The members of my modern languages faculty at Winifred Holtby School in Hull and I spent many an hour observing teaching and learning in English, mathematics, the sciences, the arts, physical education, and I shall be forever grateful for witnessing the masterclasses that enabled us to become better teachers. Not better teachers of the subject, but better teachers of children.

As is so often the case, when new policies are launched, projects are started, programs are developed and implemented with the best of intentions, the one thing that gets forgotten, or ignored, is the continued professional development of teachers. It is almost as if teachers are taken for granted and assumptions rule. Policymakers and governments need to understand that in order to keep raising the quality of education, providing a continuous, high-level investment in the quality of teaching and the creativity of teachers is a must. This applies, of course, to the introduction of the national curriculum in 1988, of which the modern-foreign-languages-for-all policy was a part, many initiatives before that, and since. Nationally, we have seen the introduction of the Curriculum for Excellence in Scotland, which is now struggling because of the lack of consideration for generous continuous professional development. Internationally, the National Education Plan in India, such an admirable and exciting attempt to put things right and move education well into the 21st century in that country, is in danger of suffering the same fate. On the horizon, there is the introduction of artificial intelligence into schools. Already it is clear that the investment in the development of our teaching professions will not match the potential of the technology. It is also important to stress that short-termism and sticking plasters are not a solution. Every time we see these important developments, we need to immediately ask ourselves: What does this mean for the teaching professions, and who will our teachers be? It pays to research and discover what happens elsewhere. In Australia, paid or part-paid sabbatical leave for teachers and non-teaching staff to develop new skills, conduct educational research, study for a new qualification, or travel abroad is relatively commonplace, after a number of years of service. Some independent schools in the United Kingdom are exploring options like this as a means to upskill and retain their teachers. The benefits of schemes like these are manifold, for the individual, for the schools, and of course, for the children. There is an argument to formalise this kind of thinking and, in doing so, to be courageous and pursue a long-term vision – to offer all children the very best schooling and education by empowering the teaching professions to be their best. I believe that the terms and conditions of employment of both teaching and non-teaching classroom professions should change to a 4 + 1 formula – for every four days teachers and non-teaching classroom colleagues apply their trade, they should have one-day preparation, evaluation, upskilling, and development time. This time should benefit the individual professionals, the school, and most importantly, the children. This is also how impact should be measured, focused on the development and the competences of the children – no more just teach-and-test. Because we should want the very best for our young people. Pie in the sky? I would rather have pie in the sky than no pie at all. Unaffordable? Firstly, that is a matter of priorities. If, as a society, we want the best, we have to pay for the best. Secondly, and commonly, the thoughts around affordability of public services are a result of our obsession with low taxation. We can't have the highest schooling quality for our children paid for by the lowest taxation levels – the calculator does not work that way. And thirdly, the pandemic of the early 2020s surely taught us that nothing is unaffordable if it is important. In addition to exploring teachers' terms and conditions of employment, I would advocate, for example, in the use of technology, that we should very seriously look at remunerating our older students to support the learning of the younger ones. My 18-year-old daughter will forever be better at TikTok, BeReal, Instagram, iPhones, iPads, et al. than her teachers. They, in turn, can then forever excel at content creation, continuous assessment, awe and wonder, and of course, safeguarding. As the world around us evolves, so should our thinking about education, schooling, teachers, and learners.

What has happened since the introduction of the national curriculum in England all those years ago can, in my view, unfortunately best be summarised as follows: further centralised control linked to a teach-and-test culture within an accountability framework that includes school league tables based upon testing what the government wants children to be taught. The creation of league tables ranked schools based on a one-size-fits-all model, devoid of context. These tables only provided a partial picture, missing the nuances of each school's unique circumstances. In football terms, this is akin to placing the old Macclesfield Town side by side with Manchester United without Financial Fair Play Regulations and pretending they are equals. Living a lie in other words – context ignored. All this is linked to and further controlled by the introduction of a national inspection framework led by the Office for Standards in Education, Ofsted. The system, over time, has been politicised, with little regard for the individual child and her or his future and for the teaching professions and their well-being. The latter is, of course, exemplified by the tragic suicide of primary school headteacher Ruth Perry in 2023. The coroner concluded that her school's Ofsted inspection "likely contributed"[5] to her death. None of it all makes a real difference to the lives of children, especially those who live in circumstances where they are up against it. All the so-called evidence that suggests it does is not really independent, and that particular song is sung loudest by those who have held the position of Her or His Majesties' chief inspector. Key appointments of positions that were there to safeguard independence, neutrality, and fairness became political, invariably supporting the governments of the day in their wishes. Ofsted itself is like using polaroid photographs to look at A and B, instead of a sophisticated satellite navigation that gets children to better places in life. A friend of mine compared Ofsted to a seagull: "They swoop in, shit on you, and swoop out again." *Outstanding* means "outstandingly compliant." We can have extensive conversations about schooling and education without mentioning the word *child* once. The accountability seems to have shifted from serving the people it was meant to help to serving the system itself.

As for the national curriculum in England, there has been little or no relevant change, and it has most certainly not moved enough with the changing times. Political tinkering has, of course, taken place by a succession of governments, including in my own subject. One year, modern foreign languages was compulsory for all; the next we were even debating an introduction into the primary phase. Soon thereafter, the whole thing became optional, a decision not driven by vision or conviction but by supply and demand and by economics. This crude political behaviour somehow always takes me back to this quote from the 1989 film *Dead Poets Society*, by the leading character John Keating, played by the incomparable Robin Williams:

> We don't read and write poetry because it's cute. We read and write poetry because we are members of the human race. And the human race is filled with passion. And medicine, law, business, engineering, these are noble pursuits and necessary to sustain life. But poetry, beauty, romance, love, these are what we stay alive for.

Languages were my love, my beauty, my poetry.

It puzzles me to this day that internationally so many schools are still looking at aspects of the English education system as the holy grail, including the national curriculum, examinations, and Ofsted. When it comes to schooling, they look at the independent sector with all its privileges, including exemptions from the national curriculum and the Office for Standards in Education. Hype over substance, and as such, what I can only describe as educational colonialism continues. It is time for those governments and schools to think of themselves as more visionary, more value-driven, more principled, more of these times, and most importantly, more child-focused. From there, change for good will flow. The new National Education Plan in India and the potential of the Knowledge and Human Development Authority (KHDA) in Dubai are evidence of this. As is the Beaconhouse School System in Pakistan, whose advisory council I am privileged to chair. The Beaconhouse School System has risen from its modest beginnings in 1975 as Les Anges Montessori Academy to become a major force in the education world. The Beaconhouse group has over 315,000 full-time students and is possibly the largest school network of its kind in the world, with an ever-expanding base already established in Malaysia, the Philippines, the United Arab Emirates, Oman, Thailand, and Pakistan itself, of course. Beaconhouse has grown into an international network of private schools, imparting distinctive and meaningful learning to students all the way from birth to postgraduation through Concordia Colleges and the Beaconhouse National University. Its role in and influence on the overall education provision in Pakistan cannot be underestimated. The Beaconhouse of today is thus much more than just a stand-alone school. Across its network, it caters to the education and training needs of a large and diverse group of individuals of varying ages, socio-economic backgrounds, and nationalities. It has become an international force for good.

In accountability terms, globally, governments' schooling key performance indicators tend to follow four- of five-year election cycles as opposed to the cycle that is the 12 or so years that individual children are schooled. The experience of my youngest daughter, Imogen, over a 14-year period, including her A-level years, has contained four general elections, five prime ministers, and the aforementioned ten secretaries of state. The accountability, in broad terms, is to the system, not to the children, and a long-term vision is so obviously lacking. The aim seems to be to top the annual international Programme for International Student Assessment (PISA) league table, without giving a thought to which way PISA is leaning. Governments that are in charge for, say, three parliamentary terms still only plan for three times four-year sessions as opposed to taking the longer-term 12-year view. In addition, it seems to me that in countries that, in democratic terms, constitute a two-party state, such as the United States and United Kingdom, there is historically and culturally a lack of compromise and consensus as to the future vision of schooling, as well as society as a whole. It is either-or. It is my way or no way. "There is no such thing as society,"[6] or there is. All this is, of course, ultimately to the detriment of children as citizens of those countries and of the world.

Schooling is, in fact, artificial. It is a narrow framework that has been designed around teaching rather than learning, operating only within certain times and places and to a particular methodology. And it is getting narrower. Schooling as we know it is also out of date, or at least past its best-by date. It has lost purpose and is increasingly struggling to provide answers to why questions. The connect between schooling and the real world is disappearing at an alarming rate, despite the fact that, in so many other ways, we are more connected than ever.

Wherever I travel in the world, I meet children and young people, and when I do, I always ask the one question: "Why do you go to school?" The answer, I would say, in at least 80 per cent of all cases is, "Because I have to." This is across the ages, across the genders, across the ethnicities, and across socio-economic contexts, in every country and every city, from the United Kingdom to the United States, from Mexico to Mumbai to Moscow. The answer is, of course, a sad answer. It is an answer without narrative, without purpose, without much of a future or hope, and without passion.

On a personal note, I can relate to this all too well. My primary school, Pius X Lagere School, in my hometown of Echt, was a good experience. My teachers knew me, and I liked them, especially Meneer Jutten and Meneer Vincken. The teaching itself seems, from memory, to have jelled with my curiosity and learning style, which was what we might now call experience-based. There was much exploration, contextualising, and purpose, just like there were many why answers and "for examples." There was a great deal of trust between the teachers and the learners.

One experience that stands out and has stayed with me all my life was a school visit to Rotterdam. I was 11 years old. In 1968, Rotterdam was a booming post–Second World War city. It was the home of Europoort, then the largest and busiest port in the world. It was also a city that had recovered from the bombings of the Second World War, when it was virtually razed to the ground, not least because of its geographical and industrial position and importance. We did, of course, travel past Ossip Zadkine's statue *De Verwoeste Stad*, The Destroyed City, which so poignantly reminded us of the events of some 28 years earlier. The 6.5-meter-high sculpture depicts a stylised human figure leaning against a tree stump. The figure holds both hands aloft, with its head thrown back, as if crying in grief, and a gaping hole in its chest and abdomen. The absence of a heart is said to symbolise the destruction of the centre of Rotterdam. My school visit to Rotterdam was history, geography, and human.

Standing at Rotterdam Centraal Station, examining the departure boards with all the far-flung destinations where both passenger and mainly goods trains would travel, was an experience that filled me with awe and wonder. We must remember that this was in the day when travelling far was not yet the norm, and when the Iron Curtain provided a barrier beyond which imagination struggled. Nevertheless, there, on this departure board, were these names, from memory: Berlin, Warsaw, Moscow, as well as, of course, Brussels, Paris, Rome, and many more. A curious 11-year-old boy's dream. I wasn't to know then that only 12 years later, as a student of German language and literature, I would, between Kassel in West Germany and Erfurt in East Germany, cross that very same Iron Curtain into the then German Democratic Republic to study at the Pädagogische Hochschule Dr Theodor Neubauer in Erfurt Mühlhausen and meet one of my all-time literary heroes, the East German novelist and essayist Christa Wolf.

Later that evening, after arriving back in Echt, I remember so clearly getting back home and going up to my room to find my school atlas. In it I found and marked all the places I had seen on those departure boards at Rotterdam Centraal Station. Over time, I marked many other places – places I, for some reason, liked the sound of, like Shanghai, or places whose names I had read about or had seen on television, like Cairo, São Paulo, and Venice. *De Grote Bosatlas* was my equivalent to Alice in Wonderland's wardrobe. I still have that atlas somewhere, in my attic. In the many years since that school visit to Rotterdam, I have had the pleasure and the privilege to travel to many countries, 64 at the latest count, and work in over 40 of those. In 2023, I had to renew my passport because there was no more room for stamps. I have been lucky. I have promised myself that when I eventually retire, whenever that may be, I will find my old atlas and compare the marks I made in it all those years ago with the stamps in my passports.

I believe that my curiosity related to all things travel was fed during that school trip to Rotterdam. I also believe that my interest in places, their histories and cultures, and their people, of course, is related to that visit. I know that from then onwards, human geography and history became two of my favourite subjects of study. They still are. Connect. Extend. Challenge. My youngest daughter is about to embark on her university studies: Spanish and Italian at Oxford University. She and I agree that the spirit of Rotterdam lives on.

Of course, not everything in primary school was plain sailing. In my last but one year, my report card read 5 out of 10 when it came to my behaviour – apparently, I talked too much in class. I remember the disappointment I felt – as a pleaser, I had let my teacher down. My parents subsequently exercised more of their hands-on approach. The disappointment, however, outweighed the physical pain.

Religious instruction was a subject delivered by the local Roman Catholic priest. The Bible and the Roman Catholic catechism ruled. As a primary-aged child, I liked the stories from the *Old Testament*, but in the same way that I liked Jacob and Wilhelm Grimm's *Children's and Household Tales*. Wonderful, scary, a little unbelievable, and constantly making me question.

Despite the omnipresence of the Roman Catholic Church in all aspects of life, from quite an early age, I really could not get on with the God thing. As a child, I could never understand why, if God were so almighty and so brilliant and kind, the world was in such a mess. Why did so many people die in the Second World War, including those from Echt? Why the famine in Bangladesh? The war in Vietnam and that image of a 9-year-old Phan Thi Kim Phuc? I could also not understand why questioning was a sin. Then, when I was 12, after my grandad died, I lost what little belief I still had.

The story of Adam and Eve is wonderful; it intrigued me. It is a good story, scary in parts – I don't like snakes – but it was also contrary to many of the things I had learned. "There were Adam and Eve and their two sons, Cain and Abel," said the priest. "And that is where we all come from." When I politely questioned this, which presumably was interpreted as a matter of morality and ethics, all hell was let loose. More of my parents' hands-on approach followed. This time, however, there was anger. From then on, God and I definitely started heading in different directions. Although I sometimes count myself lucky that it was not Noah's ark we were studying – the inclusion of animals could have been the end of me.

The move to my secondary school, the Bisschoppelijk College Echt, was an experience that, for me, in many ways, left a great deal to be desired. With the benefit of hindsight, I think that perhaps I was not yet ready to move on. Why do all children of a certain age make this move at the same time? The contrast with my primary school was painfully big. Many different subjects taught by many different teachers. My world felt compartmentalised, each compartment with slightly different norms and expectations. The consistency had gone, as had, to a significant degree, the personal touch. More of my father's bullying to boot. Connect. Extend. Challenge. Hard to come by. Except for three subjects, three connections with the real world, and of course, three brilliant teachers: German, English, and slightly strangely, history.

Connect. Extend. Challenge. In history, this was the teacher, Meneer Mersch. His approach was to start in the present and, from there, like a history version of Agatha Christie's Hercule Poirot, to find your way back to origins and culprits. It was all slightly strange, unusual. Meneer Mersch was Belgian, like Poirot. He took us from the 1973 front pages of *De Volkskrant* or *De Telegraaf* about the oil crisis and car-free Sundays back to the British Empire and the Middle East, or from Leonid Ilyich Brezhnev to Karl Marx, Friedrich Engels,

Das Kapital, and the slums of the city of Manchester. I love detective stories, and I love being part of the investigation. To this day, I cannot resist Marple, Morse, or Brunetti. Meneer Mersch made us detectives.

German and English were my favourite subjects.

Every Thursday after school, I would cycle to the local record shop, Goossens, to pick up a copy of next week's top 30, alongside a copy of the popular music magazine *Muziek Express*. The magazine published, amongst pop news and gossip, the latest hit parade lyrics. "Where have you gone, Joe DiMaggio? Our nation turns its lonely eyes to you."[7] Lyrics were learned off by heart in bedrooms all over the country. "Mrs. Robinson" became my favourite song. Others turned to "(Sittin' on) The Dock of the Bay," "Hey Jude," "Those Were the Days," or "Born to Be Wild." But much more happened. Who is this Joe DiMaggio? He was married to Marilyn Monroe. She was in *Some Like It Hot*. Which album is "Mrs. Robinson" on? *Bookends*? What does that mean? Where are Simon and Garfunkel from? New York? They were originally called Tom and Jerry. After the cartoon? What else have they written? And so it goes. Curiosity has never killed a cat. Many years later, I applied this lesson learned to my teaching, at Taverham High School and elsewhere. But this time in German. The effect was not quite the same, of course. English-language music is a worldwide phenomenon transcending borders, whereas German-language music is much more geographically restricted. However, for some of the young people I worked with, German singer and musician Herbert Grönemeyer's "Bochum" became their version of my "Mrs. Robinson."

Every weekend, I and countless others would listen to that week's top 30 presented by Felix Meurders on radio Hilversum 3, record the songs as well as possible on a reel-to-reel tape recorder (it was so annoying when Felix started to speak before the end of the song), and check how well we had learned the lyrics of by heart. English was cool. "What's that you say, Mrs. Robinson?"[2]

In addition, in the Netherlands, many television programs were of English or American origin and were subtitled in Dutch. The same applied to the cinema. Invariably, and mostly unintentionally, you picked up bits and pieces of the language and, indeed, the accents. From Bud Spencer and Terence Hill, Bonanza, and Batman, Flipper, Mr Ed the Talking Horse, the Flying Nun, and Ivanhoe, to the BBC News and, of course, Coronation Street. English was cool, indeed.

Unlike with history, the why answer with English did not come out of school. It lived in the real world. My English teachers saw this and used it, brilliantly. Especially Meneer Heijnen. Somehow, over time, he made the journey from the top 30 and the *Muziek Express*, to Graham Greene's *The Quiet American*, via Bob Dylan, Joan Baez, Vietnam, Woodstock, and protest songs seem like common sense and the most natural thing to do. I saw the purpose, got the point, and was hooked. I still am.

German was different yet again. More immediate and more intense. Almost natural. The vicinity of my growing up, my dialect, everyday life, cycling to visit my relatives across the border in Breberen or Saeffelen. My mother and her mother spoke better German than Dutch. On my father's side, there was a German-born grandmother and her brother, Onkel Karl. I understood and could confidently speak the language from a very early age. I understood the why too.

Before the top 30 and the *Muziek Express*, there was Heintje Simons. Heintje was born the son of a coal miner who had to retire because of silicosis, reducing the family to near poverty. The family opened a small café, where Heintje used to sing along with the jukebox, a sort of early karaoke. When he was 11, he entered a local singing contest. He beat 30 competitors to win the contest. Producer Addy Kleijngeld heard about him and went to audition him at his home. After hearing only a few notes, he took him on as a client and became his manager. What a story! Heintje became famous as a child singer, with hit song "Mama" (written by Cesare Andrea Bixio, Bruno Cherubini, and Bruno Balz), and as a child actor, with his appearances in numerous German films in the 1960s and early 1970s. The *Frankfurter Allgemeine Zeitung* said of him, "No one is bigger in German show business." His 1967 recording of "Mama" sold over 1 million copies and was awarded a gold record. The following year, his debut album, *Heintje*, went on to sell over 2 million copies, resulting in a platinum record award. His sales in 1968 and 1969 alone totalled over 10 million. To cap it all, Heintje Simons was from Bleijerheide near Kerkrade, 30 minutes from where I lived; he spoke my dialect and was just about two years older than me. Heintje to me was one of us. What was not to love about Heintje, the boy who sang in German? I have a vivid memory of me sitting on a Vadah bus, travelling to my grandparents on my mother's side, singing to Heintje's songs to myself. "Heidschi Bumbeidschi" was my favourite, completely in a world of my own. As I got off the bus in Koningsbosch, to be met by my grandfather, everyone on the bus applauded. What was not to love about Heintje Simons? And so German was cool first.

Initially, at secondary school, I struggled with German. I was much better and more confident than the teachers recognised. Teaching was to the middle, from the book, and took no account of the qualities individual learners brought to the table. It was boring. And I rebelled. As a consequence, I was sent out of lessons regularly but, no doubt to my teachers' annoyance, still got full marks in tests. Those teachers in my early years at secondary school put me off my favourite subject because they never made the effort to get to know me and personalise what they were doing accordingly. Looking back, with the benefit of hindsight, I think they were lazy. And at the very point where I was about to switch off completely, Meneer Beurskens happened, gave me a book, and introduced me to Heinrich Böll. The rest is history, and I became a German teacher because of him. More than 50 years later, he is still with me. "If you are a teacher, 50 years from now someone will mention your name. Just let that sink in."[8]

Maths could have been another favourite, but it was not. Living where I did at that time, so close to the Belgian and German borders, real or applied maths was part of everyday life. In Maastricht, for example, were waiters serving drinks and food at the Vrijthof carrying at least three purses: one with Dutch guilders, one with Belgian francs, one with German marks, and often there was a fourth with British pounds sterling because of the many British Armed Forces bases in the region. The same skills were part of the life of everybody else who nipped across the border for petrol, daily shopping, or for any other reason. The purpose for maths was there for all to see.

"Pythagoras in boots" was how Johan Cruijff was described by David Winner, author of *Brilliant Orange – the neurotic genius of Dutch football*. I adored Johan Cruijff, wanted to be like him. I would have happily spent my days learning about Pythagoras, triangles, turns, and total football. Instead, my maths lessons consisted of "If A is 2, and B is 3, what is C?" I didn't care. I didn't understand the question. And I certainly didn't know what use this might be to me, ever. Connect. Extend. Challenge. Absent without leave. Real maths was a thing of the future.

Many years later, my then 11-year-old daughter, Imogen, visited KidZania London for the first time with two of her friends. When children have checked into a KidZania, they receive a boarding pass to take them into the city built for children. They also receive 50 KidZos each, the KidZanian currency. Once inside, children can open a bank account and receive a KidZania bankcard. In order to open such a bank account, the children have to work and earn first, as 100 KidZos are required for the bank to agree on the account with the child. The aim is for children to experience for themselves the culture of work, earn, save, and spend. Except, of course, that children are champion at beating the system. Creativity and innovation reign. I discovered much later that my daughter and her two friends essentially broke the bank. That went something like this: Two of the girls would give their 50 KidZos each, received on entry, to the third girl, who, in turn, would go and open her bank account. She would then withdraw 100 KidZos and give these to the second girl, who would open her bank account, withdraw 100 KidZos, and give these to the third girl, who would also open her bank account. Three bank accounts opened. No work-and-earn. Real maths.

My chemistry at school is a vague memory of periodic tables. My music was a catalogue of listening to Emerson, Lake, and Palmer's *Pictures at an Exhibition* and writing down what we felt. In geography, my atlas became a collection of names to be learned by heart, as opposed to a book of dreams.

These experiences, good and bad, stayed with me and influenced me much later in life, when I was the teacher. German exchanges and longer-term work experience stays, day trips, and other visits, the planning of these involving the young people and their families, all became a part of me, the teacher. "For example" became the most important two words of my teaching; they are the start of stories that give context to abstracts and make learning visible.

The former mining town of Mechernich is located in the district of Euskirchen in the south of the state of North Rhine-Westphalia, Germany. It is located in the Naturpark Nordeifel in the Eifel hills, approximately 55 kilometres from Cologne. In 1983, this Germany was West Germany. The Städtisches Gymnasium Mechernich, now Gymnasium Am Turmhof, was, and still is, the partner school of Taverham High School. In 1983, that partnership was just 1 year old. The key drivers of the partnership in Mechernich were English teacher Franz Josef Hilger and his religious studies colleague Ulla Henk. At the Taverham end, it became me.

In the early 1980s, many schools organised day trips to Boulogne or Calais if they taught French. Exchanges, staying in families, were rarer. German was very much a distant second when it came to studying modern foreign languages. Visits to and school partnerships with Germany were also trickier: It was further away, at a time when flying was still not the norm and mostly far too expensive.

Very often, school visits to the European continent were seen as a little bit of a jolly, an end-of-term, or even end-of-year, outing. It struck me very early on that there was far more potential in school partnerships and subsequent friendships between young people. From my personal experience, this could be a very important answer to many children's why questions.

My first exchange visit to Mechernich was in the summer term of 1984, when some 20 Taverham High School young people joined me on the ferry from Harwich to Hoek van Holland, and then a train journey to Cologne, where we were met by my German colleagues. The short coach journey to Mechernich ended in the school car park, where our young people were greeted by their German friends and their families.

There was an extensive program, including visits to Cologne and Aachen, the local open-air museum in Kommern, and participation in lessons in school. The return visit to Norwich in the autumn of 1984 was similar: a visit to London, a guided tour of Norwich, roller skating in Bury St Edmunds, and a visit to the Rowntree Mackintosh factory, with free chocolate thrown in to boot and, again, lessons at the school.

It was clear to me, however, that we could do better and provide more purpose and better answers to the why question. The solution would lie in the person-to-person connection and the actual visits being an important part of this relationship, but not the be-all and end-all.

Letter- and postcard-writing became part of the curriculum menu, based on knowing our friends better. From birthdays to hobbies, from pets to family members and other friends, from favourite subjects to favourite teachers, everything was thrown into the mix to make the pairings better and more purposeful. The planning for the visits involved the young people and their families, as well as other members of the Taverham High School community. It was ongoing.

The result was that, within a few years, the numbers would rise to 50 participants or more from each school annually, staying for two weeks in families in Mechernich and Taverham. We were also flying – with Virgin from London Stansted to Maastricht, and then onwards by coach to Mechernich – three countries in one morning. Visits for the English young people were moved to wintertime, during carnival week, when often there would also be snow. Carnival itself was a cultural experience, and sledging, tobogganing, skiing as well as skating, and hills, of course, were, for many of our Norfolk young people, something new. In 1986, we even took the Taverham High

School Sport Aid event to Germany and jointly raised funds for the Band Aid Trust. In school, special lessons would be planned, and at Taverham High School, that resulted in Shakespeare experiences by Richard Taylor, local geography by Paul Nevens, and local cookery by May Nay, drama by Colin Denn, religious studies by Lesley Milne, amongst many others. The exchanges had become part of the school culture, not just a modern languages jolly.

An almost-natural development followed. Young people from both Taverham and Mechernich started to ask whether they could visit each other during school holidays, especially in the summer. Family visits happened, and the Trimester Aufenthalte were born.

The age range for the exchanges was from 11 to 16. If, from about the age of 14, it became really clear that our young people were very committed to learning German, clearly enjoyed it, had aptitude, and maybe were even thinking about studying German post-16, the conversation was now heading towards longer-term stays. Similar conversations were developing in Mechernich. The year 1987 saw the first Trimester Aufenthalte – stays for up to a whole term. This included going to school, participating in lessons, catching up with work in other subjects, a programme of visits, and the ultimate test, work experience.

It goes without saying that competences in the use of the foreign language grew exponentially, as did the joy of learning. Even more importantly, the young people's confidence grew in equal measure. A good many of the participants in the exchanges and the longer-term stays ended up studying German or English post-16 and even into university. Most, of course, did not. They took their experiences and their enhanced confidence with them into the rest of their lives. The purpose of these experiences is, of course, not to serve the subject, but always to serve the young people. Personally, I am still in touch with a good number of the now not-so-young people, both English and German, and indeed with my teaching colleagues. A life reward in itself. An unexpected long-term outcome of this approach was that, many years later, during a conference in Kuala Lumpur in Malaysia, my all-time favourite pupil professed that he had become a teacher because of me, amongst a few of my Taverham High School colleagues. I had become to James Neill what Meneer Beurskens was to me. "If you are a teacher, 50 years from now someone will mention your name. Just let that sink in."

There are times when I wish I were still organising exchanges now. One of the downsides of the project in the 1980s was that communication between the young people was both slow and expensive. Telephone calls between households could cost a small fortune and therefore could not be relied upon as a regular and frequent means of staying in touch. It had to be letters and postcards. Once the letter was written at either end and subsequently posted, it could take up to a week for it to arrive with its intended recipient. You then had to hope that he or she would reply as swiftly as possible, and even if that were the case, this could still take another week or so. It was a frequent observation by the young people that they had often forgotten after three weeks what they had written in the first place. Oh, how to run such a programme now, with emails, WhatsApp, Facebook, TikTok, Instagram, you name it, at your disposal. The potential for instant communication is phenomenal, and I am envious of those current teaching colleagues working with young people on this and in this way. Of course, as it was in the 1980s, safety always comes first. I do fear occasionally, however, that in the 2020s, the controlling nature of the system, the lack of trust, with an almost overemphasis on health and safety, is getting in the way of the opportunities, the quality of the experience, the fun of things. Perhaps in schools, in that respect, we need to begin to think about "wilding the tame"[9] a little.

Wilhelmus "Wim" Marinus Antonius Jansen was a Dutch professional football player and manager. As a midfielder or defender, he spent most of his career at Feyenoord Rotterdam, winning honours, including the European Cup, now Champions League, in 1970. He earned 65 international cups with the Dutch national team and played in the teams that reached the 1974 and 1978 FIFA World Cup finals. Wim Jansen was also one of Johan Cruijff's big football friends. In his biography, *Wim Jansen: Meesterbrein*, Yoeri van den Busken quotes Jansen, in conversation with Cruijff, reflecting on youth development:

> We learned to play football on the streets. There you learn what body control is. If you fell twice, you were in pain. That you had to avoid. You had to be cleverer, escape with the ball from bigger players. On today's beautiful pitches you are not troubled by this anymore. Therefore you don't develop that aspect naturally anymore and it has to be included somehow in training. . . . What we did on the streets, I call natural education. At Feijenoord, from the age of ten I received taught education. Nowadays, we must make sure that at the clubs is combine the natural and the taught [education]. The earlier we start with this, the better.

Jansen accepted this change as a result of progress and societal change. He never complained about it, as in proclaiming the good old days to be better, but he saw that the education of the young talent needed to be adapted according to the times. He saw that as natural progress. In our schooling system, we have never really made that adaptation. We have too often stuck with the good old days. Perhaps that is one of the reasons our schooling is struggling with progress and the introduction of new technologies, especially with trust related to children's independence in learning and their natural capability to educate themselves, to learn from experience.

I took the approach with me to my next job at Winifred Holtby School in Hull and beyond. It informed the basis of my work as education director in Wythenshawe in 1999 and as adviser for modern foreign languages in Manchester and Salford, including the introduction of French, German, Italian, and Spanish into primary schools in the early 1990s. The power of finding answers to why questions through experiences and personal connections can never be underestimated.

Education, in contrast to schooling, is not a boxed-off area that you dip in and out of when needed. Connect. Extend. Challenge. Education is the university of life, from the second you are born until you pass away. It is what you experience outside of any school – at home, at work, with your family and friends. It is the foundation of self and something so individual to each of us that it cannot be replicated from one person to the next. Education, in my mind, is very often where learning is made visible, where things become real, and where that reality itself has purpose.

"Whatever the question, education is always the answer."[10] I met Archbishop Desmond Tutu on 7th October 2016 at a beach restaurant overlooking Table Mountain in Cape Town, South Africa. It was his 86th birthday. I had been invited to join the family for a birthday lunch by Thandeka Tutu, the archbishop's and Auntie Leah's daughter and my friend. "Come to the annual birthday lecture," she said, "from wherever you are." I was in Abu Dhabi. Having missed my connection in Doha, I arrived in Cape Town somewhat deflated – I had missed the lecture. "It doesn't matter. Just freshen up and get a taxi to the On the Rocks restaurant in Blouberg, on the beach." So here I was. I had arrived at this restaurant, on the beach, overlooking Table Mountain. As I walked in, the empty chair was next to the "Arch." It was mine. We talked, and he laughed his laugh. I told him he was my hero. We shared fish and chips and vanilla ice cream.

When I asked him about the post-apartheid reconciliation process, which, at the request of his friend Nelson Mandela, he chaired, his answer was, "Whatever the question, education is always the answer." And when I asked him whether I could borrow that phrase, he said, "You can have it." Education is everything we do and everything we are.

There is no doubt in my mind that the better schooled we are, the greater our ability and opportunity to educate ourselves and to be educated. Yet we must always see schooling as a means to an end, not as the end itself. The former is life, the latter politics.

There is also no doubt in my mind that here is a point of equity and equality. I think it is fair to say that the more advantaged we are as children, the greater the chance of, in conventional terms, being successful at school. It is also fair to say that the less-advantaged we are, the greater the chances that in the schooling system we will be less successful in the same conventional terms. We must, at this point, also remember that being advantaged or disadvantaged is not the choice that children make. They are both the innocent bystanders and the victims of circumstance.

I play this game at conferences where I say to people, "I'm going to give you a word, and I want you to have two pictures in your head. One is a picture from the 1920s. And one is a picture from the 2020s." Do this now as you are reading. I say "aeroplane," and you think of that plane in the 1920s and that in the 2020s. You wouldn't get me in that plane from the 1920s if you paid me! I then repeat this with the words "car," "hospital," and "telephone." Over that 100-year period, they all look very different in your mind's eye, right? I then say "classroom." Apart from the number of children in there and the fact that there is now a whiteboard, rather than a blackboard, not much has changed. The children face the front, listening. The teacher is at the front, teaching. Hands still have to go up, permissions sought. Toilet visits still need to be asked for and are often frowned upon. Everything feels factory-like: controlled mass schooling for controlled mass employment.

The purpose of schooling in the 1920s, and for many years that followed, was to create a well-schooled workforce, not a well-educated society. It reminds me of a quote by my favourite comedian, the Glaswegian Billy Connolly, who said:

> At school I mainly watched pigeons screwing on the roof. I finished school when I was 14. The gates of the school opened, and

the gates of the Clyde shipyards opened at the same time. We automatically went from one into the other.

We are now in an age where there is no Industrial Revolution–style mass employment anymore, no need for that mass schooling. Much of our lives is personalised and will become so evermore. Our children will be all sorts of "entrepreneurs," from social entrepreneurs to business entrepreneurs, to personal entrepreneurs writing their own narratives of the possible. Yet we still teach, or governments would like us to teach, as if we were in the first, as opposed to the fifth, Industrial Revolution. In my mind appear more images of Pink Floyd and Alan Parker's *The Wall*. In England, in particular, since the academisation from 2010 onwards, this drive towards strict uniformity seems to be in vogue with the powers that be. It goes against everything else that goes on in our world, and especially in the increasingly personalised world of our children. As the late Sir Ken Robinson said, we "teach creativity out of children," and we do so with this archaic view of favouring being uniformly well-schooled over personally well-educated.

It was in my Children's University days that I visited a brand-new secondary school in the southeast of England, a so-called private finance initiative school. The architectural design of the school was clearly from a blueprint. It all looked very familiar. Brand-new, high fences, intercom systems to get in, and signage on the path that said, "Walk this way." Having walked that way, via at least two intercom buzzers, once inside, one would find an enormous reception space with a desk a long way away. Behind the desk were people in what seemed like uniforms. "One flew over the cuckoo's nest," I thought. As I turned around, there was a notice on the wall that said, "No children." The principal came to greet me, and I asked him whether they were getting any more in or whether they had run out altogether. He replied that the children had a separate entrance. "Upstairs, downstairs," I thought. After a guided tour around what felt like a very sterile environment, I was lucky enough to have lunch with a group of young people from the school. I asked them about the school and about the fence. They didn't seem to mind the school but were certainly not enthusiastic in any way. "Why do you think the fence is here?" "To keep us in, to stop us from leaving" was the answer from quite a few of the young people. I told them the story of Dunblane and Andy Murray and the shooting in March 1996, when 16 primary-aged children were murdered in Dunblane Primary School in Scotland. It was after that that fences made an appearance nationally. It was interesting to me that the young people had not connected their own safety and well-being with the fences. I was pleased to leave the school, wondering what role in the community it played and how it enabled its young people to connect, extend, and challenge. I could not help thinking that what the school needed were longer tables, not higher fences. Uniformity also stretches into architecture and design. One size fits all, with our children and young people being just another brick in the wall.

"The aim of teaching is not to produce learning but to produce the conditions for learning; this is the focal point, the quality of learning."[11]

If schooling is about being taught, *education*, in its widest sense, is about learning. Learning by thinking, learning by doing. It is about joy and fun, experiences, and purpose; about standing up, falling down, and standing up again; about trial and error; about skills, character, and being "street-wise." Learning is a continuous journey of discovery, of trials, tribulations, errors, and successes. This learning often involves something that is personally significant, meaningful, or memorable to the learner. In this context, I often share my Wythenshawe and Manchester Airport black-tie dinner story with a smile on my face. I think it was Aristotle who said, "We are what we repeatedly do." Excellence, then, is not an act, but a habit.

"We are still only in the foothills in what we know about learning," so wrote David Perkins, a Harvard professor, in the 1990s. What we do know, however, is that learning is not a simple linear progression. It is, in fact, a messy business, occurring in sudden bursts of insights, "Eureka" moments, or quiescent periods, and sometimes regressing to earlier mental models or skill levels. This uneven process applies equally in sport, art, and music, where skills never develop along a neat, step-by-step line. Learning is marked not only by periods of consolidating and rehearsing but also by forgetting and losing touch. Much of the knowledge that has been apparently acquired has often been stored in inaccessible places, from which we can't quite retrieve what we think we know. Equally, a lot of what we have learned needs to be discarded, because it is, or was, only half-formed, ill-conceived, simply wrong, or is now outdated. What we do know is that emotions play a central role in everything we learn, and that the more powerful the emotion, the stronger the mental linkages that wire together in the brain. We know that learning is active, playful, exploratory, and deeply satisfying when we feel we have conquered a skill, negotiated difficult intellectual terrain, or made our learning visible. Learning is its own reward, and it is only in school that it appears to require grades or other incentives to make it work. We also know that for this learning to happen, the conditions need to be right, congenial, and conducive to effort and inquiry. In seeking out as well as evaluating learning, there are six key questions – the 5Ws plus H, the where, when, who, what, why, and how.

In school, the where, when, and who have largely been taken for granted – learning as situated in classrooms, between 9:00 a.m. and 4:00 p.m., with teachers teaching and young people being taught acquiring knowledge. The main emphasis has traditionally been placed on the what and, to a lesser extent, the how. The why tends to be seen as too difficult a question and as too much of a distraction from simply getting on with it, covering the ground of a demanding taught, nationally prescribed curriculum, its constantly expanding boundaries attempting to encompass the best that has been thought and said, deeming this as essential for the life of the mind and, to a lesser extent, the body and soul.

"Over 85 per cent of learning occurs outside the school. . . . Habitats outside the classroom – out there in the wild – are where the best learning might take place. It is certainly where most learning might already be taking place. So it is important that we all try to get out there in the wild with our children as they adventure into exciting virgin territory . . . remagicatising the world!" so said my friend the internationally renowned museologist and educationalist Dr James Bradburne, former director general at the Palazzo Strozzi in Florence and the Pinacoteca di Brera in Milan. Just as much of what we learn in school is soon forgotten, much of what we learn outside school can often stay with us longer and prove of greater long-term value. There is a growing acknowledgement among researchers and policymakers that schools are only a partial solution to the challenge of education, and that motivation, often through purpose, and enrichment need to be nourished from other sources. Children come to school with very different reserves of social and intellectual capital. Some come to school with a very rich stock of capital from families in which they are taken places, in which there is a lot of talk, questioning, explaining, finding out, with parents grasping opportunities to stimulate thinking, create knowledge, and grow intelligence. Many children, however, enter school with little resource to fall back on and without the resourcefulness to make sense of their classroom experience. Schools alone simply cannot – and I believe should not – fill the knowledge, skills, and attitudinal gaps. They should connect, however, and extend, and challenge.

In informal learning, the where, the when, and the who become pre-eminent. The people we learn with, and from, take centre stage – peers, friends, parents, significant others. Our learning is highly sensitive to time and place, to learning moments which remain in memory, closely tied to the social contexts in which they occurred. Nor is the what necessarily known in advance but catches us by surprise and is all the more valued for its spontaneity and emotional impact – the "wow" factor. Awe and wonder. Rotterdam Centraal Station and my *De Grote Bosatlas.*

Experiences and connected learning reverse the order of the 5Ws plus H. It starts with the where and builds its learner-centred curriculum – its what – around unique environments which offer children and young people a different kind of portal into learning – content in places and experiences which can help boost, rather than diminish, self-belief and self-confidence. As well, for example, as art galleries, zoos, parks, farms, aquariums, libraries, and museums which adults and children visit for essentially educational purposes, there are many less-obvious places for learning, such as local youth clubs, restaurants and hotels, shopping malls, sports clubs, theme parks, offices of any kind, ports, railway stations, or airports. And then there is the internet, of course, with all that brings. While it is assumed that school is where you go to get an education, it is similarly assumed that you would only visit a train station or an airport, for example, to go somewhere else, not for an educational purpose. Yet train stations, airports, and many other places we routinely pass through have their own curriculum, often very rich but typically hidden, just like Rotterdam Centraal Station had for me all those years ago.

Through a 5Ws and H approach, experience-based learning should seek to recognise and exploit situations and stimuli which generate inquisitiveness, which sparks the desire to dig deeper, sustaining effort simply because the learning itself, the finding out, is compelling. How children and young people choose, how they decide to learn, and how learning continues underpin the 5Ws and H in three ways: self-initiated learning, which is when, out of myriad possibilities, the child decides to find out about something; self-directed learning, which is when the child has a major say in how that learning takes place; and self-sustained learning, which is when learning carries on beyond the chosen activity because it is engaging or fun or simply because learning is its own reward.

"I don't know why I should have to learn Algebra. . . . I'm never likely to go there" is an observation by the comedian Billy Connolly about his school days, which brings us to the neglected but important why question. It is a question about values, about what is worth doing, what is worth learning, and what is worth being. It is a question of purposes as well as outcomes, and about investment in a process that is of itself rewarding and empowering, so that opportunities to engage with learning out of the classroom should lead back to the more structured and sequential logic of the classroom, but with renewed confidence, a clearer sense of learning purpose, and a higher level of insight for the learner.

The genius of experience-based learning, outside the classroom, is not only in exploiting the where and respecting the what but also in asking the why and the why-not questions. Why not find ways of exploiting not only the potential resource for learning of cultural repositories, such as museums, theatres, libraries, and galleries, but also the less-evident resources of an airport, for example?

On a busy Wednesday morning at KidZania London in June 2017, some two years after its opening, I noticed three schoolgirls sitting outside the newspaper activity, which was sponsored by the *Metro* newspaper. As it turned out, they were three 10-year-olds from a school in the northwest of England. The girls were excitedly looking at and comparing their own newspaper front pages, a tangible outcome of their hard work as a reporter. As I sat down with them, I asked each one of them how they liked English at school. The answer was not as enthusiastic as I might have hoped for. They clearly liked it but had some serious misgivings. Particularly when it came to writing. They said that writing mostly was not creative but instead very prescriptive, that teachers' commentary was in red pen and felt mostly negative, that is, correcting mistakes. Rarely was a green, blue, or even amber pen used and positive feedback given as to what they had done well. It was clear that writing was not their favourite. Understandably, I think. When asked about their own *Metro* front pages, however, the tone changed, and the excitement upped several gears. All the ideas were their own; they walked around KidZania, interviewing other young people, and with their and their parents' or teachers' permission, they had taken photographs, drafted and authored their stories, checked and corrected each other's work, and suggested improvements and amendments. They were very happy with the outcome and said they would be very proud to show their parents and grandparents what they had done. Making learning visible works – it is difficult to show and tell a grade. There is a lesson in here about connect and extend. All three girls also told me that the school has its own newspaper and that, next Monday, they would go and ask the headteacher how they could become involved. They would show her their *Metro* front pages. Connect, extend, and challenge too.

The key principle to be observed in thinking about environments for learning is how the environment allows children and young people to build on what they already know. While it is often difficult in a classroom to assess and cater for the prior learning of 30 individuals, there is greater time and space in an environment outside school to recognise and discuss the different launch pads from which children's learning can take off. In relation to the airport example, some children will have travelled by plane, some many times, some not at all. Some will have read books or comics with plane and airport stories or seen one of many films, usually dealing with crises and disasters. Some will have watched the news, also tending to focus on dramatic events. Some will have watched a reality programme dealing with the mundane aspects of airport life, stress, bad manners, and missed flights. All these offer useful starting points for discussing misconceptions, as well as the nature, origins, and potential bias of different information sources. Stimulating learning environments help children mine a wealth of factual information, but the emotional aspects also play an important role. Airports and their intimate connection with flying arouse a host of feelings and can never be approached neutrally or with cognitive distance. In common with all learning, it is crucial to grasp, and to exploit, the emotional engagement with the subject and to keep asking the question of how we can capture the spark and fan the flame.

From personal experience, Manchester Airport offers an elaborate range of educational programmes for different ages. Even in the days of the Wythenshawe Education Action Zones, this was the case. In those days, these covered topics such as information systems, internal communication systems, marketing, maintenance, noise monitoring technology, and of course, climate change–related matters. There were suggestions for a range of activities, such as designing a welcome leaflet, creating an on-line information system, and reporting of a critical incident, as well as for extended problem-solving case studies, such as, in May 2003, how to manage 45,000 fans from Turin and Milan arriving at, and later departing from, Manchester Airport for an AC Milan–Juventus Champions League final at Old Trafford or, more generally, how to decide what range of tasks needs to be managed to turn around a flight arriving from Stockholm with 200 passengers so that it departs again on time.

There were also tests of imagination. This was the hidden curriculum of Manchester Airport. Children's and young people's questions once they had made the connection. Although they lived next door to the airport, for many of our children, the connection became real when they visited, saw, heard, smelled, and met the people who made the airport into what it was.

How does an airport work? How many different kinds of jobs are there in the airport? Who manages an airport? What does airport management entail? How are take-offs and landings managed so that planes don't crash? How can you know if a plane 300 miles away will be on time or not? What do you need to know and learn to become a pilot, a member of a cabin crew, a baggage handler, a police officer at an airport? What are the surprise jobs at an airport? There are doctors and nurses, a priest, truck drivers, ambulance drivers, police, chefs, and teachers. There is a prison, a bank, a medical centre, and a place of worship, as well as a centre for teaching – of cabin crew, pilots, engineers, and others. Where do planes travel to? What countries are those cities in? What languages are spoken there? What else do we know about those countries? What do we not know? Why do people travel there? What different purposes might people have in visiting those countries? What interest of mine might take me there? For a holiday? For a sporting event? Where are the next Olympics, and how would you get there, and how long would it take? What places are familiar through Champions League football, such as Manchester, Madrid, Moscow, or Milan? Or the Eurovision song contest? Can we track the flight path on a map? Where are airports located in relation to major urban centres? Why? What time is it in other world cities? Why are times so different? What currencies might people need, and how do exchange rates work? How does money get bought? How many flights are departing in the next hour? How many would that make in a day? How many would that make in a year? What might be the total number from all British airports? What is the likely statistical chance of a plane crashing? What percentage of planes arrive on time? What is the average length of delay? How far away are different destinations? How long does it take to get there? What, then, is the average speed? If Starbucks claims there are 87,000 possible combinations of drinks, how many different drinks and drink flavours do they need to have? On a plane, what happens to the wee and poo?

"There is always one moment in childhood when the door opens and lets the future in," so said Graham Greene. For me, in Wythenshawe, it was important to see the children and young people make connections with what they already knew, or thought they knew, to see them challenge some of their own preconceptions and misconceptions, and to witness them extend the reach of their imagination and creativity. In this there were three key ideas that encapsulated the essential features of these thinking routines: Firstly, connect – how does this experience connect with what you already know, what you are good at, or what you believe? Secondly, extend – how does this experience extend your thinking, your skills, or what you believe? And thirdly, challenge – how does this experience challenge what you already know, what you are able to do, or what you believe? Translated into the Wythenshawe context, firstly, now that you have experienced the airport as opposed to just live next door to it, is it as you expected? Secondly, now that you know more, do you think about it differently? What do you believe or think of it now? And thirdly, what does this thinking differently mean to you? For example, are there now jobs that you aspire to that you previously thought were out of your reach? Can people from Wythenshawe fly planes? Connect. Extend. Challenge.

It is important to sit back and think long and hard about a longer-term aim to create a better education for every child.

This thought process starts with some old but key questions: What are we trying to achieve? For whom? By when? To what standards? And why? We know that what unites successful provision everywhere is a focus on excellence and purpose for every child, regardless of socio-economic contexts, gender, ethnicity, or geography. It is this that should inform which aspects to keep in our current systems and where to innovate to create a better and more equitable provision for all. A key question has to be how we can better connect the best of schooling with the experiences out there so that education makes sense to all, so that learning becomes a satellite navigation system to better places in life.

While we should not throw out babies with bathwaters, we must also recognise that the global pandemic of 2020 and 2021, COVID-19, drove an urgency to implement faster new models of learning and innovate beyond the conventional four-walled classrooms. At the same time, the pandemic has shone a light on, and indeed widened, many of the inequities in school systems globally, from the learning environment at home to access to devices, internet, and high-quality schooling. There is not yet any clear evidence of a concerted political will to take on the challenge of fixing long-broken delivery models and making 21st-century education better for and accessible to all – in other words, to put the money where the mouth is. This is something electorates globally will need to urgently consider. Going back to 2019 and pretending nothing has happened is not really an option.

I would like to invite educators and policymakers to consider with me a number of basic, pragmatic principles and ideas to start (re) building an education and, by implication, schooling provision that will begin to better serve the needs of our children, our adults, our communities, our societies, and yes, our economies, and although this may seem overwhelming, the time to start reimagining the future of our children's education is always now.

Get the basics right. Every school system must get at least three basic components right. Without these there, we disable children, preventing them from reaching the heights they are capable of and they want to reach. Firstly, core skills. Children need a strong foundation in literacy and numeracy. You cannot live as well if you cannot read or write, or be as creative if you cannot do your sums. You cannot innovate without knowledge. Provision needs to ensure that knowledge is being adopted in both remote and in-person environments, and thereby, the use of technology becomes a further key life-skill. Secondly, high-quality teaching and learning. Children learn best from people. Who the teachers are must be open for debate; academic experts, artificial intelligence experts, project managers, extra-curricular experts, other children, role models, et al. The definition needs reassessing. While greater use of technology in education may be inevitable, technology will never replace the great teacher who uses the latest technologies to bring awe and wonder to the learning table. Every system must develop and support all teachers, especially as they learn new skills for remote and hybrid learning. Thirdly, performance measurement. We need to measure what we value. It is hard to achieve excellence without data on current performance and benchmarks to aim toward. However, data should be used primarily to inform – to direct support to the children, teachers, schools, parents – not to punish. Data should include information about the whole child, insights, and engaging expertise from outside the schooling arena, such as market and academic research, for example, leads to better understanding. School systems need better, broader, appropriate assessments and better tools to help them help each child succeed.

Allocate resources equitably to support every child. Globally, there are significant inequities between countries, yet funding is insufficient to close the gap to universal enrolment, let alone to universal high-quality education. Achieving the Sustainable Development Goal[12] "to ensure inclusive and equitable quality education and promote lifelong learning opportunities for all" will require a substantial increase in investment in the children most at educational risk. Within countries, the pandemic has laid bare once more the inequities of access to high-quality education. Those inequities emerge even before school attendance begins. Instead of helping low-income and disadvantaged children narrow the gap, the current funding mechanisms in many countries widen it. Change will mean a move away from "[t]he definition of insanity: doing the same thing over and over again and expecting a different result."[13] This applies to funding, teaching, access, boundaries, ownership, leadership, et al.

Rethink school structures and policies. Education systems now have an opportunity to rethink the school structures that were forged in the 18th century. Perhaps events of the early 2020s can be a catalyst for innovation. The list of educational innovations and possible interventions is long, but we should not just experiment with our children's futures, yet equally, we don't want to be held back any more by inertia or continue with failed projects. Bold education systems can take an agile and research-based approach. Smart systems will also expand their partnership networks, including non-governmental, societal, and cultural organisations, collaborating with academia to bring the best of learning science, with employers to create linkages to the workplace, and with the business world to access funding. All school systems must challenge themselves to reshape their models to deliver better education to every child, recognising that, within this, one size does not fit all and valuing local contexts. The school of the future is one not full of the latest technology but full of the very best people, whoever they may be and whatever their tasks may include, to serve the children. As a variation on a theme, it takes a community to raise a child. The school of the future is more than a school. In all this, trust will be key.

Support children holistically. The correlation between mindsets and academic performance has long been clear, but the shift to remote learning put it into stark relief. Children with high levels of self-motivation, persistence, and independence have continued to thrive, while others, often from disadvantaged contexts, have struggled. Similarly, the emotional toll of events of the early 2020s has raised awareness of the need to address anxiety, depression, and other mental and emotional health issues as a precondition to helping children learn. Good schools are more than a school. In a good school, "every child is everyone's responsibility." Good schools address the whole child, helping them develop skills and awareness that go beyond what they need simply to find work. Good schools play a critical role in helping children learn how to become effective citizens, parents, workers, and custodians of the planet. More than ever, we need to enable and empower good schools.

Harness technology to scale access. Research tells us that just handing out devices to children does not lead to improved learning. The lockdown of the early 2020s reminded us that lecturing on a video call is rarely a substitute for face-to-face learning. The challenge is not just to adopt new technologies but to incorporate them in ways that improve access and quality for all. This needs to be built up from the individual children and their contexts, thus enabling and then empowering them.

Move toward experience-based learning. Experience is everything. For our children to connect with the purpose of schooling and education, we need to, of course, provide knowledge and understanding. But how? And why? We need to utilise what is available to us – in terms of technology, for example, but also in terms of all that says that not all classrooms have four walls, locally, nationally, and globally. My work at both the Children's University and at KidZania exemplifies this. We are the facilitators enabling children to join the dots and recognise that experiences are "the appliance of the science," "the theory into practice," "the why answers," and often, "the awe and wonder." Every experience is a "for example," and every "for example" is an experience. We need to empower children to make sense of the world as agents of their own change and guide them to discovering their own inspirations and aspirations. Then, we need to support them in finding their roadmaps and help them get there, from an early age. For this to be achieved, we need to become our children's allies of empowerment. And when we do this, we will find ourselves in a world where not every classroom has four walls, where the environment becomes a teacher. Should we not collectively draw up a list of experiences, outwith school, we believe our children are entitled to by, let us say, age 7 – and then again at 11, 14, 16? Should we not aim to create learning cities, learning communities, and learning families, remembering also that virtual is actually real? To all involved, the value of the connection between being taught in school and experiences out there will soon become very clear – believe me. We need to make experience-based learning and partnership our modus operandi, *purpose* our watchword, high standards and a sense of achievement our aim, and our children's well-being and preparedness for tomorrow our promise. As school systems invest in solutions for remote and hybrid learning, they can plan for a future of this blended, personalised learning in and out with the classroom, utilising "the environment as the third teacher."[14]

I believe that the age of 11 is particularly significant. It marks a crucial transition period, coinciding with the end of primary education in many countries, leading to the very different and less-personal world of secondary schooling, to sometimes losing old friends and having to find new ones, and on top of everything else, also encompassing the onset of puberty for many. Growing pains in so many ways. Reaching the age of 11 presents an opportune moment for us to reflect on what our children have encountered and consider what they still need to explore. By fostering a collective vision and working together as schools and communities, we can ensure that our children have diverse and enriching experiences throughout their educational journey. Whenever I visit schools and enter the staffrooms, if I can, I grab a whiteboard pen and start writing down my list of ten experiences I believe every child is entitled to have had by the age of 11. I intentionally leave a rubber next to the pen, as I expect people to rearrange, debate, and even erase some items. It serves as a catalyst for meaningful discussion, and one we desperately need to have. So here's my list of ten things to do before you are 11.

First and foremost, have a lot of fun! This tops the list because childhood should be filled with joy and laughter. The order of the following points is arbitrary. Embrace the multiple uses of the internet. Recognise that the internet is not just a single entity; it is a multitude of virtual environments that can complement real-world experiences. Alongside this, a visit to a museum, gallery, theatre, or musical performance is essential to expand children's cultural horizons. Before turning 11, every child should engage in acts of kindness and charity, making a positive impact in the world. Additionally, they should create something tangible that they can be proud of, whether it is an artwork, a story, or a science project. Encouraging their entrepreneurial spirit by exploring innovative ideas and turning them into small projects is also valuable. To broaden their perspective, they should experience a glimpse of the future by visiting a workplace or a university. Stepping foot in another country and immersing themselves in a different culture will foster global understanding, at least online, but preferably in person. Finally, they should explore their own capital city and visit their seat of government to understand the decision-making processes that affect their lives. These ten experiences represent a well-rounded set of adventures and opportunities that can shape children's growth and development. However, it is important to remember that this list is not exhaustive, and each child's journey is unique. The aim is to inspire discussion and encourage us all to reflect on the experiences we want our children to have before they reach the age of 11. Imagine a child walking out of an experience, beaming with excitement, and confidently declaring, "I'll be back!" That's the kind of impression we want to leave on young minds. In my opinion, before reaching the age of 11, children should also have exposure to social media and social networking. I know – I can almost hear the collective gasp. But let us face it: They are already engaging with it, and it is better to guide them safely now and teach them how to enjoy it responsibly. Alongside this, we must enable children to explore and believe in a world of possibilities, igniting their curiosity and empowering them to follow their dreams. It is through these experiences that they discover the endless potential within themselves. Let us ensure that children have the opportunity to explore, learn, and shape their own narratives and find purpose through doing so. We cannot expect our children to reach their potential by only experiencing life within the confines of school. If we want children to dream big, we need to empower them to find out how.

Help children become future-aware. We must aim for children to understand that learning is a satellite navigation system to better places in life, locally, nationally, and globally. Therefore, we need to introduce into education and schooling early opportunities to be aware of the world around us and the futures it may hold – let us, for now, call it futures awareness. Every year, the world of work tells the world of education that what is being produced does not meet the necessary requirements in terms of skills and competencies. Our schooling now does not cater for the requirements of today, let alone tomorrow. Our education systems are based on the requirements of the past. Every economic age has its core asset, and in our time, this is knowledge and understanding, skills and character qualities. Events of the early 2020s have accelerated automation in the workplace, as in everyday life. School systems need to help children adapt to these changes and other impacts of rapid digitisation, from ethical standards and cybersecurity to the impact on health, forensics, and almost every other part of society, including the economy. In the digital era, educators need to expand their understanding of what it means to be literate in the 21st century: not replacing traditional learning, but complementing and enhancing it. With the speed of change in the digital era, all those who teach must also increasingly be critical partners in helping children develop life and work-ready skills and write their own narrative of the possible. We live in a world that is strangely contradictory. On the one hand, ever-speedier global access to knowledge, news, events, and more, with an increasing need to be able to research, analyse, and judge. On the other hand, ever-narrowing schooling curricula and testing, ever-greater emphasis on overprotection in the name of health and safety. No wonder our children find themselves at times confused. How on earth will they acquire the skills to make informed decisions, take calculated risks, learn from their mistakes? Should we not move towards a more free-range learning approach and include risk? Without elements of calculated risk, self-confidence is below where it might be, and surely, we will be wondering in years to come why our supply of entrepreneurs – calculated risk-takers by definition – has dried up.

Measure what we value, as opposed to merely valuing that which we can measure. This, of course, will include national tests and assessments. Nobody should be so naive as to think otherwise, whether we agree or not. Additionally, however, we must recognise insights that arrive from elsewhere. My global KidZania research and the Children's University research undertaken by Cambridge University are such examples. As is, for example, a remarkable film produced by my friend the Australian Genevieve Bailey titled *I Am Eleven*. The film weaves together deeply personal and, at times, hilarious portraits of what it means to sit at this transitional age. The young minds provide us with powerful insights into their worlds, from Jitter in India and Goh in Thailand, to Giorgio in Bulgaria, Luca in Germany, Kim in the United States of America, and so on. In this day and age, information, data, and insights are everywhere and serve us with a unique opportunity to learn and know our children better. For a long time now, it has been on my mind to construct a barometer of childhood which will give us a global overview of the status quo and what it means to be a child at a certain moment in time. The findings of this research should also be segmented at all sorts of levels, geographically and personally, including, of course, age, gender, race, and socio-economic contexts. This *Imaginarium of Childhood* will give us an annual overview, a comparison with the past, longitudinal insights, and most importantly, stepping stones to improving the lives of our children.

Invest in teachers and teaching. While education experts recognise the importance of great teachers, teacher preparation and development still fall short in many systems. That has to change, starting with creating more linkages between teacher training and local schools, much like the linkages between medical schools and hospitals, to anchor learning in real-world practice, led by the experts, as well as by grasping the opportunity to reimagine teacher training and development more fundamentally by leveraging advanced technology.

The role of the teacher requires rethinking and redefining to include facilitation, programme leadership, partnership development, and resource procurement and management skills. This thinking is part of the long-term 4 + 1 concept I proposed earlier – for every four days teachers and non-teaching classroom colleagues apply their trade, they should have one-day preparation, evaluation, upskilling, and development time. In addition, school systems should free teachers to spend more time on high-value activities that require deep teaching expertise and relationships. This might also involve new roles, such as learning assistants to help children and families adapt to remote learning. Longer-term systems might consider a more radical unbundling of the role of the teacher, enabling individuals to take on more differentiated roles that play to their strengths, preferences, and areas of expertise. What is critical to any successful educational transformation is that the place education holds in all societies needs to be given greater priority and higher status, and that the teaching professions are held in the highest possible esteem, made tangible by recognition and respect and a remuneration commensurate with the responsibility of leading our young people into new and better futures. At the start of the 2023–2024 academic year, I was invited to give a keynote address at the University of Cumbria to some 200 teacher training students whose first day of their journey it was. Part of the question-and-answer session at the end of my keynote focused on the status of the teaching professions. I was asked the question "Do you believe that teachers should be held in the same high regard as doctors and lawyers?" My answer was, "No. It needs to be higher. Remember that without teachers, there would be no doctors or lawyers."

For a final thought about education and schooling, and teachers and learners, let us go back to David Winner and *Brilliant Orange – the neurotic genius of Dutch football*, when he compares two great Dutch football icons and managers: Louis van Gaal and Johan Cruijff.

> Philosophically, the key difference may be that while [Louis] Van Gaal advocates, the same football as [Johan] Cruijff, he remains convinced that his players need him to play it. If football is physical chess, then Louis sees himself as the grandmaster and his players as the pawns. Cruijff, by contrast, aims to educate intelligent, talented players to become independent minded individuals, who will then instinctively make the right choices and collaborate effectively with teammates. In other words, while Louis sees the role of the

manager as supreme, Johan wants to develop footballers who make the manager superfluous.

Schooling and education. Where do I stand? Next to Johan Cruijff, of course. Always.

Notes

1. Source: *Cambridge Dutch–English Dictionary*.
2. Vanessa Langley, headteacher, Arbourthorne Community Primary School, Sheffield, United Kingdom.
3. Gail Borden, inventor, United States of America.
4. Anne Frank, Jewish girl who kept a diary (1942–1945), the Netherlands.
5. *Ruth Perry: Prevention of Future Deaths Report.* Courts and Tribunals Judiciary of England and Wales, 2023.
6. Margaret Thatcher, prime minister (1979–1990), United Kingdom.
7. From "Mrs. Robinson," a song by Paul Simon and Art Garfunkel, 1968.
8. *The Epic Classroom* – Trevor Muir
9. Professor David Perkins, co-director, Project Zero, Harvard University, United States.
10. Emeritus Archbishop Desmond Tutu, Republic of South Africa.
11. Loris Malaguzzi, founder of the Reggio Emilia approach, Italy.
12. United Nations General Assembly.
13. Albert Einstein, theoretical physicist; winner of the Nobel Prize in Physics, 1921.
14. Loris Malaguzzi, founder of the Reggio Emilia approach, Italy.

CHAPTER

4

"Technology, bloody hell!"

This is the chapter I was not going to write. After all, technology is integral to everything we do. It is a fact and natural part of life. It is, at times, brilliant. It is everywhere. It is in fact so everywhere that we mostly take it for granted. It is also, in many ways, really nothing special. It is part of humanity. Part of human development. Of learning and teaching, in school and out of school, in the real world and online. And always has been. It is also something with which our children and young people are more confident and more familiar in many ways than we grown-ups are. What's the problem? Well, in one sense, there isn't one, and in another there is. The technology in itself is fine. Actually, it is much more than that. It is wonderful, it is unbelievable, and it enables us to do so many things so much better. There is excitement, awe and wonder, incredulity, pride, and of course, relief when it works. But – and it's a big *but* – at the same time, technological development and the speed thereof are making us behave differently. That in itself is also nothing new, but the pace, the variety, and the multitude of technological development are something to think about, as are the potential engagement and interaction levels and their consequences. Of course, the technology story will never end. Its awe and wonder will never end, its potential will never end, its capacity to change lives for the better will never end, and the risk of it being in the wrong hands will never end. Our human worries about technology will never end either, I suspect. On balance, however, I would much rather be with it than without it. Technology and its use, rightly or wrongly, are causing us concerns, especially, of course, when it comes to our children and young people. So here we are. Perhaps we need wider reflections and different thoughts, continually.

"Football, bloody hell! I can't believe it." The quote is by legendary Manchester United manager Alex Ferguson, now Sir Alex, from a post-match interview after the 26th May 1999 Champions League final, in which United surprisingly, very narrowly, and very last-minute defeated Bayern Munich at the Camp Nou in Barcelona to complete a historic treble – English Premier League, English FA Cup, European Champions League. Since that evening, the quote has been used as a title for podcasts, radio and television programmes, and memes, as well as being the title of Patrick Barclay's biography of the great Scot. As someone who watched the match, I had no fingernails left. As someone who witnessed that interview, I heard excitement, awe and wonder, incredulity, pride, and of course, relief.

"Technology, bloody hell! I can't believe it." My excitement, awe and wonder, and incredulity when I am confronted with the latest advancements in technology, especially where these apply to education, potential and aspiration. The relief and pride come when I can eventually get things to work. In football, the genius lies in the execution, not in the name of the game itself. In technology, the genius does not lie in the technology per se; it lies in the people who recognise the difference that can be made, almost entirely to the lives of others. The genius of technology lies in the human capacity to better lives, all lives. Technology, per se, is overrated. In itself, it serves little purpose except to show what we are capable of. It is like the car that can travel at 250 miles per hour in a country where the roads are so congested that nobody can travel very much faster than 60 or 70 miles per hour at best. That kind of technology is about showing off. It is the look-at-me technology.

The Kalinga Institute of Social Sciences (KISS) is the largest tribal institute in the world, providing food, accommodation, healthcare, and all the basic necessities of life absolutely free to some 80,000 poorest of the poor tribal children to pursue their studies there, from early years to postgraduate, as well as vocational training. KISS, as a unique experiment to eradicate poverty through education and the use of education as a tool to empower the underprivileged section of society and provide sustainable employment, is being hailed as an example and a success across India and, increasingly, globally. KISS has recently been declared a "Deemed University" by the Ministry of Human Resource Development of the government of India. In India, "Deemed University" is an accreditation granted to higher educational institutions by the government. According to its definition, the accreditation indicates "an institution of higher education, other than universities, working at a very high standard in specific area of study," and the accreditation grants "the academic status and privileges of a university." With this, KISS has become the first tribal university in India and in the entire world. It plans to educate 2 million Indigenous, tribal children over the next decade and is in the process of setting up branches in ten further states in India, with the support of the respective state governments. Working with its founder, the social entrepreneur, educator, and philanthropist Dr Achyuta Samanta, I have learned how creatively translating a vision into reality, thinking big on a number of key fronts, needs to join up. Technology, and its use for good, is one of those key fronts, in terms of communication and connectivity, content development, the learning agenda, personalisation, awe and wonder, and most importantly, equity and social justice. Not grand. Not blingy. But pragmatic, and purposeful. Real yet aspirational. And above all, contextual and relative to who the children and young people are, to where they are at, and to how technology can help them move on and up. Achyuta Samanta was born to Anadi Charan Samanta and Nilima Rani Samanta in the village of Kalarabanka in the Indian district of Odisha in 1965. His father died when Achyuta was 4, and he grew up in abject poverty with his widowed mother and seven siblings. However, he persevered and, at the age of 22, after receiving his master's degree in chemistry from Utkal University, joined the teaching profession as a chemistry lecturer in a college in Bhubaneswar. At 25, he embarked on a journey that would change his own life and the lives of hundreds of thousands of people. With just 5,000 Indian rupees, the equivalent of 45 British pounds sterling, in his pocket, he started KISS and KIIT, the Kalinga Institute of Industrial Technology, in two rented houses. After the long journey from then to now, he has more recently developed the Kalinga Institute of Medical Sciences, the Kalinga Institute of Dental Sciences, and the Kalinga Institute of Nursing Sciences, besides an attached 2,600-bed state-of-the-art hospital and a cancer care hospital. He developed the first smart village in Asia, the Kalarabanka Smart Village. Achyuta Samanta's life story is one of incredible inspiration and hope for all, but especially the poorest of the poor, and his commitment to technology for good, writing positive narratives of the possible, reflects that. There is no doubt in my mind that his work and that of his many colleagues and friends exemplify the role technology can play in narrowing gaps and so in creating a fairer and better world. It is my privilege to know him and work with him in an advisory capacity to keep further developing education as a satellite navigation system to better place in life – for all. In this, the role of technology for good will no doubt continually grow.

This technology that arises out of a combination of need and curiosity, out of a desire to make things better, is the technology we should pursue. It is the technology that is not about faster but that is, first and foremost, about better. It is the technology that is linked to our human values. Technology for good as opposed to just good technology. And this technology for good becomes extraordinary when it is combined with genius – the technology of "what if?" Of that, of course, there is no greater example than Leonardo da Vinci, as we can witness to this day in the wonderful *Museo Nazionale Scienza E Technologia Leornardo Da Vinci*, the Leonardo Da Vinci Museum of Science and Technology, in the Italian city of Milan, where da Vinci's technological thinking has been brought to life, from submarines via hospital operating theatres to flying machines. The modern three-point safety belt was perfected by Sweden's Volvo engineer Nils Bohlin in 1959, and its patent given for free to the world. The invention has been credited with saving at least a million lives worldwide. Technology for good and kindness, hand in hand. The story of the children's author Roald Dahl and the invention of the Wade-Dahl-Till, or WDT, valve is a very different, very personal, yet equally significant example. The Wade-Dahl-Till valve was developed in 1962 by hydraulic engineer Stanley Wade, Roald Dahl, and neurosurgeon Kenneth Till. In 1960, Dahl's son Theo developed fluid on the brain after being struck by a car. A standard implement was installed to drain excess fluid from his brain. However, this hollow tube or shunt jammed too often, causing pain and blindness, risking brain damage, and requiring emergency surgery. Till, a neurosurgeon at London's Great Ormond Street Hospital for Children, determined that accumulated debris in the ventricles could clog the slits in the shunt, especially with patients such as Theo, who had bad bleeding in the brain. Dahl knew Wade to be an expert in precision hydraulic engineering, from their shared hobby of flying model aircraft. With Dahl coordinating the efforts of the neurosurgeon and the hydraulic engineer, the team developed the new mechanism. As Till reported in the medical journal *The Lancet*, the invention was characterised by "low resistance, ease of sterilisation, no reflux, robust construction, and negligible risk of blockage." By the time the device was perfected, Theo had healed to the point at which it was no longer necessary to implant the shunt in his skull. However, several thousand other children around the world benefited from the WDT valve before medical technology progressed beyond it. The co-inventors agreed never to accept any profit from the invention. Necessity, the mother of invention and technology. And then, of course, there is Achyuta Samanta's story. Technology, in the end, is a human story.

    These days I write with a fountain pen, again. Technology. For me, in writing terms, this is another journey back in time. It takes longer to write with the fountain pen. I feel as if it is making me take more care and giving me more time to consider and think about what to write. And how. We make choices, including where technology is concerned – we are mostly in charge of what we do and how. In my primary school days back in Echt, I learned to write using a very old-fashioned and cheap type of fountain pen – the dip pen. Our desks were wooden, the ones you see at antiques fares now. With a lid and, to the right, an inkwell. The "to the right" bit was very important in a Roman Catholic primary school. We were only allowed to write using our right hand. The left hand, after all, was the hand of the devil. Those who were left-handed found themselves in a bit of a predicament. You were told, and told off, in no uncertain terms, that being left-handed really was not a good thing. It was anti-Catholic and anti-Christ. You were forced and taught to use your right hand, and punished if you didn't. In the name of God, you were told how to use technology. Ballpoint pens came in later. BIC was the name. In 2024, proudly, the accompany reminded us in an advertisement how, over the many years, its pen actually hasn't changed. BIC is still BIC. BIC's main purpose, to me, at that time seemed to be that it was far less smudgy than the dip pen and the inkwell, and that it was faster. With the benefit of hindsight, I am convinced that being less smudgy was a very good thing, but I am now less convinced that being faster was equally good. I am not sure that my writing became better or, indeed, more legible as a result of the ballpoint pen. I think it probably became less recognisable, more doctor-like, if you wish, and more rushed in terms of expressing thought processes. Faster does not necessarily mean better. Time may be money, as they say, but time is not necessarily quality. Surely, technological advancements should serve quality more than efficiency. It should always be about making things better. This, for me, is the debate about good tech versus tech for good. Ballpoint pens weren't particularly welcomed by all either, by the way. This was a technological development that challenged the status quo, and it took quite a while before its use in schools in the Netherlands became accepted. In schooling and education, we do struggle with change of the technological kind. The explosive reaction to the inclusion of the calculator into children's lives has only been exceeded by that of the introduction of artificial intelligence. In both cases, it was an invention too far, the world gone mad. The whole world was going to be dumbed down, and all children would cheat. Perhaps that says more about us as grown-ups and our trust in children and teachers than it actually says about technology.

In the late 1990s and early 2000s, not long after I started as the director of the Wythenshawe Education Action Zones, interactive electronic whiteboards became all the rage. And every teacher wanted one. The solution to all our problems. Then, like now, that was, of course, not true. What became quite obvious quite soon was, however, that these same teachers were not entirely clear as to what they wanted the whiteboards for or, indeed, of what they were capable. And why should they know? Their enthusiasm was an expression of wanting to make things better, and that, for me, was enough. In the end, we decided that we would utilise the expertise of our own quality development teachers and the professional trust that teachers Zones-wide had in them. We acquired half a dozen portable electronic whiteboards, which travelled with our quality development teachers into classrooms and were used as an integrated part of learning and teaching and, before that, of course, the planning. Calling these whiteboards *portable*, incidentally, is stretching the imagination some distance. We gave it the necessary time and resource to ascertain what our next steps would be. Patience was a virtue. Quite some time after that, we started the acquisition of interactive electronic whiteboards for many of our classrooms, confident in the knowledge that now they would make learning and teaching better for all and not just be used as a white version of a blackboard.

All these stories, in their own way, relate well to the use of technology in schooling and education, then and now. We, at times, need to look for ideas, answers, and solutions outside of our domain – observe and learn elsewhere, and marry that with the knowledge and skills we already possess. If it makes learning better, and teaching, of course, then let us use it. This will take time, agreed values and principles, a very significant and ongoing investment, not just in the kit, but much more importantly in the people – our teaching and non-teaching colleagues, our children, and their families. Technology in education is about making it better, excitement, awe and wonder, incredulity, pride, and at times, relief. It is not per se but part of a bigger plan, a hybrid 2.0, where we will be able to seamlessly connect between the virtual and real worlds utilising artificial intelligence and all the magic that can bring, where real personalised learning can become the norm rather than the exception. It will also take us, over and over again, to the question of who the teacher is, and we will need to paint outside the frame to find the answers. Parents, carers, the wider community (including the world of business), and of course, the young people themselves all have a co-educator responsibility, and some will be able to exercise this in the area of technology and learning, to make it better. The story goes that in 1908, when asked about customer input in the development of the Ford Model T, the American founder of the Ford Motor Company, Henry Ford, famously said, "If I had asked people what they wanted, they would have said faster horses." There is clearly sometimes also something about the mindset of those at the forefront of technological inventions and development that screams empathy, self-confidence, and determination. Parts of that self-confidence, empathy, and determination, as well as calculated risk-taking, should travel with the new technology to its users. There are plenty of Henry Fords out there.

Technology is a funny thing. It is everywhere, and always has been. In everyday life, however, we just take it for granted, don't even notice that it's there. In the morning, I turn on the coffee machine, and the news on television, then my wife leaves to work in her car. I use my laptop, and my mobile phone; I order the shopping online, do the washing. And so it goes. I am not really interested in the technology itself, in the how it all works. I was never a child who took things apart, and I certainly was never the child who put things back together again. I have no idea about engines, big ends, and all that. I am not interested either. Many years later, in the early 1990s, information technology advisers everywhere would immediately revert to rams and bytes if asked the simplest of questions and would tut and shake their heads in a similar way to a plumber when he has a look at a stop cock. I thought rams and bytes were part of the American football Channel 4 had recently started to screen. The advisers often didn't advise; they merely confused instead. I just need to understand how technology works for me. And I believe that one way or another, and to a greater or lesser degree, this is what most people's relationship with technology is. I believe that, by and large, in everyday life, our relationship with technology is quite good, comfortable even.

Too much of a good thing. It is all in the balance. All in good time. Of course, there are concerns about young people and the use of technology. This particularly relates to social media, but also in general to the amount of time that they can spend staring at screens. There are, of course, also safeguarding issues, and concerns about whom they might be communicating with. Although any of this, of course, does not just apply to young people – it applies to all of us. And whilst it is important to recognise that, in educational terms, the environment is the third teacher, that can, in virtual environment terms, easily be too much of a good thing. Balance matters. There are also concerns, quite rightly, about the mental and emotional well-being of young people in relation to social media and the amount of online contact opportunities there are. I, too, suffer from social media-itis. I use LinkedIn as my professional network; Facebook and Instagram to stay in touch with friends and long-lost family members; X, formerly and more fondly known as Twitter, as my letting-off-steam space that also, at times, drives me mad – it is there that occasionally I can feel my anxiety rise to the surface. I sometimes worry that technology and its development and innovation are speeding ahead too fast for us as human beings to keep up emotionally and mentally. And that this, in itself, causes anxiety and affects our wellness. And of course, there are bad people online, just like there are in real life. At the same time, I disagree with those who think that the solution is to ban the technology or access to it, including mobile phones, in schools. They, too, have a role in our education and in our schooling. If I were teaching now modern foreign languages, I would be urging the youngsters to bring their mobile phones into the classroom, fully charged, so that we could communicate with our exchange partners, wherever they might be, via WhatsApp, via FaceTime, or by other techie means – in the target language, of course. The excitement, I promise, would be tangible, and learning would be purposeful and full of awe and wonder. And fun. In 1886, Carl Benz applied for a patent for this vehicle powered by gas engine. Patent 37435 may be regarded as the birth certificate of the automobile. My grandfather recalled the first car in his village, with somebody walking in front of it with a red flag to warn of its imminent arrival. We now have pedestrian crossings and traffic lights, speed restrictions, speed cameras, satellite navigation; we have fines and points on licences, seat belts, and child seats. We have not stopped using the car and started walking again. We have adapted to remain safe. In that sense, progress cannot be denied, and it would be unwise to do so. We cannot unknow what we know. How we cope with technology and how we utilise it in terms of learning and teaching are up to us. How we behave around it is our decision. Blaming the technology per se is cowardly and completely the wrong thing to do. In the summer of 2019, I was asked to give a keynote address to a very large gathering of parents and teachers at the Skolkovo Business School in Moscow. I was asked, as part of the speech, to share my thoughts on the role of technology in the lives of our children. In the question-and-answer session that followed, one father very firmly told me that when his teenage children came home after school, they would immediately disappear into their rooms, where they would then engage for far too long with their technology, which included a television, a laptop, an iPad, and their mobile phones, as well as various online gaming gizmos. His concern was that he was no longer communicating with his children, and for that he blamed the technology. I asked him who had put the television in his children's rooms and who had bought them the laptop, the iPad, the mobile phones, and all the other bits and pieces, to which he replied that he and his wife had. I asked him how many times he had knocked on his children's doors to see how they were, to go and chat with them, to talk about what they were doing, or to join in. The answer was none. I also asked him whether he had put the televisions in their rooms so that he could have exclusive access to the big one in the lounge. Blaming technology is easy and lazy. It is like blaming cars for drink-driving. It doesn't add up.

It feels to me that our main concerns around technology and our children and young people do lie in the areas of interaction and engagement. Perhaps they should, truthfully, also lie in the area of our inability to cope with this as grown-ups. Like the father in Moscow, we want our children to have everything without being educated ourselves about the positives and the negatives. And about our role, of course. And when the ostrich policy doesn't work, we will need to think and react differently. Not against, but with. Not in isolation, but together, playing our part as the villager in raising the child. We also need to trust our children more. In every aspect. When I do knock on my youngest daughter's door and go in, I, more often than not, find her studying. There is a book and there is paper; there are pens and pencils; there are headphones or earphones, a mobile phone, an iPad, and a laptop, and no doubt her music coming from somewhere, and sweets. Sometimes I go in just for the sweets. "How on earth can you work like that?" is a question my parents would ask when I had paper, a book, pens and pencils, and a cassette recorder playing my music. It is tempting at times for me to ask the same question. But then I remind myself that my daughter works hard, is a high achiever and a very successful attainer, that I can trust her blindly, that she trusts me, and who on earth am I to question in 2024 her modus operandi?

Whilst we seem to struggle with the interaction and engagement, we are much happier about the technological developments that provide us with insights and data, which, in turn, influence our thinking and acting. Technology provides analytics from all sorts of places, including organisations, such as the Children's University and KidZania. On a personal level, my youngest daughter and I follow each other on the tracking app Life360. It means we know where we are and that if anything is wrong, we can get there as quickly as possible. It makes us both feel better, safer, and more comfortable. The minute she feels uncomfortable with this, it goes off, of course. I love the part of technology that puts our minds and hearts at ease. Technological advancements in healthcare are literally unbelievable. Within my lifetime, the first heart transplant was performed, and the patient, Louis Washkansky, lived for another 18 days. Nowadays, we are able to support people in an incredible array of ways, including technologically developed prosthetics and implants and, of course, extended life expectancies for many. It is a privilege to watch every four years the Paralympics, which gives such joyful evidence of what, utilising technology, we are capable of. I marvel at the world of sport, which demonstrates time and again how to use technology to enhance performance. The more and the better we know, the better the data and the insights, and the more we can personalise and plan. In the world of football, this is, at top level now, also used in the development of young players at, for example, Ajax Amsterdam's and FC Barcelona's youth academies, as well as at the Qatari Aspire Academy. Johan Cruijff, Pep Guardiola, Sir Alex Ferguson, Arsène Wenger, Bolton Wanderers Football Club's former manager Sam Allardyce, and many other top managers introduced technology, often first experienced in American college sports, to measure the lifestyles of their players, including sleep and diet, all to enhance players' capacity to perform.

We have a long way to go in education and schooling, but we should not shy away from technology and the benefits it can give us to know and personalise for our children better. We need to look elsewhere for answers if we can't find them on our islands. Our good schools, which are more than a school, will need the technology, data, and insights to support their young people and communities so that they, too, can better enhance their children's capacity to perform. Of course, this is academically, but if this in our poorer communities means tackling health and well-being, providing food or warmth, we need to invest accordingly, in inverse proportion to opportunity. If you are hungry, you can't play, or learn, and you certainly can't achieve as well. Before, however, we can personalise, we must know and understand. The role technology and the insights it can bring us can play in this must not be underestimated. Personalisation of the individual can also lead to a form of personalisation of the organisation in which they are being schooled and educated. These insights, in turn, can influence organisational planning, even policies and funding formulas, in inverse proportion to need. In this area, too, the influence of technology can be as important as we dare it to be.

In the end, and all things considered, however, as an educator, to me the excitement and incredulity of technology are about awe and wonder, about writing a better narrative of the possible with our children, about technology being in the hands of good teachers, about dreaming, and about flying. It is "to infinity and beyond" in educational terms, to quote *Toy Story*'s Buzz Lightyear. If I were a child at school now, the technology would, inspirationally, be my atlas, there at my fingertips, and, aspirationally, make me travel wherever I wanted to, artificial intelligence permitting, with my grandad. "Technology, bloody hell!"

They say that every cloud has a silver lining, and what a cloud *2019 novel coronavirus* or *coronavirus disease* – as it has been termed by the World Health Organisation – was. In technology terms, I am certain that in years to come, we will talk about "bC" and "aC" – "before COVID-19" and "after COVID-19."

Early 2020: An educational 999 or 111 emergency call, or whatever number wherever you are. The *2019 novel coronavirus* announced itself with a vengeance. Lockdowns followed quickly, more so in some countries than in others. Children and young people were at home, just like that. The response from schools? Immense! Almost overnight, schools were able to cater for their children and young people online. And where online was not possible, creativity, innovation, resilience, perseverance, and care prevailed. Anyone who, looking back, says otherwise needs to remember better and, as they say these days, "needs to give their head a wobble."

Dr Arunabh Singh, director of the Nehru World School in Ghaziabad, Uttar Pradesh, India, told me the story that for those children who did not have reliable, if any, internet access at home, a brilliantly simple alternative was thought of. School buses, normally used to transport the children considerable distances to and from school, were now being used instead to transport their work to them in the morning and collect it late afternoon. The school's teachers would then comment on this work in writing, and it would subsequently be returned with further learning tasks the next day or so. There will be many such stories in every country, every village, town, or city, and in almost every school. In addition to work being couriered backwards and forwards, there are stories of breakfasts still being available for collection, and care equally being available aplenty. Whilst many countries quite rightly applauded their nurses and doctors, I feel that, sadly at times, they perhaps forgot to do so for their schools.

After a good six weeks or so of lockdown, I received a call from my friend Dr Mary Ashun, principal of the International School in Accra, Ghana. Mary being Mary, an innovative force to be reckoned with and with an energy as if she were "on Duracell batteries," was excited to discuss her plans post-COVID-19 for the school as a consequence of the lessons she had already learned.

In the context of her school and her children, Mary had observed that online learning for some young people was hugely beneficial for shorter periods of time. In her mind, she was particularly focused on the 15-to-18 age range. She started to formulate the idea that post-COVID-19, her older youngsters would probably come to school physically for around four days per week, or slightly less. The remainder of the time, they would be at home, and online. Her idea was that, in that time, with the school they would develop a system of surgeries whereby, at appointed times, the young people would meet on a one-to-one basis with their subject specialists to delve deeper into the subject matter – a kind of Oxford University tutorial approach. She felt that, to the context of her school and its young people, this was an opportunity not to be lost. That, I suppose, was an example of Mary being Mary. There have, no doubt, been many changes, small and big, in schools everywhere. It is such a shame, with the benefit of hindsight, that the opportunity for change for good was not seized upon, not coordinated. At government levels, we found that we lacked vision, we lacked the expertise, and we lacked courage.

When push comes to shove, the question becomes whether we do have the courage of our conviction. Talk about education 0 to 99 properly, for all? Embrace life-changing opportunities? Think differently? Or do we conveniently go back to 2019 and pretend that the next two years never happened? I found that rush back to the past quite disturbing. Erasing silver linings seems to me to be not clever, lacking in vision, and it demonstrates an absence of courage. It also said a lot about those in charge at the very top. Blind instead of visionary. Cowardly instead of courageous. Opportunities lost.

Not all organisations were as ready to respond to the emergency and as resilient as schools. For years, I had urged KidZania head office to develop an interactive online presence alongside its physical ones. To no avail. The thought was not entertained, despite the additional opportunity of reaching many more children and young people globally who did not physically live near any of the existing KidZanias or, if they did, could not afford them. At KidZania London, in partnership with the then government and the private sector, we had even trialled such an online presence. The arrival of COVID-19 simply meant that, globally, all KidZanias closed and, thereby, in the process, disconnected from its aim to get children ready for a better world, as well as, of course, deserting the children when they probably needed them more. Post-COVID-19, if it weren't for the brilliance and sheer determination of the local KidZanias, from Doha to Dallas, via Istanbul, and from Moscow to Mumbai, who know their communities like good schools do theirs, there would be far fewer KidZanias in existence now.

Is technology improving our qualities of life? Or is it making us busier by making us more visible, more accessible? Are we programmed yet to say "no"? Are we clear enough about the boundaries, expectations, and what is right and wrong, as well as good and bad? In the "real world," we have more or less well-established procedures, expectations, and subsequent behaviours. Our "real" days start and end at set times; the weekends are ours, and so are our holidays. But is that also the case in the parallel "online world"? Do times change? Have our procedures and expectations been adjusted? Our behaviours? Are we sending emails in the evening, and when we do, when do we expect a response? When does the recipient feel the response is due? Are there mixed messages? This all needs working out, collectively, realistically, and fairly. How is that going? When, in the late 1990s early 2000s, I worked at the Wythenshawe Education Action Zones, with an office at Manchester Airport, there was pressure for me to have a work computer at home and a work mobile phone. I gave in in the end but did question whether if my chairman rang at ten o'clock at night, it was all right for me not to answer the phone. And therein lies a problem. There are no doubt times when boundaries have become blurred and expectations have become norms. Some years later, when I was working as an adjunct fellow at the University of Adelaide in Australia, I witnessed how things could be looked at differently. It was not uncommon when, at 4:30 in the afternoon, university colleagues would lock their work mobile phones in their desks and go home. When I questioned this, the reply was: "It is a work phone. It's home time now. And in the very unlikely event of an emergency, the university has my home number, anyway." Balance mixed with a healthy dose of common sense. I loved my time in Adelaide. It is, at times, also good to see that there are occasions where technology doesn't win, despite concerted and often expensive efforts. I and my son Tom, for example, are very happy that Kindle and all the technology like it, in the end, never outnumbered the book. Looking ahead, it is undoubtedly the case that we must enable and empower our children to take greater charge of writing their own narratives, including drawing boundaries, in order to arrive at a better work–life balance and a better well-being.

There are many questions that, for now, remain mostly unanswered, but eventually, we will get there. These things just take time, observations, research, evaluations. How good can learning using technology at early years be? And how healthy? What about real lifelong learning – 0 to 99? Will the use of technology enable us to do this much better and near seamlessly? Can we enhance communities involving technology, and thereby the lives of at least some of its constituents? For example, can we make lonely, often older, people less lonely in this way? Our children could spend time teaching them how to FaceTime or WhatsApp. Good technology for good by good young people. Can the use of technology help us tackle inequalities in everyday life, not just in policies and on paper? Can it democratise? Can it enhance our feelings and thinking aesthetically? As well as competences, can we better our online *us*? Online respect, online courtesy, online decency, values, and principles around online behaviour that we can all subscribe to – be good people in both worlds. The use of technology as a key life skill: What we very many years ago rather strangely have started to call the 3Rs – reading, writing, and arithmetic – have, by many, been viewed as the most important components of education. Is there not now a case to be made for the inclusion of technology as a key life skill, or at least the application thereof? The 3Rs and 1T? I think so.

Selfishly, the technology that flowed out of COVID-19 has made my life better and has arguably made me healthier. Before the pandemic, there were months when I literally felt that I lived on aeroplanes. If there was an urgent need for a meeting, pretty much anywhere in the world, I would pack my suitcase, fly there, and do what I had to do. I remember, on one occasion, flying from KidZania head office in Mexico City to KidZania Dallas in the USA, and from there, via Hong Kong, to Kuala Lumpur, to speak at the BETT Asia conference. If you take the number of miles, the amount of time, and the time zones involved, you will understand how tiring this at times was. I remember arriving in Kuala Lumpur and literally being totally disorientated for the first few days. There was, of course, technology pre-COVID-19, but Skype and other platforms didn't really do the trick. The technology, although it at times worked, too often got in the way of the flow and became a point of frustration. Post-COVID-19, my life changed. Most meetings started to happen online, sometimes even conference inputs. I was in a position to begin to work out what worked for me and what didn't. Meetings, formal and informal, interviews, even workshops for me work online most of the time. Keynote speeches don't. In the years that followed 2020, I found myself working from home most of the time, yet thanks to the technology, I could still be here, there, and everywhere, but without being all over the place. The technology worked, and it has no doubt improved my work–life balance and my well-being. I see more of my family and provide proper daddy day care for our two little dogs. No doubt this change does not just apply to me, and no doubt the technology that flowed out of COVID-19 has also done our planet a favour in this respect. There were, of course, also many mishaps and many funny stories. Tie, shirt, slippers, and shorts. The latter invisible, of course, until I needed to get up because Richard, the postman, knocked on the door to signal that he had left a parcel. And in the rush I forgot that the camera was on. Tie, shirt, slippers, and shorts were not that good a look, I found out.

There is also no doubt that my children's lives have changed post-COVID-19. My youngest daughter's experience of the use of technology in schooling and soon at university is significantly enhanced from what was her world before 2020. And of course, young people have the capacity, the ability, the motivation, and the in-built courage to adapt, make the most of these opportunities, and enjoy them. My eldest daughter's working life has also been, I think, positively affected. She no longer has to undertake the long commute from her home in Kent into the centre of London on a daily basis. She and her colleagues decide what happens, when, where, and how, and a balance, I believe, has been arrived at. Anna probably averages three days per week in the London office and works at home for the other two days. Fridays is, more often than not, the day she chooses to be at the Edelman offices, because there is the opportunity after work to then socialise with friends and colleagues. The best of both worlds. She also feels that this arrangement enables her to do more, to do it better, and to be well. This is, of course, where professionalism and mutual trust form the foundation of all that blossoms.

There is also a rather strange phenomenon that has entered my world. And no doubt everybody else's too. I now have good friends I have never met face-to-face. My American friend Mark Sylvester, with whom I meet monthly for about an hour when we put the world to rights, is now very dear to me, and I know that feeling to be mutual. We have started calling ourselves the *Elder Council*, based, I suppose, on Walter Matthau's and Jack Lemmon's fictional grumpy men in the 1968 film *The Odd Couple*. I met my Indian friends Ritu Malhotra and Anit Gupta what feels like a very long time ago, and we, too, occasionally catch up online. The support of both Anit and Ritu whilst I was writing this book has been invaluable. Yet until very recently, in Doha and Delhi, we had never met properly, face-to-face, that is. There are many other new such friends too. I am quite getting to like this new form of friendship, somewhere much nearer to the real thing than to Facebook, yet still online.

All this also makes me wonder what the lives of our children might look like in the years to come, building on my own experiences but looking into their distance. After lots of reading, talking to futurists et al., trying to imagine, watching television and films, and thinking things through, I recognise that there is a picture that wants to emerge.

By 2054, when a child born in 2024 is 30 years old, technology and, inevitably, artificial intelligence will be a fundamental part of daily life, seamlessly integrated into almost every aspect of living. Maybe . . .

The day begins with an artificial intelligence–personalised morning routine. Artificial intelligence–controlled environments will track sleep patterns and adjust the wake-up time to ensure they are fully rested. Smart windows will adjust lighting to simulate a sunrise, while sound systems will play customised music or a podcast to start the day. Artificially intelligently powered mirrors in the bathroom will provide health insights, such as hydration levels or skin conditions, offering tailored recommendations and cures. Wardrobe selection will be managed by artificially intelligent recommended outfits based on weather, activities, and style preferences. Meanwhile, appliances in the kitchen will prepare breakfast based on dietary needs and preferences, with health-conscious suggestions designed to fuel the day ahead. Take it or leave it?

In 2054, artificial intelligence will revolutionise work environments. Spaces, using augmented reality and virtual reality, will replace today's video calls, creating a more interactive and immersive work experience. Artificial intelligence will handle mundane tasks, like scheduling, data analysis, and decision-making. Artificial intelligence–powered tools will take abstract ideas and turn them into fully developed plans, like designing a new product. Their work–life balance will also be artificial intelligence–driven, with systems that monitor stress and suggest breaks or physical activities to maintain well-being. Artificial intelligence will optimise time management, helping workers stay productive without burnout. Transportation will be fully automated. Take it or leave it?

In 2054, shopping will be a blend of virtual and physical experiences, with artificial intelligence offering hyper-personalised recommendations. Autonomous drones will ensure quick and seamless delivery of goods. Entertainment will also be personalised by artificial intelligence. Content like movies, music, and games will be tailored to mood, preferences, and even social trends, creating fully immersive experiences. Artificial intelligence–generated virtual environments will help people connect with friends and family through holographic meetups, no longer limited by physical distance. Social interactions will also be shaped by artificial intelligence, with people attending virtual events, concerts, and gatherings, where artificial intelligence ensures they feel present and engaged, even across vast distances. Take it or leave it?

Health monitoring will be constant, thanks to artificial intelligence–powered wearables tracking everything from heart rate to mental well-being. Artificial intelligence will provide real-time feedback, helping people maintain health goals by adjusting nutrition and workout plans based on personalised data. Routine health diagnostics will be handled by artificial intelligence, identifying potential health issues before symptoms appear, reducing the need for physical doctor visits. Mental health will also be supported with artificial intelligence–driven mindfulness routines and stress management exercises. Take it?

In 2054, as evening approaches, artificial intelligence will help wind down the day by adjusting lighting, temperature, and sound for optimal relaxation. Before bed, AI will help review the day, offering insights into productivity, health, and well-being, suggesting improvements for the next day. As bedtime arrives, artificial intelligence will adjust the environment for optimal sleep, ensuring users wake up feeling refreshed. I wonder what they will dream of. Good night, all. Leave it?

Firstly, I am not so sure how much artificial intelligence is familiar with the quirks of human behaviour. Adjusting the wake-up time for any human is difficult enough. And surely, even on the artificially most intelligent bathroom mirrors, there will be toothpaste marks and hair gel. Similarly, I cannot imagine for a minute my children's wardrobe selection being managed by anything or anyone but themselves. I am, of course, all in favour of revolutionised work environments for our future generations, but I had hoped that our society would be one where our children, and our children's children, would perhaps work less for, relatively speaking, greater rewards, and not merely financially.

All my children, and their friends, manage their own shopping experiences very well, both online and physically. And the same can be said for their entertainment. I am sure that, in all this, technology will play a very significant role, but I strongly suspect that it will be a secondary one, and that the personal aspects will take top spot. While new forms of social interaction, and new kinds of friends, have to be welcomed, I still hope that future generations will be able to meet in restaurants and bars and go on holiday together. Perhaps there will be "artificial intelligence–free zones"?

There is no doubt in my mind that in health and well-being, artificial intelligence will play an enormous part, not least analytically and diagnostically. But for whom?

Somehow, in these futuristic forecasts, I miss words like *happiness* and *joy*, *company*, and *positivity*. I think it's interesting that aesthetics and the arts rarely feature in futuristic forecasts, along, of course, with the joy and all the awe and wonder they bring. I also wonder what 2024 child and 2054 grown-up these predictions are modelled on. Somehow, I don't think that these are the children that Desmond Tutu so often referred to, from Soweto, or Bianca Senna; from the favelas of São Paulo or, indeed, Achyuta Samanta; from the slums of Mumbai. I am all for "futuristic." But in the end, I have to conclude that my musings and research, reading, talking to futurists et al., trying to imagine, watching television and films, and thinking things through lead me to mostly leave it, and there are only few aspects of it where

I happily and enthusiastically would take it. I think I would like to leave it to our children and our children's children. I trust them to make a much better and fairer job of things. Interesting thoughts, though.

As a teenager, even as a child, and certainly as a young adult, I have to say, whatever technology that was at that time – newspapers, television and radio news, cinema news even – brought to me and my contemporaries the news of the world. John F. Kennedy, his brother Robert, Dr Martin Luther King, Alexander Dubček and Jan Palach, Fidel Castro, and Che Guevara; who Anne Frank was and how she died; the Holocaust and *Wo warst du, Adam?*; Neil Armstrong and his journey to the moon. It also brought the 1968 student demonstrations and *Woodstock*. Our news sources were limited and sporadic and, at the same time, orchestrated to certain times of the day. The six o'clock or eight o'clock news. It wasn't constant, instantaneous. We knew what we knew. There were no thoughts about conspiracy theories, about not landing on the moon, about fake news. We trusted what we were given. Rightly or wrongly. We had no alternatives, no real choice. What, in 2025, is the role of technology in truth and in trust? Information overflow, from everywhere. Is technology a help or a hindrance? Or does it steal our time and push us into decisions before we have the opportunity to make up our mind properly? Does it empower our children to better search for the truth, who they are, and their humanity? Their values and their purpose? Their identity? What is the moral and ethical purpose of technology? Is this a new journey of discovery? And a better one? Answers in a WhatsApp message, please! But in any case, let's watch this space and be our children's scaffolding and safety net. Some things don't change, and neither should they.

And finally, for this chapter at least, technology is, of course, also personal. Very. More than we realise until we stand still and think. Technology brings us so much joy and, in many ways, so much freedom. We can now do and enjoy things pretty much wherever we go, at whatever time. And more safely. I can be in touch with my friends and family, literally not even at the touch of a button. I like that feeling very much. We can enjoy what technology brings on our own, or together with friends and family. It allows us to make many more and different memories. There are probably no more than a dozen photographs of me when I was a child. Now, on our phones, we can make memories every second of every day and keep them to enjoy and remind us whenever we wish. When I first moved to the United Kingdom, there were three or four television channels, and they all dutifully ended at around midnight with a test card and the national anthem. Music was accessible only in set places, the lounge, the kitchen, your bedroom, if you were lucky. Now, everything is with us 24/7. Technology allows us to be us in so many ways. Uniquely and personally us. Television, radio, the cinema, online – technology enables and empowers us to have very special, often shared, experiences. For me, from radio and reel to reel players, via cassette recorders and the Dutch weekly music television programme *TopPop*, to vinyl, compact discs, and downloads technology to my mobile phone, they have all, at some point in my life, allowed me to enjoy music, increasingly, when and wherever I want to. Imagine all the music you would never have heard. I have laughed and cried, learned lyrics off by heart, and sung along, badly. The connect to this day is immense. Technology has allowed me to have my life story in songs. There are many. Simon and Garfunkel's "Mrs. Robinson" of course, learning lyrics, and "Drive" by the Cars at the Live Aid concert. "Heidschi Bumbeidschi" and Heintje Simons in my early childhood; "Stop Making Sense" by Talking Heads, big suits in the 1990s; Herbert Grönemeyer's "Bochum" on Taverham High School's German exchanges; Miriam Makeba, Hugh Masekela, Ladysmith Black Mambazo, in conversation with Desmond Tutu. Personally, much more importantly still, technology has allowed me, whenever I want, to remind myself of and to remember those dearest to me through music, something I rarely talk about – it is within me. My technology allows me to be private. My wife's song, more than any, is Roberta Flack's "The First Time Ever I Saw Your Face." There is nothing more to say. Adele's "Someone Like You" is the song of my eldest daughter, Anna. With it in 2012 she won her secondary school's talent competition after a few years of trying. I drove to the local supermarket, Morrisons, and bought all the flowers in store, the proudest dad in town. "Con te partirò," or "Time to Say Goodbye," by Andrea Boccelli and Sarah Brightman was played many years ago in a Venice seafood restaurant when a waiter said to Tom, my son: "I can see that your father loves you at least as much as I love my son. And that's more than words can say." It is tattooed on my heart. Tom, however, barely remembers. Such is youth and such is life. I love him for it. Our story. Lewis Capaldi and his "Before You Go" once made me cry in the back of a taxi in Qatar, not long before my youngest daughter started her university life – I was thinking of an empty house without her. Empty. Quiet. And tidy. It is my and Imogen's song. She was the last one to leave home. I stand on my hill and wave. I could tell similar stories in films, in television programmes, in black and white and in colour, online and in many more ways. "Technology, bloody hell! I can't believe it."

And the role model we are! KidZania Manila, the Philippines – July 2018.

"Es doe mer gelökkig bös" – *as long as you are happy*. Looking up to my grandad (wearing my Honorary OBE) at the British Schools in the Middle East conference, Bahrain – March 2017.

February 1988: my last Taverham High School and Städtisches Gymnasium Mechernich exchange visit. In the then West German capital Bonn with our headteacher and my *All-Time Teacher Eleven* Manager, Mrs Jean Daines [red arrow], our amazing young people, and me [orange arrow]. Behind the camera, taking the picture was my favourite pupil, James Neill.

Shakespeare per i Ragazzi. Wythenshawe goes to Italy. Piazza Santa Stefano, Bologna – May 2004. "Our lives will never be the same[1]".

---

1 *Romeo and Juliet*, William Shakespeare.

Manchester Airport, United Kingdom. Between Terminals 1 and 2, on the Skywalk, is the Wythenshawe Education Actions Zones legacy: "More than!"

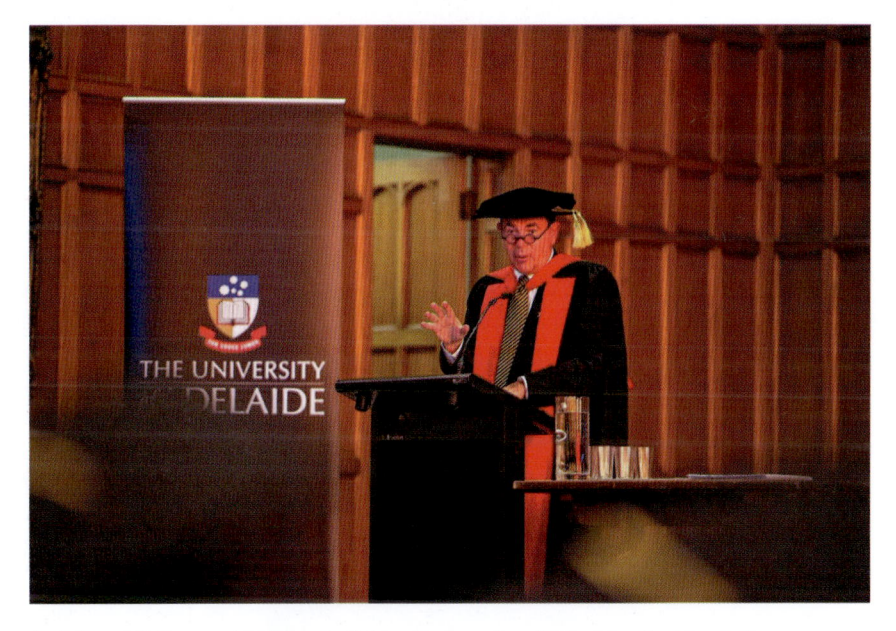

As Adjunct Fellow and Children's University founding CEO at the first Australian Children's University graduation, the University of Adelaide – November 2013.

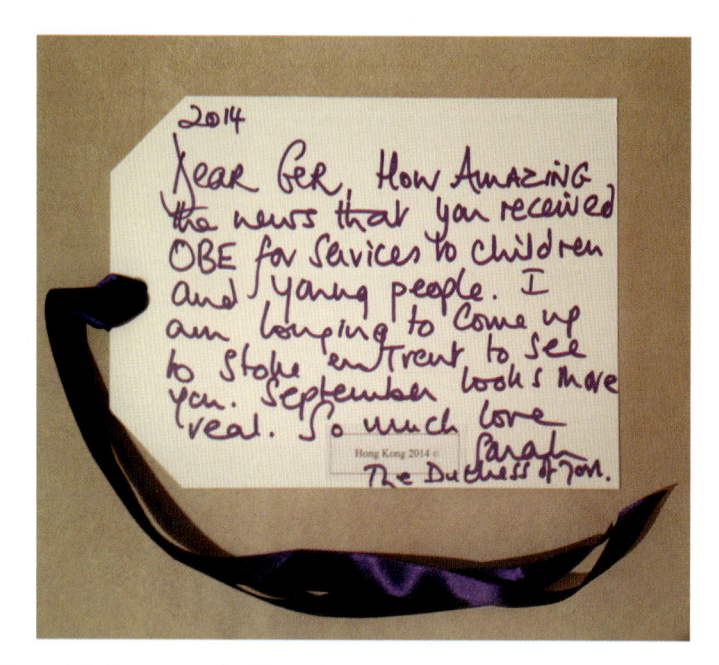

Congratulations on my OBE from Sarah Ferguson, the Duchess of York – June 2014.

For my wife. Always. The Shard, London, United Kingdom, with my honorary OBE – June 2016.

My first ever big keynote address: the Aula Magna at the University of Bologna, Italy – May 1993.

Talking creativity creatively, with my friend Sir Ken Robinson – January 2016.

QUDWA Conference, Doha, Qatar, with OECD (Organisation for Economic Co-operation and Development) Director of Education and Skills Andreas Schleicher – September 2017.

"Whatever the question, education is always the answer". Sharing vanilla ice cream with the Emeritus Archbishop Desmond Tutu on his 86th birthday in Cape Town, South Africa – October 2017.

At the Instituto Ayrton Senna, with Ayrton's niece and Marketing Director Bianca Senna in São Paulo, Brazil – May 2018.

As the banner said in 1985: "Ethiopia: Bob's your uncle"! Meeting again, with Sir Bob Geldof talking Blue Peter badges and catching up. This time I was the VIP. London, United Kingdom – January 2018. "Nobody made a greater mistake than he who did nothing, because he thought he could only do a little[2]".

---

2 Edmund Burke, Irish statesman and philosopher.

One of many reunions with former Taverham High School pupil (my favourite) and then International Director for GL Education James Neill at BETT Asia, Kuala Lumpur, Malaysia – March 2018.

At the United Nations Head Quarters in New York, United States of America, as part of the World Innovation Summit on Education (WISE) with Secretaries General Kofi Annan (1997–2006) and Ban Ki-moon (2007–2016) – September 2018.

Making the CNN news in Chile – May 2019.

Name no longer needed – Kuala Lumpur Airport, October 2019.

Measuring what we value – Father's Day 2020.

Christmas duty calls – December 2021. Father Christmas and his helpers Florence and Connie. Arbourthorne Community Primary School, Sheffield, United Kingdom.

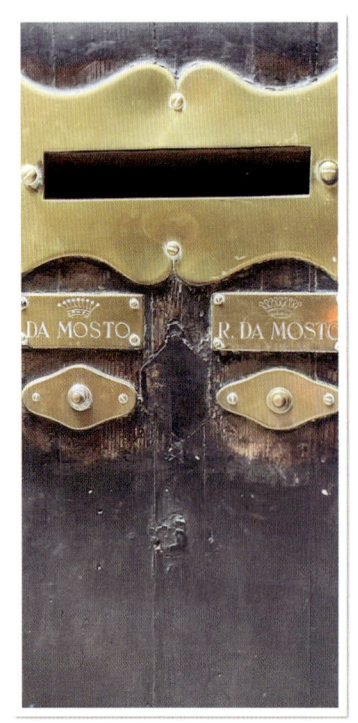

Exploring possible post-COVID-19 learning outside the classroom journeys, at home with author, film maker and BBC television presenter Francesco Da Mosto: "As many times as I went out, was as many times as I got lost. But I was never lost. I was always somewhere in Venice" – August 2020.

From Birth To Boardroom. Views with the benefit of hindsight. Since 2020, the online environment has rocketed in importance – July 2022.

CIIE Conference, Monterrey, Mexico – November 2021: Post COVID-19, face to face again.

DIDAC India Conference, Bengaluru, India – September 2023.

With my friend Carla Rinaldi in Leicester, United Kingdom, at the Independent Association of Prep Schools – March 2024.

Still putting out fires at KidZania Doha – April 2024.

His Highness Sheikh Hamed bin Zayed Al Nahyan after the 2024 Majlis Mohamed bin Zayed Lecture, titled Reimagining Early Childhood Education. The lecture took place in the Majlis Mohamed bin Zayed venue at Sheikh Zayed Grand Mosque [in the background] in Abu Dhabi – June 2024.

Receiving a copy of the Kalinga Institute of Social Sciences (KISS) India founder, Achyuta Samanta's biography of his mother, *My Mother My Hero* – September 2024.

Contemplating, and swiftly rejecting retirement with my good friend Dr James Bradburne in Reggio Emilia, Italy – June 2024. James is a global leading expert on children learning in museums and galleries. We both advise the Fondazione Reggio Children and our mutual friend Carla Rinaldi.

Eating vlaai (cake from Limburg) with my cousin Jac at my other grandparents' house (Oma en Opa van de Bosch), in 1962. We would meet again in August 2024, 62 years later. Much older, a little wiser, more experienced, and more able to set aside the negatives in our past. Adults feuding hurts children. Without technology and social media, this happy reunion would have been very unlikely.

Experience is everything. Travels with my children: with Anna on top of the world at the Burj Khalifa, Dubai – May 2018; drinking a Sling with Tom at Raffles Singapore – November 2012; and on top of the world again, this time with Imogen in West Kowloon, Hong Kong – August 2017.

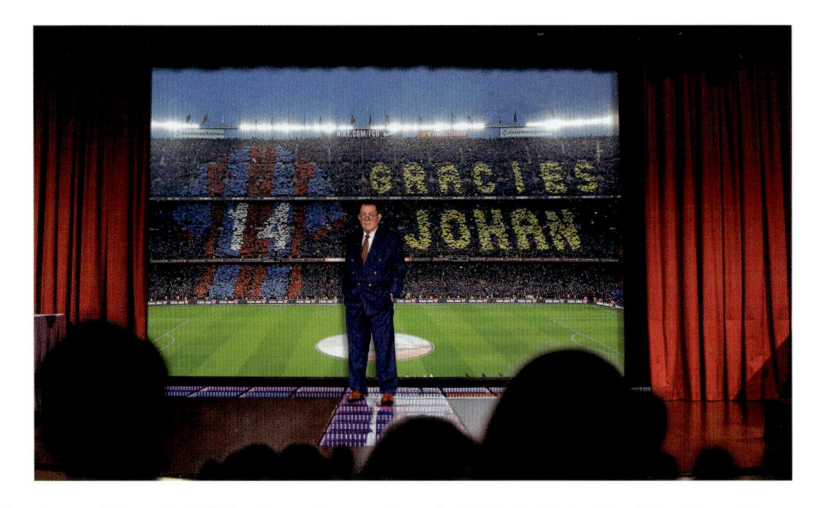

Thank you Johan Cruijff, for the role you played. KidZania Doha (and the Camp Nou, also known as the Estadi del FC Barcelona, Spain) – RIP, 24 March 2016.

In 2025, the Sheffield Teaching Hospitals will be my home from home for significant chunks of time. And my beacon of hope. I thank my lucky stars for Professor Hopper, Dr Darby and Mr Patel, for David Frith, my main cancer nurse, and for the rest of the National Health Service's Sheffield branch. And I thank my lucky stars, of course, for team Graus! – January 2025.

CHAPTER

5

The role we play

"Every child is everyone's responsibility." Arbourthorne Community Primary School is my favourite school in the world. The mantra belongs to its headteacher. The implication is that we all have a role to play. "It takes a village to raise a child."

I like the concept of "favourite." It requires our heads and our hearts. To me, *favourite* means, to quote the *Oxford English Dictionary*, "a person or thing that . . . is especially well liked." My favourite food is white asparagus from the Limburg province of the Netherlands. My favourite place on Earth is Venice, Italy. My favourite friend is Carla Rinaldi, president of the Fondazione Reggio Children, again in Italy. My favourite country is Italy! My favourite song is "The First Time Ever I Saw Your Face" – the Roberta Flack version. My favourite book is Antoine de Saint-Exupéry's *The Little Prince*. My favourite person on earth is my wife. My two little dogs, Florence and Connie, are joint first, as are my three children, Anna, Imogen, and Tom – all for very different reasons. That, too, is possible. My favourite teacher is Meester Beurskens, my German teacher. My favourite pupil is James Neill – he is especially well liked and has been a friend for life.

Having favourite pupils does not mean exercising favouritism in a professional sense, of course. Those who believe that do not understand education or schooling and clearly suffer from a lack of trust in the professionalism of all those connected with teaching children. It does mean, like in every other walk of life, that you meet people whom you get on with better than with others. These are often encounters of like-mindedness and like-heartedness. I have been very fortunate to encounter many young people wherever I have been who I loved teaching and whose company I liked. It would be difficult to list them all, but they certainly include Frazer Scott, Richard Ward, and Lynette Brock, née Upton, from my Taverham High School days; the miracle of social media has meant that we are in touch again, occasionally at least, after all those years. There are many others, of course, with whom I am no longer in touch. And there is my now-friend and former pupil James Neill. There is also still his sister, Rachel, and his dad. The fact that we got on so well, and still do, is also a family affair, I suppose. In turn, my family and I were very happy that James could attend the award ceremony, at which I was made an honorary Officer of the Most Excellent Order of the British Empire in 2016. All these young people had in common that they were kind, were caring, would roll up their sleeves to lend a helping hand, or went the extra mile. They would turn up voluntarily for extra lessons, they would enquire after the others' well-being, and they would remember birthdays. They were often a shoulder to cry on for their peers and friends. They would bring up the food they had cooked in Mrs Nay's home economics class to my classroom for lunch. They were, more often than not, also part of a school that was small enough for us to know all the children and for them to know us. They were all clever in their own way, and they were all funny, very funny. I suppose that all of us who work with children have our own stories and memories.

Wank is a small town in southern Germany, in Bavaria, near Garmisch Partenkirchen and Schloß Neuschwanstein. I had never heard of Wank, at least not as a southern German town. The very funny, very clever young people I was involved with in a project about knowledge of German-speaking countries, *Landeskunde*, did, however, discover the existence of the small town. After a lot of research, the project was presented both in the form of a report and a display in the library at Taverham High School. I, as their teacher; my head of department, David Harding; and the headteacher Mrs, Daines were invited to the preview. Whilst admiring the beautifully presented work, I noticed an asterisk next to a small town: *Wank*. The asterisk was accompanied by a footnote, which, translated, read as follows: "As the state of Bavaria is a predominantly Roman Catholic area, on a Sunday all the Wankers go to church." In language learning, there is a stage of self-confidence that often expresses itself through humour and as a result of trusting relationships. I thought this was clever, slightly cheeky, confident, and very funny. As did Mrs. Daines. She did remark, however, that before the public viewing, that particular aspect of the display ought to be removed. And it was. By the young people themselves, of course. Favourite moments, favourite pupils.

My favourite school is Arbourthorne Community Primary School – it is there that I am Father Christmas.

The district of Arbourthorne is part of the city of Sheffield in the north of England and is located in its southeastern part. It is classed as the city's most deprived community[1] and is in the 10 per cent most deprived neighbourhoods in the country. The school has around three times the national average of pupils eligible for free school meals. To me this is reminiscent of my times working with schools on the Bransholme, Lower Broughton, and Wythenshawe estates in Hull, Salford, and Manchester, respectively. There is, of course, in all those communities, clear evidence of the link between educational outcomes and place-based disadvantage. A complex ecosystem of factors and interrelationships between school, home, and community shapes individuals' life chances and determines socio-economic and geographic outcomes. Schools can and, in my view, should play critical roles in deprived urban, and rural, areas through both their educational functions and their community engagements.

Arbourthorne Community Primary School, led by its headteacher, Vanessa Langley, is committed to positioning itself at the heart of its community. The school has a long history of innovative thinking to engage families to get involved, such as the development of the Red Robin House, a redundant, since-converted caretaker's house, now life skills centre for children and families – it was also a place to keep warm and be fed in the winters of 2022 and 2023, when many families had to choose to either eat or heat because of the cost-of-living crisis, at least in part caused by Brexit. In 2018, the school co-launched an initiative called *An Even Better Arbourthorne*, a partnership with the Centre for Innovation in Voluntary Action and other external community organisations, including the Urban Institute at the University of Sheffield. The school also serves free bagels for breakfast and dongles into homes where there is no internet; grows its own community food in polytunnels; has community fridges, which are stocked with support from local supermarkets; runs cookery classes; employs parents, and an artist in residence who takes children to London, the capital city that is theirs too, and to theatres and a restaurant, to museums and the coast – ten things to do before you are 11. It has *Sparkle and Shine* assemblies, works on aspirational programmes with Sheffield High School for Girls, a local independent school, such as *SHINE* and *Cool to Be Clever*, thus widening the field of experiences and alumni, and with the universities of course; it has a partnership with the Fondazione Reggio Children in Italy, it takes children on summer outings, has an annual formal awards evening, and a netball team; it has children who act in plays and play instruments in music performances, who play football and learn Latin – they even have their very own Father Christmas. It asks, "Who do you want to be like?" instead of "What do you want to do when you grow up?" It is values-driven. The school supports its parents and is theirs and the community's go-to place when life is dark and overcast. It puts the child in the middle of everything and builds personalised scaffolding so that every child can go as high as they can – it also has safety nets to catch them. Of course, Arbourthorne Community Primary School gets good results and is Ofsted-good, both because of what it does and because of who it is. The children in value-added terms make wonderful progress – *wonderful* being better than *outstanding*. The school supports and understands the whole child. In simple terms, if, as a child, you are cold, hungry, unhappy, or many other things – never your fault – you cannot function, let alone succeed with flying colours. We may all be in the same storm, but we find ourselves in very different boats. It is about scaffolding and safety nets. "All grown-ups were once children, but only few of them remember it."

The school is very clear about its expectations and how every piece of the jigsaw, from children, parents and carers, teachers, and other colleagues to partners and the wider community, contributes to the overall successes. Everybody gives their very best. That's it. This simplicity and clarity remind me of Josep Guardiola Sala, commonly known as Pep Guardiola, FC Barcelona ball boy, player, captain, manager, winner, and Johan Cruijff disciple. When he was appointed Barcelona manager in 2008, his first address to the first team contained the following:

> I won't tell you off if you misplace a pass, or miss a header that costs us a goal, as long as I know you are giving 100 per cent. I could forgive you any mistake, but I won't forgive you if you don't give your heart and soul to Barcelona. I'm not asking results of you, just performance. I won't accept people speculating about performance, if it's half-hearted or people aren't giving their all. This is Barça, this is what is asked of us, and this is what I will ask of you. You have to give your all.[2]

It is every time I visit the school that I am reminded why it is my favourite. On top of everything else, for the children the school is a haven, a home. As you walk through the door, greeted courteously, respectfully, and with a smile, doors are opened for you, and at every turn you are welcomed and asked how you are – all by the children, of course. There is a positive work ethic and joy in the air, and relationships are wonderful. Displays are welcoming, bright, and shiny, positive, encouraging, aspirational, representative of the school's values, and they involve the children at every point. There is a vending machine from which you can obtain books via a token that is an award for being a star. The headteacher's office is at the front of the building, with an open door. Of course, it is not perfect – not all the time, anyway. Thankfully.

What is in evidence in such abundance in the school is the role we play as adults in the children's becoming me. And how this, in turn, grows into an organisational culture, into an organisational role model. We lead by example, and our example is mirrored and followed and becomes the norm, in turn feeding our core values: *We are a team. We care. We aim high. We are thoughtful. We have a voice. We are respectful. We have self-belief. We are determined.* When I say "we," I mean all those who are part of the school community, including children, teaching and non-teaching colleagues, parents and carers, external partners and volunteers, visitors to the school, Father Christmas, and the headteacher's husband. I love the school that much that I married the headteacher, or so the joke goes. After school, at weekends and during the school holidays, Vanessa Langley is Mrs Graus. Interest declared! We all have our role to play.

As adults, we bear a responsibility for the role we play in children's lives, for they consciously and subconsciously watch and emulate our behaviour. We need to bear that responsibility better, more clearly, as a higher priority, as a strategy to make our schools better. The role we play needs to be written into every job description; it needs to become the modus operandi to live our values and make them visible. Every action we take, every word we speak, and every decision we make have the potential to shape the beliefs, values, and attitudes of the younger generation. Therefore, it is crucial that we embody qualities and behaviours that we wish to see reflected in them. By being kind, compassionate, and respectful, we can inspire them to cultivate these qualities within themselves. Our responsibility lies not only in providing guidance but also in being people who demonstrate integrity, resilience, and empathy, as well as a positive work ethic and, intrinsically, a will to make the world a better place. Through our actions, we have the power to shape a future generation that is compassionate, responsible, and capable of creating positive change in the world. When this becomes an organisational culture – if you wish a chosen organisational role model rather than individual efforts – we make visible a way society can be. In this aspect, too, Arbourthorne Community Primary School is more than a school.

From the earliest of ages, the role we play in the lives of children holds immense power, as they are intelligent, perceptive, and impressionable human beings. In early childhood particularly, children are often likened to sponges, soaking up everything around them. We must remind ourselves that sponges soak up dirty as well as clean water. Our actions and behaviours serve as templates for them to emulate and learn from. It is crucial that we recognise the impact we have and strive to set positive examples. By exhibiting kindness, empathy, respect, beliefs based on values, and positive attitudes, we foster an environment conducive to their growth and development. Conversely, negative behaviours can leave lasting scars – I often use the Australian public service commercial *Kids Copy Our Behavior!* made by the Western Sydney University to exemplify this.[3] Whether consciously or subconsciously, children absorb and imitate what they observe. As caregivers, parents, teachers, and mentors, we must collectively embrace the responsibility of shaping their characters by embodying the qualities we seek to instil in them. The role we play is about values, principles, and behaviours. This includes, amongst many, other things, right and wrong, respect, kindness, positive attitudes, work ethic, truth, trust, transparency, and also, very importantly, the appreciation of aesthetics, beauty, awe, and wonder. And happiness, of course.

Through this, we become role models, Not all of us, not all to the same children, or at the same time. Becoming a role model is a bit like the wand in the *Harry Potter* books: it chooses the wizard.[4] We know that a role model is someone who should set a positive example for others, particularly children. We know that they possess qualities and behaviours that inspire and motivate others to emulate them. They can be parents, teachers, community leaders, national and international figures, celebrities, or even fictional characters. We know that the focus is on their overall being and the positive impact they have on others. But there is more. Like the wand chooses the wizard in the *Harry Potter* books, more often than not, the child chooses the role model, for better or for worse, from its experiences and its own view of the world. The role model is about more than the role we play. It is about who we would like to be like.

"Mrs Poole," "Mrs Poole," "Mrs Poole." Mrs Poole was a teaching assistant at Mottram St Andrew Primary School in the late 1990s and early 2000s. Mottram St Andrew Primary School is a small village school in leafy Cheshire where the personal touch was very important. Mrs Poole, above all, was the teaching assistant of my eldest daughter, Anna. Up to the point of meeting Mrs Poole, on her very first day at the school, Anna was a "Daddy," "Daddy," "Daddy" girl. "Look, Daddy!" "What's this, Daddy?" "Can I have . . . Daddy?" "I love you, Daddy." When Anna returned home after her very first day at school, her first words were "Mrs Poole." Her third, fourth, fifth, sixth words were also "Mrs Poole." For me, this was a new experience, and I wasn't sure how I felt about "Mrs Poole this" and "Mrs Poole that." Mrs Poole, incidentally, was everything you, as a parent, would want a Mrs Poole to be. She was kind, generous, patient, wonderful with children, in her own way bringing the best out of them and, through all this, making sure that they couldn't wait to be back the next day for more. The wand had chosen the wizard.

I wonder whether Mrs Poole really ever knew how important she was to Anna and what tone she actually set. In the role they play, everyday role models have a significant influence and hold immense importance in the lives of children in the early stages of childhood. These role models, which certainly included Mrs Poole, serve as a consistent source of inspiration, guidance, and encouragement for children. They provide a consistent framework for behaviour and values, shaping the way children perceive and interact with the world around them, and teach children important life lessons, helping them develop essential social and emotional skills. By observing and emulating the Mrs Pooles of the world, children learn how to navigate challenges, set goals, and make responsible choices. Moreover, their presence contributes to the development of positive self-esteem and confidence in children from the earliest of ages, as they witness their characteristics, accomplishments, and abilities. They serve as beacons of inspiration and guidance throughout their formative years.

As we grow older and become more experienced, into our teenage years and beyond, our role model choices become more deliberate, at times more complex. For me, firstly, of course, there was, and is, my grandad – Opa. Always. My other personal, chosen role models have varied enormously over time. From the fictional Floris, a Dutch Robin Hood–style good guy, to Robin Hood himself; to Bud, who owned Flipper; to *Bonanza*'s Little Joe; to *Till der Junge von nebenan*; and to Willy Vandersteen's Suske, of course, of *Suske en Wiske* fame. In real life, there were Anne Frank (I wanted to be able write like her), Heintje Simons (I wanted to sing like him), Dr Martin Luther King (I wanted to be able to speak like him), Christiaan Barnard (I wanted to save lives like him), and Johan Cruijff, of course – I wanted to play the game of football like him and be longhaired and rebellious like him. At various points during my childhood and youth, I wanted to be like these people and characters. In many cases, I still do. Looking back, I now also realise that I at no point saw that first and foremost Anne was a Jewish teenage girl, or that Martin was a Black American, as an obstacle – it genuinely never occurred to me, I am happy to say. I saw who they were and what they could do. I was also lucky, I guess. Censorship was not something I was aware of, which meant that I and my teenage contemporaries pretty much had role model access to whatever and whoever was out there. In the Netherlands in those days, society was liberal, and the church's censorial reach was increasingly limited to pulpits in half-empty buildings. Jan Wolker's 1969 erotic romantic novel *Turks Fruit* was ours to read and could be found on most schools' reading lists. When the Paul Verhoeven–directed film was released in 1973, Monique van de Ven and Rutger Hauer respectively became every Dutch male and female teenager's poster girl and boy. I suspect that in countries like the United Kingdom and the United States, this may have been somewhat different. When shortly after its publication in 1986, Bob Geldof's *Is That It?* autobiography was suggested by some to be placed on the English literature A-level list, there was an outcry. In the 21st century in the United States of America, "certain" – whatever that means – books are now being banned and withdrawn from reading lists. Who thinks it a good idea to ban books, school and children's books at that? They will be burning them next. Perhaps Professor Henry Walton Jones Senior, fictional father of the fictional archaeologist and action hero Dr Henry Walton "Indiana" Jones Jr. should be another of my role models: "Goose-stepping morons like yourselves should try reading books instead of burning them!"[5]

As time has passed, I still see Anne Frank as my role model, but now well beyond her writing abilities. I still want to be able to speak like Martin Luther King, but I now also want to behave like him, and Mahatma Ghandi. My admiration for those working in healthcare is, I suppose, in some way, connected to my admiration for Christiaan Barnard, who performed the first human-to-human heart transplant operation on 3rd December 1967 at the Groote Schuur hospital in Cape Town. Johan Cruijff's sublime footballing skills are now outweighed by his leadership qualities that go well beyond the game of football itself – although I do have to confess that, even now, at the age of nearly 68, I cannot walk past a football without trying the Cruijff turn – almost always badly. Robin Hood is also still there, and I am pleased to say that later in life, I have driven many a finance director to despair by insisting on "Robin Hood policies": at KidZania, for example, schools from disadvantaged areas paid significantly less than did their more affluent counterparts, who, in turn, actually subsidised the KidZania experiences of their less-fortunate contemporaries. As far as books and Henry Jones Sr. are concerned, "[i]f you only read the books that everyone else is reading, you can only think what everyone else is thinking."[6] Context matters more and more as experience grows. Other role models have come at various times, and a few have also gone again, but not Dutch prime minister Joop Den Uyl; Christa Wolf; Welsh actor Richard Burton; South African president Nelson Mandela, and United States of America President Barack Obama; Desmond Tutu – naturally; German Chancellor Angela Merkel. "Wir schaffen das. We can do this," her statement made during the 2015 European migrant crisis, described as a core slogan of the German concept of Willkommenskultur.[7] In 2015 and 2016, Germany, a country of about 80 million citizens, took in about 1.2 million asylum seekers in total (compare that to the just under 20,000 asylum seekers who entered the United Kingdom).

What, however, happens when the wand chooses the wrong wizard? What if the wrong role model is chosen? Every generation has its own experiences, good ones, not-so-good ones, tempting ones. In my case, the good ones included the first man on the moon; the oil crisis of the 1970s and car-free Sundays, including riding our bicycles on the motorway; the 1974 football World Cup Final, being the best and still losing; Live Aid; the Tony Blair UK election victory in May 1997; "Things can only get better," and they did; in 1990, Nelson Mandela walking out of the Victor Verster prison; and then spending time with Desmond Tutu many years later. The confusion, unrest, and uncertainties of the years around 1968, for me, were a tempting experience.

In continental Europe, the late 1960s and early 1970s were times of unrest, demonstrations, uprising even. From Berlin, via Paris, to Rome, and even Amsterdam. Rudi Dutschke and Daniel Cohn-Bendit, German and French student leaders, respectively; the Sessantotto in Italy; and the Kabouters, or Gnomes, in the Netherlands; university occupations; strikes; transforming economies; the Cold War; the war in Vietnam; and on top of all that, in West Germany and Italy, a generation that was still coming to terms with their parents' and grandparents' war, World War II, and the concept of their Kollektivschuld.[8] Evidence of a distaste and discontent is evident with traditional societies. Whilst in most of Europe the unrest was the result of ideological, cultural, economic, and generational clashes, in Italy and West Germany, the causes went deeper and were personal. *Wo warst du, Adam?* Heinrich Böll's 1951 novel *Where were you, Adam?* is about the question about society's responsibility for its actions and symbolises the zeitgeist of those born after 1945. The children's question to their parents and grandparents was literally that: Where were you? At the same time, they saw those who were fascist collaborators now also in important positions in the new Germany. And Italy. And the United States of America. The news coverage of the demonstrations and riots was relentless, albeit that, in those days, there was no 24-hour news, no internet, no social media. "The youth of today." Many impressionable Rolling Stones- and Bob Dylan-loving teenagers were hooked. I was fascinated, curious. With hindsight, it felt as if we understood the anger.

As the protests slowly wilted, after initial hopes of fundamental change, the resolve of a few hardened. The Rote Armee Faktion, or Red Army Faction (RAF), also known as the Baader-Meinhof Group, named after its founders, the journalists Ulrike Meinhof and Andreas Baader, emerged in West Germany in those late 1960s. While it is not directly derived from the 1968 student revolts, the movement did have roots in the broader sociopolitical climate of that time. The RAF was a left-wing militant group that believed in armed resistance against what they perceived as historical capitalist imperialism and state repression. *Wo warst du, Adam?* At the same time in Italy, the Brigate Rosse, or Red Brigades, emerged in the wake of the 1968 student revolts. "One man's terrorist is another's freedom fighter."[9] To a rebelling teenage boy, there was a naive element of romance and excitement in this, not much different to television's *Floris* and *Robin Hood*, or Che Guevara, one of the poster boys of that time. With hindsight, what was missing was Google – personal fact-checking was almost impossible, and so the fairy tale lived on. The bubble burst when the murders started: amongst many, the aeroplane hijack murders in Somalia's capital, Mogadishu, and the murders of Siegfried Buback, the attorney-general of West Germany; Jürgen Ponto, the head of Dresdner Bank; Hanns Martin Schleyer, then-president of the West German Employers' Association – all leading members of West German society, all former Nazis, all executed, without trial. Faced with reality. I remember those names to this day. The difference between *Floris*, *Robin Hood*, and Baader-Meinhof.

In Italy, the story of the Brigate Rosse was very similar. Every time I stand on Piattaforma 1 at Bologna Centrale, Bologna's railway station, as I have done many times, including with Wythenshawe primary school children, I am reminded of that time in the late 1960s, the 1970s, and the early 1980s. In the morning of 2nd August 1980, at 10:25, a time bomb hidden in an unattended suitcase detonated in an air-conditioned waiting room at Bologna Centrale, which was full of people seeking relief from the August heat. The explosion collapsed the roof of the waiting room, destroyed most of the main building, and hit the Ancona-to-Chiasso train, which was waiting at that first platform. Eighty-five people, including children, died, and over 200 were injured. The huge crack in the waiting room wall has been left as a reminder, alongside the names of those who died. It was found to be the work of the neo-fascist group Nuclei Armati Rivoluzionari, not as first and for a long time suspected the Brigate Rosse. Same difference.

In the end, of course, for me at least, the wand chose the right wizards. But I do understand how easy it would be not to. "Every child is everyone's responsibility."

If we see the role we play firstly as inescapable – we play a role whether we like it or not – and secondly as one of upholding values, living them, leading by example, walking the talk, as something we also collectively do, and we see role models as the chosen individuals within that framework of behaviours, like the wand chooses the wizard, we also need to have a closer look at what we mean by heroes, legends, celebrities, et al. We have become, I feel, very liberal, very loose in the use of words like *hero* and *legend*. There are times when we would do well to consult an old-fashioned dictionary and remind ourselves of the origins of the words we so easily attribute to people, especially to social media, "famous for 15 minutes"[10] celebrities.

In summary, the role we all play is a fact of life and one of upholding values. This does include, as we have already seen, right and wrong, respect, kindness, work ethic, truth, trust, transparency, and also the appreciation of aesthetics, beauty, awe, and wonder. A *role model* is someone who is chosen because he or she sets an example for others, particularly children. They possess qualities and behaviours that inspire and motivate others to emulate them. Role models often exhibit integrity, empathy, perseverance, and other desirable traits. They can be anyone within the experience field of the child, even fictional characters. The focus is on their overall character and the impact they have on others. A *hero* is someone who goes above and beyond to help others, often in the face of adversity or danger. They are seen as courageous, selfless, and morally upright individuals who perform extraordinary acts. Heroes are typically known for their acts of bravery, such as rescuing people from perilous situations or fighting for justice, often supporting the underdog. While they can serve as role models, not all role models are considered heroes. *Superheroes* are fictional heroes with extraordinary or superhuman powers who use this special strength to do good things and help other people. And finally, a *celebrity* is a person who is widely recognised and famous, typically for their achievements in entertainment, sports, or other fields. Their fame often stems from their talent, skills, or public persona. Celebrities enjoy significant public attention and may have a large following, but their influence on children can vary greatly, as can their longevity. Some celebrities may serve as positive role models, using their platform to inspire and make a difference. It is important to consider the values and behaviours of individuals in these different roles when assessing their impact on children.

I have only truly ever met one or two people who to me are all four: playing their role, a role model to me and many others, and a hero. They are celebrities too, reluctantly. The wand choosing the wizard applies to grown-ups too.

BBC One, 09:00 p.m., the Nine O'Clock News, 23rd October 1984. A Tuesday unlike any other. "Dawn . . . it lights up a biblical famine . . . the closest thing to hell on earth. . . . [D]eath is all around."[11] The report about famine in Ethiopia, first broadcast nearly 40 years ago, is one of a handful of television news reports that changed the way we view the world. Michael Buerk's words and the accompanying images led to the greatest single global outpouring of charity and sympathy in the late 20th century, as Bob Geldof's the Band Aid Trust, the "Do They Know It's Christmas" single, the Live Aid Concert, and Sport Aid galvanised a world stunned. In turn, it led to a generation of celebrities for whom the causes of the under-developed world, and Africa in particular, would eventually become a necessary accessory to their careers. George Clooney's involvement in Darfur, Salma Hayek's in Sierra, Angelina Jolie as a United Nations ambassador, Bono's and Luciano Pavarotti's charity concerts would all have been unthinkable 40 or so years ago were it not for the bandwagon begun by Michael Buerk's report. It also led charities to transform themselves into business-like aid organisations, and the establishment of overseas aid departments in every Western government. Charity was replaced by aid, sympathy by activism. Turning a blind eye was no longer really possible. Michael Burke's BBC news report and Bob Geldof's subsequent response embedded themselves into my generation's conscience. And into that of Taverham High School.

Wednesday, 24th October 1984, Taverham High School. Morning briefing took place every day at 08:45 a.m. in the staffroom before the teaching day started. It was the responsibility of the deputy headteacher, Brian Copelin, to coordinate what were mostly operational matters – who was absent, who was visiting the school, important matters we needed to know about things that had occurred in the lives of our children, any other business. Under "any other business," I could not help but raise the Michael Buerk BBC news broadcast from the night before. I suggested that, as a school community, we had a responsibility to do something, anything, as long as it made a difference. Everybody agreed. The long journey to collectively making a difference had started, and more than once it felt like the blind leading the blind. Everything we did was new, at least to us. Following Bob Geldof, we had a role to play.

"The most inspirational person of my educational years taught me that we are all equal. A sponsored walk with penfriends on an exchange trip in Germany led by Dr Ger Graus for Live Aid still makes me proud of the determination for change we all had and have," so said former pupil and now underwriting team manager at Countrywide Richard Ward. Kindness and a sense of humour were two of Richard's greatest attributes, even as a young teenager at Taverham High School. I happily and humbly take the compliment, though.

By the time I left Taverham High School in March 1988, we had raised in excess of £10,000 for the Band Aid Trust, more than any other school in the country, regardless of size. Assemblies, raffles, auctions, donations, fasts, jumble sales, non-uniform days, sponsored breakfasts and runs, cycle rides and even canoe journeys into school, a sponsored walk during our German exchange with our friends from the Städtisches Gymnasium Mechernich, and of course, our sponsored Sport Aid run in May 1986, which took over the whole of Taverham, stopped traffic, and brought everybody out of their houses and into the school. The run itself raised over £7,000. It is worth reflecting what a wonderful effort all this was. A small rural school with some 500 children and its teaching and non-teaching staff raised more than £38,500 in today's money. Even more importantly, however, as Richard Ward indicates, we played our role in changing mindsets and *heartsets*.

Where to start? It took a while for us to get our act together. Ironically, that was exactly what was also happening at the Band Aid Trust headquarters, based at the back of Debenhams on Oxford Street in London. Eventually, I found a telephone number, and I rang. Penny Jenden, who was Band Aid's director, answered the phone and, after a lengthy conversation, passed me on to a number of other people who had turned up in a volunteering capacity. We grew our relationship from there. There was something wonderful about the organisation. On a day-to-day basis, they were dealing with some of the world's most prominent politicians, presidents and prime ministers, musicians, journalists, and reporters; they were constantly on the news, and yet they always found time to work with us, to be kind and respectful, to guide us, and to listen. It was as if nobody was more important than the next person. With hindsight, a little bit like Arbourthorne Community Primary School, the Band Aid Trust felt like an organisational role model, reflecting the values of those behind it.

When Saturday, the 13th of July, arrived, Live Aid day, everything felt unreal. I remember television screens pretty much wherever you went with the live broadcasts from Wembley and, later, Philadelphia. The public had been invited to become activists, not just to donate, but to participate, to be angry, to talk, and to become part of the solution. I truly believe that the Band Aid Trust, on that day, redefined the charitable role we can play. This redefinition had started from the moment the trust was formed. Bob Geldof was omnipresent, arguing as much for change as he was pleading for donations: "Give us your fucking money now!" When the Christmas single "Do They Know It's Christmas" was released in December 1984, the public reaction was extraordinary and wonderful in equal measure. I remember in Andy's Records, a local music store in the centre of Norwich, people buying 10 or 20 copies of the single, keeping one and giving the rest back to the store for resale. Food stalls and street vendors would charge what I can now only describe as a Band Aid tax and donate this straight to the cause. The words "Will you sponsor me?" were heard everywhere. Michael Buerk's news report and Bob Geldof's reaction had sparked a public warmth that was rare in a political climate where the then prime minister Margaret Thatcher had declared that "[t]here is no such thing as society." She was wrong.

Looking back now, everything feels like a timelapse. So much was going on, so many people wanting to become involved that the whole thing very quickly expanded beyond Taverham High School, into the city of Norwich itself, and into the University of East Anglia. Andy's Records – that store again – donated free singles, maxi singles, and albums for auctions and raffles, and when artists were performing at the University of East Anglia's Student Union, the store gave us even more so that these memorabilia could be signed and auctioned. Our friends at the University of East Anglia's Student Union supported us time after time. Talk Talk's drumsticks, Suzanne Vega's albums, Big Country's T-shirts, Jesus and Mary Chain, Alison Moyet, John Martyn, Marillion, Echo and the Bunnymen, Squeeze. . . . We received messages from Bill Wyman, Midge Ure, and Bob himself. Later, local businesses printed our Taverham High School Sport Aid T-shirts at cost price. Food sold on the Sport Aid day was donated for free. The police and St John's Ambulance Service turned up free of charge. Local shopkeepers did what they could to support, and even the press got behind us.

Following on from Live Aid, Sport Aid was a sport-themed campaign for African famine relief held in May 1986, involving several days of all-star exhibition events in various sports and culminating in the *Race Against Time*, a 10-kilometre fun run held simultaneously in 89 countries. Timed to coincide with a UNICEF development conference in New York City, Sport Aid raised £30 million for the Band Aid Trust and UNICEF. The event was organised by Sport Aid chair and founder Chris Long, Bob Geldof, and John Anderson, head of Global Special Events, UNICEF. At 15:00 UTC on Sunday, 25th May 1986, runners around the world ran, jogged, or walked 10 kilometres, having collected sponsorships or donations to support African famine relief charities. That day, nearly 500 children, teachers, non-teaching colleagues, governors, parents, brothers and sisters, wives, husbands, partners, and others, including the staff from Andy's Records, ran the Taverham High School *Race Against Time*. Those who couldn't run or walk cooked, marshalled, sold drinks, helped with the set-up and with the tidying afterwards. Christine Green, our Latin and classical studies teacher, counted the pennies, every single one of them. In our lives, this is a day that will never be forgotten. We all played our role, but nobody more so than Bob Geldof – role model, hero, reluctant celebrity. Live Aid and all that followed left many marks. It certainly contributed in a very big way to Taverham High School becoming much more than a school. It also meant that, since, I have never been able to listen to "Drive" by the Cars again. In a hut backstage before the concert, Bob Geldof had shown David Bowie a film compiled from newsreel footage of the Ethiopian famine, shot by the Canadian Broadcasting Corporation. David Bowie, in tears, offered to drop a song from his main set to show the video. As he left the stage, Bowie announced, "Lest we forget why we are here, I would like to introduce a video made by CBC Television; the subject speaks for itself. Please send your money in." The music the video was set to was "Drive" by the Cars.[12]

We met for the first time at Television Centre in London for an episode of the BBC One children's television programme *Blue Peter*. The date, Thursday, 12th February 1987; the time, 04:30 p.m. Bob Geldof was there with his dog, Growler; the presenters were the late Caron Keating, Janet Ellis, and Mark Curry. The occasion was to introduce three teenagers who would be accompanying Bob on a fact-finding visit to Ethiopia – they were Melanie Saluja from Longcroft School in Beverley in the East Riding of Yorkshire, and Nicola Adams and Heath Dicks from Taverham High School. Both schools were being recognised for their wonderful contributions to the work of the Band Aid Trust. I am certain they could have chosen any of many schools across the country. Our Taverham High School's Nicola and Heath were nominated by the school community as two young people, amongst so very many, whose commitment had been role-model-like. I met Bob again many years later, at the education show BETT in London, on 24th January 2018, where we were both speaking. It fell to me to introduce him onto the stage. I had been given a whole list of instructions and accomplishments which I was to mention as part of my introduction. However, he and I had caught up beforehand and ended up discussing our *Blue Peter* appearance and, of course, our *Blue Peter* badges. Naturally, Bob Geldof has a gold one. My introduction, in the end, simply mentioned Sir Bob Geldof, Live Aid, the fact that we were on *Blue Peter* together, and that he outranked me in terms of badgeholdership. It was a delight to reconnect.

I shall be forever grateful to Bob Geldof for the changes he brought about in us, how his activism made us change the way we played our roles. I admire most his honest and direct approach, his resilience, his perseverance, his self-belief, his outspokenness, and his stubbornness; the fact that, at times, he didn't seem to give a toss about what certain people thought of him; but most of all, I admire his belief in activism. Role model activists are not commonplace. In a different way and in different times, to a different generation, perhaps Greta Thunberg is like Bob Geldof. An inspiration and a role model to many, disliked by the powers that be, a rebel with a cause.

Less of a rebel but still with a cause is the Bollywood superstar Shah Rukh "King" Khan. In India, Khan is the subject of hero worshipping on an epic scale. SRK has appeared in more than 90 films and earned numerous accolades, including 14 *Filmfare Awards*, the annual awards that honour artistic and technical excellence in the Hindi-language film industry of India. He has been awarded the civilian honour *Padma Shri* by the government of India, as well as the *Ordre des Arts et des Lettres* and *L'Ordre National de la Légion d'Honneur* by the government of France. Khan has a significant following in Asia and the Indian diaspora worldwide. In terms of audience size and income, several media outlets have described him as one of the most successful film stars in the world. Many of his films thematise Indian national identity and connections with diaspora communities, as well as gender, racial, social, and religious differences and grievances. The hero worshipping, however, extends well beyond Shah Rukh Khan's artistic exploits. His philanthropic endeavours have provided healthcare and disaster relief, and he was honoured with UNESCO's *Pyramide con Marni* award in 2011 for his support of children's education, and the World Economic Forum's *Crystal Award* in 2018 for advocating for women's and children's rights in India. His Meer Foundation empowers women and helps acid attack survivors in India. He also supports cancer sufferers, in memory of his father, Mir Taj Mohammed Khan.

Shah Rukh Khan is also connected to the two KidZanias in India, KidZania Mumbai and KidZania Delhi, both as an investor and as an educator. He takes an active interest and, whenever possible, visits both KidZanias, when the admiration for him becomes evident. Teachers, parents, carers, and children speak of his Bollywood and philanthropic engagements in equal measure. "King" Khan is admired for who he is as much as for what he does. This was never more evident than during the opening of KidZania Delhi on 26th May 2016, when his role model and hero status shone like nothing I had seen before. The story goes that there had to be two opening nights. The first one with Shah Rukh Khan in attendance, when the crowds turned out to be with him. The second opening was the following day, when "King" Khan was not there and everyone came to see the new KidZania. Like many others who have achieved fame and riches, Shah Rukh Khan made a choice, and it is that choice to be seen to be good that makes him the role model he is.

An initially unexpected by-product of the KidZania concept was the role model aspect of the supervisors, our colleagues who were running and role-playing the 60 or so activities in each of the KidZanias. "Children can only aspire to what they know exists." KidZanias are cities built for children, where young people aged 4 to 14 can experience the world of work through role-modelling and role-play, designed to inspire and empower: from inspiration to aspiration. Since its inception in 1999 in Mexico City, KidZania now has a presence in 25 cities in 22 countries on five continents, with plans for further developments in some 20 locations, including Europe, USA, Canada, China, Australia, and South Africa. Since 1999, the total visitor number globally has exceeded 100 million children. Through its commercial partners, there are more than 60 real-life professions children can learn about in a 75,000-square-foot child-sized city, as part of KidZania's experience-based approach to learning. KidZania London was the United Kingdom's first educational entertainment centre, opening in June 2015. I became its first global education director. I am convinced that, in the future, we will see many manifestations of this KidZania-style thinking and concept, both in the real world and online.

In 2015, Ken Ramirez was the managing director of Renault UK. Ken, Mexican by birth, had worked in the car industry all his life, including in Japan, where he had met his wife and where his daughter Miriam was born. Miriam had visited the KidZanias in Mexico, the Middle East, and Japan and was a fan. Her first question when the Ramirez family moved to London was, "Where is KidZania London?" The answer was "Being built." The subsequent call from Ken Ramirez that came into the KidZania London office said, "Renault wants to sponsor the automotive activity at KidZania London." Thank you, Miriam.

Changing the tyres on a Formula E replica car, wearing Renault overalls in a noisy workshop, being the engineer, was the main part of the Renault activity. It was noisy, fast, and furious, and you could almost, *almost* smell the burning rubber off the tyres. Originally, the activity was timed, and the overall winners over a period of time were given family tickets to visit the annual Formula E event in London. The KidZania London Renault activity was opened by the former four-time Formula One world champion and Renault driver Alain Prost and his Formula E driver son, Nico. The first part of the activity was about exploring the differences between an electric engine and a traditional combustion engine, an eco-activity, so to speak, that had the white laboratory coat appearance of the appliance of science.

With hindsight, analysis showed us that the staffing of the activity itself was almost entirely male almost all the time – two male supervisors in Renault overalls, tools in hand, next to a Formula E racing car. Human resources applying stereotypes. What could possibly go wrong? The fact that all this was unintentional, and without much further thought, says something in itself.

The analysis of the Renault Formula E activity as part of my ongoing global research showed, not surprisingly, in the light of the staffing analysis, that it was almost entirely male: 97 per cent of the children opting into the activity were boys, from the age of 4. It was time to experiment. Many conversations followed with my friends at the Fondazione Reggio Children, and with Carla Rinaldi in particular. For a long time, I had been telling our supervisors how important they were to the children's learning and fun aspects of the activities. The level and quality of interaction make or break the experience. But I had focused too much on the acting role of the adults and not enough on how and what the children see.

For four weeks, I parked myself on a bench outside the Renault activity. The plan became that, every day, in full Renault kits, between 10:00 a.m. and 12:00 noon, the activity would be staffed by two male colleagues; between 12:00 noon and 2:00 p.m., there would be one male and one female supervisor; and between 2:00 p.m. and 4:00 p.m., two female colleagues would run the show. It was a game of wait-and-see. Almost immediately, patterns developed, and they lasted throughout the four-week test period.

Between 10:00 a.m. and 12:00 noon, you could literally sit and watch the girls go by. You could see them look and think, "This activity is not for me." It was reminiscent of my childhood, when girls at football matches would, at best, stand on the sidelines and watch. They would certainly never participate. This was not for the girls. In that first session of the day, the activity was a boys' domain: Consistently, over 95 per cent of the children choosing to participate in the activity were boys. The change during the second session was noticeable. The one female supervisor visibly drew the attention of the passing girls: The percentages changed consistently across the four weeks to around 80 per cent boys and 20 per cent girls. The third and final session had an even greater impact. You could see a significant number of girls look and think, "This activity is for me." The average percentages over the four-week observation period landed at around 35 per cent girls and 65 per cent boys. We can only be what we can see. A key lesson from an organisational point of view is that change like this can be achieved at no extra cost; for us, this was merely a different, more empathetic deployment of existing human resources. Thoughtfulness goes a long way. We need to utilise this in many more walks of life, including, of course, teaching, both in terms of primary education in general, and also in terms of subject specialisms in secondary education and beyond. And this does not just apply to gender. The beauty of being a Formula E engineer was in the eyes of many more beholders. The role we play is seemingly often subconscious, hidden even. That, too, is in the eye of the beholder. It affects ethnicity, socio-economic contexts, geography, and more. If we put ourselves in their shoes, and when we create the right environment, we can trust the children to flourish. Empathy and trust are key. The research itself is ongoing and now, apart from the Higher School of Economics University and Oxford University, also includes Qatari universities.

Dennis Bergkamp was 17 years old when then Ajax technical director Johan Cruijff played him in the European Cup quarter-final against Malmö FF in Sweden. The story of Dennis Bergkamp's breakthrough is one of trust in youth and finds its origins in the summer of 1985, with Ajax's third coming of Johan Cruijff. Ajax wanted to appoint the club legend as their new manager, but he lacked the required diplomas. And for the record, he wasn't going to put any effort into obtaining those. As a ruse, the Amsterdam club provided him with three assistants, who did take the necessary exams and made Cruijff a technical director who helped out at the training ground. He actually was, in effect, nothing less than the manager. The Dutch FA knew there wasn't much they could do to stop it so simply decided to award him his diploma in January 1986, anyway. Cruijff turned it into a habit to give chances to young talents, with his motto that "good enough is old enough." I often imagine and wish for this vision, belief, commitment, and trust in our secondary education.

The 1986–1987 season turned out to be the beginning of an Ajax rebirth – not least because of a teenage schoolboy. In the final days of 1986, Cruijff handed the 17-year-old Dennis Bergkamp his competitive debut in the Eredivisie, against Roda JC. Then, in March of 1987, the youngster claimed his place in the hearts of Dutch fans forever. The draw for the quarter-final of the Cup Winners' Cup pitted Ajax against Malmö FF, a Swedish side then managed by Englishman Roy Hodgson. It was a good draw for the Amsterdam club, everyone agreed. Despite not being the world force they once were, Ajax should be able to beat Malmö and progress to the semi-finals. On 4th March, they travelled to Sweden for the first leg, only to find out the pitch was covered in snow. The game was cancelled at the last minute and rescheduled for Saturday, 14th March. The cancellation meant Bergkamp missed out on his European debut, so after the new date was decided, he immediately checked his diary. He was disappointed. Why? The youngster had a year and a half left at grammar school and was determined to get his diploma. The Ajax squad was supposed to travel to Sweden on Thursday, but young Dennis had an important biology exam scheduled for Friday. Cruijff respected that, but leaving his most talented youngster out of his squad was not an option. He set up an ingenious plan. Schoolboy Bergkamp could sit his exam on Friday, and then his parents would drive him to Schiphol Airport, where he got on a plane to Copenhagen with Dutch journalist Kees Jansma as his chaperone. From there, the duo was to reach Malmö by boat. In those days, Bergkamp was not yet afraid of flying, which allowed him to make a 15-minute appearance in a surprise, 1–0 defeat in Sweden. Despite not standing out, Cruijff had absolutely no doubts about his young talent and handed him a spot in the starting line-up for the return game just four days later. Not for the first time, Cruijff surprised friends and enemies by fielding an unknown youngster in a big game. Ajax finally had the chance to reach European success, after all those years, and the manager was putting his faith in a teenager who hadn't yet proved to be an asset. What was he thinking? The criticism would soon die down. De Meer, the iconic former Ajax stadium, where, as a teenager myself, I saw Cruijff et al. perform their magic, was packed with 25,000 fans who all wanted to see their team overturn the 1–0 defeat.

The pitch was, as was so often the case, absolutely abysmal, but the Ajax technicians showed that they coped with the circumstances better than the Swedish with their English kick-and-rush style. In his debut as a starter, Bergkamp played as a left winger and surprised everybody by impressing with a scintillating display that put his marker in a spin. Before the match, Cruijff told him, "That defender is an old fart, he's useless and slow – you are better than he is," or so Bergkamp explains it in his autobiography.[13] The youngster proved him right. Bergkamp's experienced teammate Frank Rijkaard would later say, "Dennis toyed with the man, leaving him colourblind." After Marco van Basten scored to make it 1–0, Aron Winter struck a second, before Van Basten sealed the deal with goal number 3. Malmö's Lindman's goal to make it 3–1 was too little too late. But Bergkamp was the talk of the town. Cruijff even granted him a substitution in the 87th minute. Bergkamp left the field to a standing ovation. As for Bergkamp's school test? He passed the biology exam he took in March and advanced to the final year of grammar school. Bergkamp continued his progression, with the first team ending the season playing a role in an Ajax cup double. The Dutch Cup was successfully defended, after Bergkamp came on as a substitute with Ajax 2–1 down to Den Haag to play his part in a 4–2 extra-time win for the Amsterdam club. He also came off the bench in the European Cup Winners' Cup final – a 1–0 win against East German–side FC Lokomotive Leipzig. It was the first of many trophies in a career which took Bergkamp to Inter Milan in 1993, and then to Arsenal, but which started, improbably, with a late flight to Sweden and trust in youth. In education and schooling, we should look and learn from others and elsewhere.

I have always liked football, ever since I was a child. In many ways, I was fortunate that as I grew up Dutch, football was seen as the best there was. Style, class, and winning almost everything there was to be won. On rare occasions, I even got to go to De Meer in Amsterdam, the home of Ajax. From the sidelines, ever so close by, I was able to admire the likes of Keizer, Neeskens, Krol, and of course, the genius that was Johan Cruijff. Johan Cruijff, with his shirt numbers 9 and then 14, was my hero, one of my role models, who I admired from afar. Endless hours into darkness, I practised his trademark Cruijff turn, and even now, if there is a ball loose somewhere and nobody is watching, I can't help but have a go. Johan Cruijff, like a Dutch Beatle, had long hair. He was different. He was different on the football pitch and off it. In an age when children and young people were there to be seen and not heard, he talked incessantly, showing little respect for authority for the sake of it, like a footballing John Lennon. He was another rebel with a cause, disliked by those who sought to maintain the post-war status quo. In his second international match for the Netherlands, a friendly against the then Czechoslovakia, Cruijff was the first Dutch international to be sent off – for dissent. Even that was cool. Johan Cruijff personalised the youthful unrest that existed in the Europe of the late 1960s. And he was truly brilliant. What was there not to like? Just like I remember those early, heady days, I also remember where I was on the day he died. On holiday in my hometown of Echt, in the chip shop formerly known as Café Friture Spee, when, whilst ordering my "Frites met mayonnaise en frikandellen," the news broke. It was 24th March 2016. Appetite gone.

Total Football (Dutch: *Totaalvoetbal*) is a tactical system in association football in which any outfield player can take over the role of any other player in the team. Dutch club, Ajax, and the Netherlands national football team are generally credited with creating this system during the 1970s. Johan Cruijff was its leader on the pitch, the conductor of the football orchestra. Total Football was all about teamwork, positioning, and space. The *Times* sportswriter David Miller christened Cruijff "Pythagoras in boots."

Johan Cruijff later became one of the world's most successful football managers and is often credited with changing the game, positively, forever. His autobiography, *My Turn*, is as much about the leadership and management of how this was achieved as it is about football itself.

It is a book I would recommend anybody to read, anybody who wants better outcomes for the people they work with and for. It is a book I believe should be in every school staffroom.

What I, after all these years, admire most about Cruijff is that almost-unrivalled trust in youth. It is something all of us who engage with children and young people should look at, from De Toekomst and La Masia, the youth academies in Amsterdam, and later in Barcelona, to his general leadership of young players. Teenagers were entrusted with leading roles in Ajax's first team, and their training was scheduled around their schooling and examinations. This was later copied by his acolytes, including Frank Rijkaard, Pep Guardiola, Arsène Wenger, Xavi. Lionel Messi became Lionel Messi because of Johan Cruijff. Imagine if we took this approach with our own young people in our education and schooling.

Parallels and similarities with education and schooling are more than superficial. If we invested our vision, energy, determination, and resources in our young people in the way that Cruijff envisaged, I feel that there would be many more winners. It is perhaps not a coincidence that, after his retirement, he invested most of his time in charitable work related to education and those less-privileged, still outspoken, still challenging authority for authority's sake, in his own inimitable way and style. In Dutch language, *Cruijffiaans* is the name for the unique language and expressions of the Dutch football player and football coach Johan Cruijff.

"Choose the best player for every position, and you will end up not with a strong XI, but with 11 strong 1s," so said Johan Cruijff.

Professionally, many of my lessons were learned from the late professors Sirs Tim Brighouse and Ken Robinson, from Ashoka founder Bill Drayton, from the Instituto Ayrton Senna, and from museologist Dr James Bradburne, amongst many others like my friend Professor Colin Beard, expert in experiential learning, Margaret Shelton, headteacher and the calm in the middle of the storm that was the then Lowry High School in Salford, David Johnston, education director in Manchester and Salford, and the late John Gretton, pillar of the Wythenshawe community and long-serving headteacher at St Anthony RC Primary School – stability matters in unstable contexts. Of course, there is Carla Rinaldi, the president of the Fondazione Reggio Children, my Édith Piaf–like friend – unassuming until her voice is heard, but she has a foot firmly in both the professional and the personal role model camps. Naturally, there is Desmond Tutu – "Whatever the question, education is always the answer" – another one of the few people who to me was all four: playing their role, a role model to me and many others, and a hero. He was an almost-reluctant celebrity too. But mostly there are teachers – my teachers and my colleagues. There were also my lecturers at the Mollerinstituut Tilburg and the Katholieke Universiteit Nijmegen, both in the Netherlands as well as at the Pädagogische Hochschule Theodor Neubauer, Erfurt *Mü*hlhausen, in the former East Germany, and at the Universität Kassel in the former West Germany. Of course, Desmond Tutu was a schoolteacher, too, as was his wife, Auntie Leah, until they were told to teach differently if the children were Black. "The mind once enlightened cannot again become dark."[14]

Many of those lessons learned were about individual brilliance, but as time went by, increasingly more became about teamwork and culture; about values, influence, and making a difference collectively; about community; about how schools inspire; about organisational brilliance.

When I was 12, I was marched, with my classmates, into the large hall at Tapton School in Sheffield. We sat in front of an ancient, black and white television and watched grainy pictures from the Mexico 1968 Olympic Games. Two athletes, both teachers from our hometown were competing. John Sherwood won a bronze medal in the 400m hurdles. His wife Sheila narrowly missed gold in the long jump. That day a window to a new world opened for me. By the time I was back in my classroom, I knew what I wanted to do, what I wanted to be. I stood for hours at my local track just to catch a glimpse of the medals the Sherwoods brought home. It didn't stop there. Days later I joined their club, the Hallamshire Harriers. Two years after that Sheila gave me my first pair of spikes. My journey started in that school hall and continues today – in wonder and in gratitude.

My fellow Sheffielder, fellow board director, and friend Lord Sebastian Coe. A middle-distance runner, Seb Coe won the 1,500 metres gold medals at the Olympic Games in 1980 and 1984 in Moscow and Los Angeles, respectively, and set 12 world records, both outdoor and indoor. He is widely considered to be amongst the greatest middle-distance runners of all time. Following his retirement from athletics, he served as a UK member of parliament from 1992 to 1997. He became a life peer in 2000: The Right Honourable, the Lord Coe, Baron Coe of Ranmore. Seb was the head of the London bid to host the 2012 Summer Olympics. After the International Olympic Committee awarded the games to London, he became the chair of the London Organising Committee for the Olympic and Paralympic Games. In 2007, he was elected a vice president of the International Association of Athletics Federations, and in 2015, he was elected the organisation's president. Seb Coe is also the chancellor of Loughborough University. And to think that it all started with two teachers, two medals, and an assembly in a school in Sheffield. "If you are a teacher, some 50 years from now, someone will think of you and say your name."

As a schoolboy, I often used to sit in my room, writing down my favourite Dutch team of the week in yet another notebook, an exercise that was as much about constructing a team as it was about finding the right players. *Fantasy Football*[15] in the late 1960s and early 1970s. It also, of course, allowed me to try to think like Johan Cruijff for a little while. Later, I began to write down my favourite all-time Dutch teams, based on more years of experience, starting with my very occasional visits to De Meer, Johan Cruijff, Johan Neeskens, Piet Keizer, and manager Rinus Michels, via the exploits of Ajax, and Willem van Hanegem's Feijenoord, to the successes of the Dutch teams of Marco Van Basten, Ruud Gullit, and Frank Rijkaard, manager Rinus Michels again, and those of Clarence Seedorf, Edgar Davids, Arjen Robben, Robin van Persie, and Frenkie De Jong. Of course, the choices are subjective, based on our experiences and preferences, but they also look at what works together. It is like building a functioning engine from all the components on the floor in front of you, Meccano- and Lego-style. Johan Cruijff could only be in a free and creative role if Johan Neeskens was his tidy-upper. Frank Rijkaard could only brilliantly build from the back, overseeing all that lay before him, if Ronald Koeman literally covered his back. Total Football.

Over the years, I have worked in and with many schools, but there are four schools I remember intimately well, those in which I worked and those I went to as a child and teenager: Pius X Lagere School and Bisschoppelijk College, both in Echt, the primary and secondary schools, respectively, where I was a pupil, and Taverham High School in Norwich, as well as Winifred Holtby School in Hull, my first two schools as a teacher. This is, of course, on top of my all-time favourite school: Arbourthorne Community Primary School. It was only recently that I started to think about my *All-Time Teacher Eleven* instead of my *All-Time Oranje Eleven*. Applying Cruijff's mantra, "Choose the best player for every position, and you will end up not with a strong XI, but with 11 strong 1s," and respecting the principles of Total Football, I can now lay my two favourite teams next to each other. One is my Dutch football team, and the other one is my team of 11 teachers I would want to see working together in every school. Both are about winning, both are about the beauty of the game, both are a joy and privilege to watch and observe.

The exercise itself? On long flights to India, Malaysia, Mexico, and Qatar, I first wrote down my football team, something I had practised since I was a young boy. I then matched the teachers I admired and the reasons for my admiration with the actual names and positions in my football team. Who was my teaching equivalent of the prolific goal scorer Marco van Basten? Who had the pace, technique, and quickness of thought of my wingers Rensenbrink and Bergkamp? Who understood and read the game like Willem van Hanegem? Who were the ultimate team players, the glue that held it all together, like Neeskens, Krol, Suurbier, and Koeman? Who had the beauty and the vision of Frank Rijkaard? Who was the safest pair of hands possible, like goalkeeper Edwin van der Sar? Who managed and steered the ship, like Rinus Michels, *De Generaal*? And of course, who was the genius Johan Cruijff, who made everything tick? Every one of my *All-Time Oranje Eleven* and *All-Time Teacher Eleven* has given me immense joy and has left their mark on me.

When I look at my *All-Time Teacher Eleven*, I am very happy. This team would do every school in the world proud and would win for every child, every family, and every community. I still call my Dutch teachers, the ones who taught me, *Meneer* or *Meester*, Sir or Master, or *Mevrouw* or *Juffrouw*, Mrs or Miss. I cannot help it. Respect. In England, it is the same for Mrs Daines. Every one of my *All-Time Teacher Eleven* has influenced me, has been an example to me, and a role model. Quite a few have been a hero too. I am better for having known them. I could, of course, have written down a squad of 26 or so, but that, in many ways, would have been too easy. Taverham High School's David Harding, my first head of department; Collin Denn, head of drama; Gordon Jenkins, head of art; Dr Angela Blanchard, head of science; Brian Copelin, deputy headteacher, all would have made the squad, as would Winifred Holtby School's Paul Kelly, head of English. And there are many others.

The exercise itself is more than a game. It questions how we think about our children, their education and schooling, and the values and principles we attach to this. It is worth doing. And it is fun. Of course, it also does not have to be football. It could be anything: netball, rugby, a drama group, or dance, you name it. It is the thought and the thinking that count.

My All-Time Oranje Eleven:

Marco van Basten
(AFC Ajax Amsterdam)
9

Rob Rensenbrink   Dennis Bergkamp
(DWS Amsterdam)   (AFC Ajax Amsterdam)
15   8

Johan Cruijff
(AFC Ajax Amsterdam)
14

Wim van Hanegem   Johan Neeskens
(Feijenoord Rotterdam)   (AFC Ajax Amsterdam)
10   13

Ronald Koeman
(AFC Ajax Amsterdam)
4

Ruud Krol   Wim Suurbier
(AFC Ajax Amsterdam)   (AFC Ajax Amsterdam)
5   20

Frank Rijkaard
(AFC Ajax Amsterdam)
3

Edwin van der Sar
(AFC Ajax Amsterdam)
1

Rinus Michels
(AFC Ajax Amsterdam)
Manager

My All-Time Teacher Eleven:

Meneer Huub Beurskens
(Teacher of German at Bisschoppelijk College, Echt)
9

Meneer Henk Jutten　　　　　　*Lesley Milne*
(Deputy Headteacher at Pius　　(Head of Year at Taverham
X Lagere School, Echt)　　　　　High School, Norwich)
15　　　　　　　　　　　　　　　8

Paul Nevens
(Head of Geography at Taverham High School, Norwich)
14

Richard Taylor　　　　　　　*Meneer Henk Vincken*
(Head of English at Taverham　(Year 6 Teacher at Pius
High School, Norwich)　　　　X Lagere School, Echt)
10　　　　　　　　　　　　　　13

David Weatherall
(Head of House at Winifred Holtby School, Hull)
4

Meneer Paul van der Goor　　*Meneer Henny Heijnen*
(Teacher of Dutch at　　　　　(Teacher of English
Bisschoppelijk College, Echt)　Bisschoppelijk College, Echt)
5　　　　　　　　　　　　　　　20

Vanessa Langley
(Headteacher at Arbourthorne Community Primary School, Sheffield)
3

Jeff Cooling
(Headteacher, Winifred Holtby School, Hull)
1

Mrs Jean Daines
(Headteacher, Taverham High School, Norwich)
Manager

The role we play

Mrs Daines is Rinus Michels. *De Generaal.* My manager. She started Taverham High School in the early 1980s. She handpicked her team. She believed in youth and trusted us. She had a vision for our children, for the community, and for us and made that dream come true. She never told us that she was right; she let us discover that for ourselves. She did not exclude children. She let us grumble from time to time. She encouraged us to go outside the box and gave us the licence to climb as high as we could. She also was our safety net. She was calm, cool, and collected. During the teacher strikes of the mid-1980s, on one Friday, our pupils threatened to walk out in sympathy and leave the school premises. I remember standing in the staffroom, looking out the window onto the car park and thinking that there was no way in which the junior strikers-to-be could be stopped. Just as the first of our youngsters reached the gate, Mrs Daines turned to our deputy headteacher and said, "Now, Brian." Brian Copelin pressed the fire alarm, and all our youngsters dutifully returned to the back of the school. Calm and order were restored. With the children, we then talked, instead of walked. Like Rinus Michels, when brilliant players left, she replaced them with differently brilliant talent. Russel Francis stepped in Peter Sanderson's shoes, Angela Blanchard into Mike Bee's, Julia Harding into Victoria "Bod" Webster's, to name but a few. Language exchanges, cultural visits, introducing modern languages for all, Sport Aid – I was more than once the beneficiary and at the receiving end of her trust. On my first day in 1983, she encouraged me to enjoy myself and to learn from my mistakes, and in early 1988, she told me it was time for me to leave. When I asked why, her reply was, "You have too much to offer. There is a risk that if you stay, you will go stale." She was generous too. Like Rinus Michels, Mrs Daines was also supportive of learning by and from experience. She continually encouraged and supported visits and exchanges, work-related learning, work in the community, and much more. In his early years as trainer at Ajax Amsterdam, the qualified physical education teacher for hearing impaired children Rinus Michels took his young players to watch European Cup matches in Brussels, Cologne, and elsewhere, for them to experience with their own eyes and ears, hearts and minds. One of those young players was Johan "Jopie" Cruijff.

Jeff Cooling was the headteacher of Winifred Holtby School in Hull. A new school in its own way following a very messy, city-wide schools' reorganisation. The school was huge, and chaos reigned. Jeff Cooling is my Edwin van der Sar – the safest pair of hands possible. Jeff was unlike Mrs Daines, but the right person in the right place at the right time. He was much more of a manager than a leader. Jeff Cooling did detail, knew where everything was and how everything worked. He saved us from scoring own goals and, in doing so, served the Bransholme children and community. Horses for courses.

Meneer van der Goor and Meneer Heijnen were my Dutch and English languages teachers. They were my glue – they stuck the bits together and answered my why questions. Dutch was not just about grammar, Erasmus van Rotterdam, *Turks Fruit*, or Harry Mulisch; it made you better at history, geography, art, and the rest of your everyday life. Meneer Heijnen brought me Bob Dylan, Graham Greene, and Coronation Street. Purpose. In footballing terms, they were what the former France and Manchester United footballer and now actor and musician Eric Cantona called "water carriers." Without them, nothing happens. Like Ruud Krol and Wim Suurbier.

David Weatherall was the head of Rudston House at Winifred Holtby School. He knew his children, sometimes better than they knew themselves. He knew their parents and carers, their homes, their lives. His insights, his calm, his kindness, and his fairness were the foundation of successful school lives for many youngsters whose everyday lives were far from easy. He told us what we needed to know and coached us into the right positions. He enabled us to teach. It is only with hindsight that I can see how important he was. He reinforced in me that the pastoral and the academic are not two separate aspects of school – they go hand in hand. Like Ronald Koeman, he more often than not went unnoticed, until you realised that you couldn't do without him. Lesley Milne was my Dennis Bergkamp. Young, brilliant, assured, a head of year at Taverham High School who, like David Weatherall, but in very different circumstances, operated in the background, made things happen so that children could learn. The different contexts of the schools meant that Lesley could, in footballing terms, go forward, be more proactive, preventative, whereas David was, more often than not, the firefighter par excellence, more protective, more defensive.

Meneer Vincken was kind. He was my teacher in the last year of my primary education. I confided in him; he knew that my home life was not great, and he looked out for me as much as he could. He was a solid teacher – he excelled at the basics, at the boring bits. Spelling, dictation, grammar, handwriting, maths, capital cities, maps – Meneer Vincken made you good at it and made you see why it mattered. He was patient. Whereas some of my *All-Time Teacher Eleven* made other teachers teach and teach better, Meneer Vincken's main expertise was to enable and empower his pupils to learn and learn better. Like Johan Neeskens, he was indispensable and a public favourite.

Meneer Jutten was sporty, pushy, with black pointy shoes, bringing the best out of the bright sparks, those in line for top grades and en route to the Athenaeum and Gymnasium. Like Rob Rensenbrink, there was only one way to go: forward, and fast. I enjoyed the challenge. Meneer Jutten taught me to learn to live with and, at times, enjoy the occasional knot in my stomach.

Richard Taylor was a giant. He was the head of English at Taverham High School. He made children love Shakespeare and poetry; he gave them confidence in themselves. I often felt that when they left his classroom, they were taller. He was funny, and slightly excentric. He drove a Morris Minor and sometimes had holes in his jumpers. Children loved him. His classroom was next to the library, and on many an occasion did I stand just outside the library, listening to Richard teach. I was so in awe of his abilities that, in my early days at Taverham High School, I felt myself become shy in his presence. He was teaching children whom I struggled with, who did not want to learn German or be in my classroom – he had them eating out of his hand. I have a metaphorical bookshelf in my mind with all the notes I took, standing outside that library, listening in. I learn from him to this day. PIP consists of: (1) Privacy: "Now that we've read the poem together, on your own, jot down the five words from anywhere in the poem that have the biggest effect on you." (2) Intimacy: "Share these in your pairs, threes. Try to explain to your mates the thoughts, feelings, questions even, that the words set off in you. Together, choose about four or five words that you think are the most important in the poem." (3) Plenary: "Okay, this pair over here. Tell us your words and, while I write them on the board, what they set off in you. . . . Other people who chose those words, do you agree with these reactions? Do any words puzzle you or raise any questions?" Richard Taylor, later in his working life, became involved in teacher training at the University of East Anglia in Norwich. Like Willem van Hanegem, he was an artist, showing others how it is done and where to go. With hindsight, my regret is my shyness around him. I could have learned so much more.

"Tell me and I forget, teach me and I remember, involve me and I learn."[16] Paul Nevens is Johan Cruijff. His subject area was geography, but he taught everyone to teach and to be a teacher, including the children. He was magic. Like Cruijff, he favoured the underdog and hated injustice; he talked incessantly, had views on most things, pointing everyone in the right direction, and like Cruijff, was invariably right. He was principled and kind. Pupils would come out of his lessons mesmerised. Like with Richard Taylor, I could only sit and watch in awe. You could have put Paul Nevens in the sports hall or drama studio with 120 children from across the age range and all would have been perfect. He would have led, directed, suggested, guided, supported, and taught; the children would have learned, taught themselves and others, and enjoyed better than with anyone else. I am a teacher because of Meneer Beurskens, I got better because of Richard Taylor and the others in *My All-Time Teacher Eleven*, but Paul Nevens is the teacher I wanted to be, more than any other.

Meneer Beurskens was a coach, a talker, making his pupils meet their goals. He is the man who gave me a book. He, like Marco van Basten, almost always hit the back of the net. He, at times, pushed me to the limit, serving generous doses of confidence at the same time. He was, more than any of my other teachers at that time, what I needed. The right man in the right place all the time. Meneer Beurskens is the reason I became a teacher. I owe him that debt to this day.

And finally, Vanessa Langley is my Frank Rijkaard. I have three headteachers in *My All-Time Teacher Eleven*: Mrs Daines, who built her school on vision and trust; Jeff Cooling, who was a truly outstanding manager, knowing that, in the context of his school, the devil needed to be in the detail; and Vanessa Langley, the headteacher of Arbourthorne Community Primary School, who sweeps all before her, who leads by example, and who is supremely adaptable to the ever-changing context of her school and her children's circumstances. In her school, where she goes, others follow. Like Frank Rijkaard, she plays the beautiful game better than most. Like with Frank Rijkaard, her versatility works wonderfully. Also, like Frank Rijkaard, she doesn't suffer fools gladly. And like Frank Rijkaard and his mentor, Johan Cruijff, she puts her trust in youth. It was Cruijff who gave a 17-year-old Frank Rijkaard his Ajax debut, and it was Frank Rijkaard who did the same for a 17-year-old Lionel Messi at Barcelona. I have seen the same levels of trust in children at Arbourthorne Community Primary School, where, for example, children gain scholarships to independent schools and firsts at university, against all odds. Here, children do fly planes, or at least some of them do. At FC Barcelona, as manager, Frank Rijkaard lived the motto "Més que un club." *More than a club*. Vanessa Langley's Arbourthorne Community Primary School is, thanks to her, "Més que una escola" – *More than a school*.

The role we play, the role models, heroes, and even celebrities, they all play their part in our lives. It is up to us to make our right choices. "The wand picks the wizard, Mr Potter."

Out of all my role models, from Johan Cruijff to Bob Geldof, from *Robin Hood* to *Floris*, and from Desmond Tutu to Anne Frank, none have been more influential or more meaningful than my teachers. My emotional attachment to my grandfather is unrivalled, the urge to kick a football like Johan Cruijff is still there after all those years, and the value that my soul-searching conversations with Desmond Tutu and my close friendship with Carla Rinaldi have in my life is difficult to put into words. However, without my teachers and those who taught me to teach, I am nothing. I believe that without brilliant teaching, we, as people, cannot be who we are.

Remember that "if you are a teacher, some 50 years from now, someone will think of you and say your name." As for me, I am proud and happy to be in someone else's *All-Time Teacher Eleven*, to have had my name said, according to James Neill, independent education consultant, former international director at GL Education, and my former (favourite) Taverham High School pupil:

> Ger was one of my most inspirational teachers while a student at Taverham High School, and his passion strongly influenced my career choice in the education sector. Having visited KidZania in London, it is clear that his leadership and passion for education are still inspiring students and colleagues alike. Collaborating and continuing to work with Ger in supporting global educational initiatives is a privilege.

Notes

1. *The [Sheffield] Star* newspaper, 26th November 2022.
2. *Pep Guardiola. Another Way of Winning. The Biography*, by Guillem Balague, 2018.
3. www.youtube.com/watch?v=fpf4F8K2to4.
4. "The wand chooses the wizard, Mr Potter," Mr. Olivander, *Harry Potter and the Philosopher's Stone*, 2001.
5. *Indiana Jones and the Last Crusade*, 1989.
6. Haruki Murakami, author.
7. Willkommenskultur, meaning "welcoming culture," is a German concept which designates, firstly, a positive attitude of politicians, businesses,

educational institutions, sports clubs, civilians, and institutions towards foreigners, including, and often especially towards, migrants.

8 German collective guilt. This refers to the notion of a collective guilt, attributed to Germany and its people, for perpetrating the Holocaust and other atrocities in World War II. Swiss psychoanalyst Carl Jung wrote an influential essay in 1945 about this concept as a psychological phenomenon, in which he asserted that the German people felt a collective guilt for the atrocities committed by their compatriots and so introduced the term into German intellectual discourse.

9 From *Harry's Game* by Gerald Seymour, 1976.

10 Andy Warhol, American artist and film director.

11 www.youtube.com/watch?v=rvPxizhicpI.

12 www.youtube.com/watch?v=9xIpHNd3hjU.

13 *Stillness and Speed: My Story*, Dennis Bergkamp, 2013.

14 Thomas Paine, political activist, philosopher, political theorist, and revolutionary.

15 Fantasy football is a game in which participants assemble an imaginary team of real-life football players and score points based on those players' actual statistical performance or their perceived contribution on the field of play. Usually, fantasy football games are based on one division in a particular country, although there are variations. Fantasy football is now a significant industry due to websites dedicated to developing the fantasy football community, and betting sites hosting their own fantasy football games.

16 Benjamin Franklin, Founding Father of the United States of America.

CHAPTER 6

More than a school – measuring what we value

The official Futbol Club Barcelona motto is "Més que un club." Translated into English, this is "more than a club." The motto, however, is not just an empty statement boasting about the stature of the football club. FC Barcelona has been very close to the Catalan people through the good and the bad times, especially in the last century, during Generalissimo Franco's Spanish rule, which effectively, and often violently, denied the Catalan people the right to be. The club was a place to meet and go to talk without fear of reprisal. It was about community, identity, and the confirmation thereof. When in 1974 the relatively recently signed Johan Cruijff named his newborn son "Jordi," after the patron saint of Catalonia, he was denied registration by the authorities because of the Franco dictatorship's ban on Catalan names. Rather than politely settle for "Jorge," the official Spanish version, he flew his family to the Netherlands and registered him there. Jordi it was. Cruijff's Catalan identity and hero status confirmed. FC Barcelona has been the flagship of the Catalan struggle throughout the years – and to many, that is what "Més que un club" means. It represents the struggle and the objectives of a community.

I know schools that are like Barça, as FC Barcelona is colloquially known. Schools that are wonderful, that, in the face of continued adversity, keep reinventing themselves for the good of their communities. Schools that are places to meet and to go and talk without the fear of reprisals. Schools that are at the heart of their communities, whose struggles and objectives they represent. Schools that are "Més que una escola," "more than a school." Schools that build scaffolding, so that their children can climb their heights, and that have safety nets, just in case. Schools that add more value than most, also in academic progress and attainment terms. Schools that see the bigger picture and understand the tiniest of jigsaw pieces. Most of these schools I know, incidentally, are primary schools. Many have the word "community" in their name, as if to wear their values and principles as a badge for all to see. These schools, to use my own phrase, walk the talk. They do what it says on the badge, to coin a phrase. All substance, little hype. "It takes a village to raise a child."

When, in the late 1980s, school mission and vision statements became a thing, many a cheeky glance was cast towards a good number of the 92 English football clubs with their Latin mottos and, indeed, north of the English border too. Latin mottos, up to then, had been the prerogative of the independent and grammar school sectors. The Blackburn Rovers motto is "Arte et labore," which means "by skill and labour." Then there is Everton's badge, which reads "Nil satis nisi optimum" and roughly translates as "nothing but the best is good enough." Manchester City's motto is "Superbia in proelia," which, as every Latin scholar knows, means "pride in battle," while the Spurs rejoice in the battle-like exhortation "Audere est facere," or "to dare is to do." Manchester United's motto is "Concilio et labore," boasting "wisdom and effort." Sheffield Wednesday is happy with "Consilio et anamis," which means "intelligence and courage," while Bristol City shares their motto of "Vim promovet insitam" – "promote your inner power" – with the city's university. Gillingham claims to be the "Domus clamantium," or the "home of the shouting men." North of the English border, the prize for non-pretentiousness goes to Queens Park, who plays at 52,000-capacity Hampden Park but is currently in the second tier of Scottish football. They meekly suggest "Ludere causa ludendi," which means "to play for the sake of playing." It is not hard to detect that here there are significant gaps between the mottos and reality. The Everton motto is, at best, optimistic, whilst Manchester City's shows no mention of Abu Dhabi oil money contributing to being proud in battle. It would be stretching things significantly too far to suggest that Manchester United has embraced wisdom and effort in recent years. My favourite has to be Bristol City's reaching out to the local seat of learning, the University of Bristol. The danger with mottos, mission, and vision statements is that they are, or have become, tokenism, that we forget to live them, that they are just there for show, or perhaps at times, in footballing terms, as a distant reminder of times long gone. In school terms, this can mean that they bear little relevance to the essence of the organisation and are often too far removed from the day-to-day realities of many of the communities our schools are at the centre of. We seem to have a thing with names and schooling. The belief seems to be that changing the name makes everything better – from "pupil" to "student" or from "school" to "academy," for example, with, as research shows, a difference to the children's lives that lies between nothing and next to nothing. All mostly hype and little substance.

Let us travel back to the late 1990s and early 2000s, to England and the south of Manchester, to Wythenshawe, and to the Education Action Zones, a setting, as we have already seen, marked by a multitude of significant disadvantages. These are complex webs of challenges and not just one isolated issue at a time. It is all a bit like the colourful cheese wedges in a game of Trivial Pursuit – here, each of the many wedges represents a different aspect of a child's life. Socio-economic circumstances, cultures, gender, ethnicity, access to and quality of education and schooling, social care and health, and exposure to crime are all part and examples of this intricate circle that can define a child's environment – never, of course, by the child's choosing.

The Education Action Zones initiative encouraged us to think outside the box in terms of tackling these disparities in children's lives. Education Action Zones were a statutory instrument,[1] charities, independent of local government, public–private sector partnerships, with the aim to improve the life chances in the most disadvantaged communities in England. We were meant to do things differently, and better – just more of the same was no longer good enough. We were last-chance saloons. A community of schools working with – and no more – the local authority, centrally funded by the government, and with local private sector partnerships making a difference. Our local private sector partner was Manchester Airport Plc and the 250 or so associated businesses it housed. We were, however, also under the direct control of the Department for Education and Skills (DfES), a forerunner of the Department for Education, which meant that what had seemed like medium- to long-term strategies collided regularly with the ticking clock of political cycles. "Of course, you can support the development of services for the youngest families. As long as the examination results at age 16 improve at the same time." My repeated argument with politicians and civil servants in England had always been this: You have had since the Education Act of 1944 to try to get it right and have very often failed. The poor, in every way, are still poor. Why would we magically get it right in just a few years? For all the efforts and all the investments over a seemingly long period of time, albeit divided into five-year or so parliamentary cycles, the system was still failing the most vulnerable children and their families. The notion that a more-of-the-same approach would yield different results, to me, seemed bizarre. It reminded me of the famous adage attributed to Albert Einstein: "Insanity is doing the same thing over and over again and expecting different results." And this is where the Wythenshawe story took an interesting turn. One where in-school and out-of-school met; where services supported the child and not the system; where, from a professional point of view, schooling met education; and where we learned about scaffolding as well as safety nets. Impact-focused partnership. Education Action Zones, at their best, were that village that raises a child. For *village*, read *community*.

Newall Green Infant School, Newall Green Junior School, and Newall Green High School were a family of schools, of sorts. Similar names, in the same part of Wythenshawe, yet functioning as separate entities, often not recognising the fact that, educationally, children journeyed through from start to finish. One day in late 1999, I came across the story where one mother had complained that she had received three separate visits from three different education welfare officers to check why her children had been absent from their schools; one was at the infant school, one was at the junior school, and one was in the high school – the oldest one often walking the two younger ones to school in the morning, or not, as became evident. The system had not allowed the connection that this was one family with three members who were "wagging it." Madness. The answer was not creating one big school group which would manage all three schools as one big unit, but it was to focus on the children, their families, their journeys, and the wider community, and it needed to be solution-driven. In partnership with the schools and the local authority, we began to look at which aspects of the work of services and resources, such as education welfare, social care, education psychology, health, crime prevention, amongst others, we could bring into the schools, with agendas solely focusing on building metaphorical scaffolding and safety nets around individual children and their families. We wanted them to safely be able to climb as high as they could or wished to. This sounds easier than, in reality, it was. To succeed, we needed to get to know our children better. "One size fits all" doesn't work, and more of the same is not good enough.

Knowing our children better is key. We never quite know what is in their baggage when they arrive at school in the morning. Often, children will come and tell us. Especially when it is about successes, achievements, and joyous experiences. From cups and medals to swimming and running, from a visit to the zoo and getting a puppy for Christmas, to just celebrating their grandparents' birthdays and their auntie's and uncle's wedding anniversary – all these things matter greatly and are happily shared. Sometimes children will come and tell us about more difficult experiences, but often, they may not tell us anything at all. They may, however, signal. It is then that our radars matter and that their trust in us comes to the fore. When I was about 8 or 9, perhaps a little older, my parents' arguing at home was becoming more and more frequent and louder. The language and tone were often violent and abusive, and always mean, unkind. I remember once hiding under the table in the kitchen, then, in the end, screaming at the top of my voice that I wanted them to stop. I remember the pain inside me. Not long afterwards, during another row, my father grabbed hold of me and dragged me in front of the mirror in the hallway. He told me to look at myself. He told me how useless and how ugly I was. He kept telling me to look. To this day, I struggle with mirrors and photographs. When, after that weekend, I got back to my primary school, Meneer Vincken, my teacher, showed that he had me on his radar. I had a shoulder to cry on and a safety net. I have no idea what was said, what action was taken or not. My parents' rowing continued. But I had somewhere to go. Going to school made me feel better.

It had struck me many years before my Wythenshawe days that, at Taverham High School near Norwich, my first school as a teacher, all adults knew the name of every child and knew something positive about every child. Not just whether they were bright, were difficult, or had some form of special needs. We often knew the names of their siblings, their pets; we knew their hobbies, their likes and dislikes, their friends or otherwise. It made for a family school where behaviour wasn't so much managed as turned into a culture, a set of values and principles that we all signed up to, almost all the time. This included the parents and the wider community. Taverham High School in those days, the mid-1980s, numbered approximately 500 young people. Size matters. By knowing the children, we, at Taverham High School, were able to personalise our provision, including the allocation of external resources and services, to their strengths, their weaknesses, their very being, in every aspect. Taverham High School educated as well as schooled. I saw this again, many years later, when I was an adviser for modern foreign languages in Manchester. The Barlow Roman Catholic High School is in the East Didsbury district of the city and, in its catchment area, includes Burnage, where, in the 1980s, the Gallagher brothers Noel and Liam, of Oasis[2] fame, lived and subsequently went to secondary school. Peter Foley was the headteacher, who knew every name of every one of his 800 or so children and, with that, who they were, who their siblings were, and often the names of their pets. I witnessed him work hard at this, because he believed that this knowing his children well would make for a better school for them. He was right. He, of course, also led by example – what Peter did was followed by his colleagues. The culture was set. In 2024, in the age of personalisation, how can you personalise if you don't know the individual and their contexts? Not knowing them takes us back to jars and lids.

In the early 2020s, my friend the then Turkish leading opposition politician and education spokesperson Sevinç Atabay argued for the return of Village Institutes to again locally contextualise, personalise, democratise, and re-secularise schooling and education across Turkey's rural communities. One of her key motives was this personalisation of education, serving and making it relevant to local communities, and taking it away from the one-size-fits-all, centrally controlled, and dogmatic approach of President Recep Tayyip Erdoğan's national conservative Justice and Development Party government. In the 2024 version of Village Institutes, technology would, of course, be a significant enabler. Village Institutes, or *Köy Enstitüleri*, were a group of small rural schools in Turkey founded in 1940 through a project led by Hasan Âli Yücel, who was the minister of education at that time. The project was initially started to train teachers. The Village Institutes were the cornerstones of the rural development projects in the post-war Turkish state. At a time when there weren't many educational institutions in most villages, they helped educate the rural populace. Village Institutes were established to meet the needs of each village's community, and of each community's member. Their approach embodied ideas of the Republic of Turkey's founder, Mustafa Kemal Atatürk, such as integrating theory and practice, focusing on the underserved, working across institutions, and a systemic approach to building a stronger society. Classical education was to be combined with practical abilities and applied to local needs. The Village Institutes had a major impact, and to this day, many people regret that they were shut down. Size mattered. There was also almost-immediate resistance against this secular and mixed education concept, of course. Traditionalists questioned these co-educational and secular aspects – key elements of Atatürk's beliefs. Powerful landlords did not appreciate the aim of educating children who could ask why questions. The decision to discontinue the Village Institutes was made in 1950 by the then-governing centre-right Democratic Party. The Village Institutes were gradually replaced by larger, centrally controlled schools. Whilst Village Institutes were initially established to provide a local and personalised education, and social and other services in rural areas, the then centre-right government decided to transition towards a more centralised education system in the interest of efficiency. Even in 2024, this all still sounds all too familiar.

For politicians, the aim of a well-educated populace seemingly often translates into a fear of losing control, whereas centralised mass schooling can, of course, achieve the opposite. The academisation in England since 2010 is another such example – it centralises control and puts this in the hands of government-approved, unelected quangos, away from democratically elected local representation. Those who suffer from these political games are, of course, the children. In England, at least, there is no evidence that this kind of politics pays educational dividends.[3]

My move from Taverham High School to Winifred Holtby School in Hull towards the end of the 1980s reinforced that size matters. This was also a move from relative affluence to significant social economic disadvantage and all that entailed. And to a much bigger school. Winifred Holtby School, at the end of Hull schools' reorganisation, counted well in excess of 2,000 children. My faculty – I was the head of modern foreign languages – at that time was the largest in the country and numbered 17 colleagues. It would be fair to say that for a lot of the time, especially at the beginning, I did not know the names of all my colleagues in the school, let alone those of the children. This was despite some brilliantly gifted and hard-working colleagues, house structures, countless meetings, and complex systems. Inevitably, the children's names you become familiar with follow a pattern: the bright ones, the naughty ones, the ones with special needs of some kind, the very troubled ones. In an area of significant disadvantage, where many children and their families were up against it, the rest all too often become "just another brick in the wall."[4] Size matters. The justification for large schools is not an educational one but is based on economics. The phrase "economies of scale" is used far too often and carelessly when it comes to children's schooling and education, especially in secondary schools. Economies of scale often have limits, such as passing the optimum design point, where costs per unit begin to increase. A common limit is having a higher defect rate. This is also why, in this regard, primary schools very often function much better than secondary schools: they are, by design, able to know and serve their children, families, and communities. It is not about the ages of the young people; it is about the size of the school and how well we know our children. Size matters. I also cannot but look with concern at secondary schooling, per se. Secondary schooling, its size, its systemisation, its economies-of-scale approach, its robotification of young people, and mass education approaches, driven by government diktat, all made so much worse worldwide, with England's academisation since 2010 as a prime example.

To me, the Taverham High School of the mid-1980s is proof of this – in a different era, I know, but the principle remains. And children themselves don't change that much – it is the world around them that changes. Mostly, it is not the young people that are the issue; it is us, the grown-ups. "All grown-ups were once children, but only few of them remember it." When, in the late 1960s and early 1970s, at around four o'clock in the afternoon my secondary school day had come to an end, I would cycle back to my parents' house, ready for my daily dose of homework. Sometimes, my journey would take me via the local library, especially when project work required more in-depth research. Having said goodbye to my also-cycling friends, at worst, an hour or so ago, I remember, the first thing I would do when back home was sit on the stairs, pick up the phone, which was attached to the wall, and call one or more of my friends, in those days not at the same time, of course. I can hear my mother now: "Are you on that phone again? What are you talking to your friends about now? You have only just left them. Do you know how much this costs?" Roll forward the clocks by some 50 years, and the dialogue between parent and child is all too similar. Except for "Do you know how much this costs?" It is much cheaper to call now than it was then. "All grown-ups were once children, but only few of them remember it." As I said, it is not the young people that are the issue; it us, the grown-ups.

The Wythenshawe project was not about economies of scale; it was about better, more targeted use of existing resources, and about finding extra bits and pieces when and if needed. We called it full-service schools. There was, incidentally, very little that was new about the concept – we did not invent the wheel. We didn't reinvent it either – context saw to that. We analysed what was needed, looked at what we already had, brought in a few missing links, made the whole thing adaptable, and most importantly, focused on the children and on nothing else. Aside from the services that were, in some way, under the control of the local authority, we also engaged with local and national charities to complete the jigsaw better. Barnardo's[5] were particularly helpful. The agendas of meetings consisted of the names of children. We also looked carefully at what was going on in the rest of the world and researched projects in places as far apart as the United States, South Africa, and Northern Ireland. Most importantly, we took almost everyone with us on our journey of personalisation, care, and community.

The outcome was that it worked. Was it perfect? No. Was it better than before? Yes. For our targeted young people, attendance improved, as did punctuality; behaviour incidences were reduced greatly; education psychologists and social workers were engaging in preventative work after about six months; health workers were actively working with the schools, as were the police; and the information flow improved massively and enabled more prevention than previously. New roles were developed, such as the full-service school's manager, and existing ones were adjusted. The professionals involved across the piece reported a greater sense of ownership and success – job satisfaction ratings were on the up. New ideas were born; confidence and creativity grew. Connected, targeted curriculum provision was developed and implemented, including the Royal Bank of Scotland Diploma. Attendance, punctuality, and behaviour do not improve because of policies; they improve because of care, patience, tenacity – *tenacity* is patience with teeth, and respect, because of good relationships between the homes and the school; because of enhanced, owned, purposeful learning experiences; because of brilliant teaching and the sweet taste of success. Everything is connected. At some point, in the early 2000s, we invented "quality development teachers," or QDTs, as they became known. Highly capable, experienced, and qualified in every way, wonderful years 4, 5, and 6 teachers who accompanied the 8- to 11-year-olds when bridging the gap between primary school and secondary school, an identified trouble spot in the Wythenshawe schooling provision. As well as accompanying the children, the QDTs worked alongside teachers in the classroom to make the quality of teaching, and thereby the quality of learning, better and more consistent across the phases. This ranged from experimenting with and implementing new technologies to focusing very clearly on the how, the for whom, as well as the what – the latter being based on much more, of course, than the mere grade or level attained at the end of primary school. Once the initial culture shock of this approach had ebbed away – "Are you coming to teach me how to do my job?" – the impact became clear for all to see. In those days before websites and social media, sharing of best practice between Wythenshawe schools and its teachers became as commonplace and as regular as the planes taking off at the neighbouring Manchester Airport. The focus of all this? The child in the middle. The key issue was that we had started to get better by purposefully, and thus better, connecting in-school provision and out-of-school services to the needs of children we had got to know better. The real difference, as always, was made in schools by brilliant people, with children, their families, and the wider community.

When I was 16, I bought myself a motorbike or, in reality, a moped that looked like a motorbike. My Tomos APN 4H – *H* for *Hippy* – was light blue with chrome and looked like something out of the film *Easy Rider*, or so I imagined. It did provide me with the new reality that meant I could, with ease, travel further away from my parents' house and do more or less whatever I wanted. *Easy Rider* beats pushbike. I earned the money for my *Easy Rider* working on farms and in the local sand lime brick factory, locally known as *de Stas*, after its owner, the very rich Meneer Stassen. Not long after my 16th birthday, I arrived back at my parents' house late, too late, and yet again, my father was waiting for me, wooden clothes hanger at the ready. This time, though, there was something different. As I came into the front door and the usual tirade was about to start, I stopped him, took the clothes hanger off him, put it on the stairs, and told him that if he ever touched me again, he would regret it for the rest of his life, or words to that effect. He never did so again. It was not long after that I moved out of my parental home into a neighbouring village, Montfort, where I had school friends and lived more or less full time with a farming family. Asparagus, gherkins, wheat, sugar beets, and pigs allowed me to earn my crust and, at the same time, finish my schooling. It also meant that I experienced something that resembled close to a home. These were happier times. At school, I had my German teacher, Meester Beurskens, pushing me towards higher education; I had a home to stay in, many friends; I captained the local handball team, earned good money, learned about the world of work and how life fitted together. With hindsight, it was here that I came across the concept of return on involvement for the first time.

The farmer Meneer Peters and his family, who took me under their wing, cared. He cared about his farm, he cared about his land and his crops, and he cared about his animals, despite the fact that these were pigs to the slaughter, to coin a phrase. He also cared deeply about the people around him, his community, and led by example. In Montfort, he was the farmer and the grown-up many wanted to be like.

There were, of course, others who did things differently. Those whose motive was driven by return on investment – battery farmers, for example. The land and crops were often not as well-looked-after, the animals less well-cared-for, and they often also were less kind to the people who surrounded them. They also somehow never seemed really content or happy. The quick-bucks brigade – "Loadsamoneys."[6] Meneer Peters's approach was thoughtful, long-lasting, focused on quality, with better outcomes for all. His sense of involvement paid greater dividends in many ways.

Return on involvement and return on investment are both metrics used to measure the effectiveness of a business's activities, but they focus on different aspects. Return on investment is a financial metric that calculates the profitability of an investment relative to its cost. It is typically expressed as a percentage and is used to evaluate the efficiency of an investment or compare the potential profitability of different investments. The formula for a return on investment is: net profit ÷ cost of investment × 100. Return on involvement is a concept that considers not just the financial return but also the level of engagement, participation, and emotional connection that customers or stakeholders have with a business. It has no mathematical formula. It looks beyond monetary gains and evaluates how involved and connected individuals are. This metric can help businesses understand the impact of their communication and marketing efforts, customer engagement strategies, and overall brand experience, as well as the impact of their approach. It allows businesses to express and make visible their commercial values, social values, and principles, to be a business for good. In summary, while return on investment focuses on the financial return on an investment, return on involvement looks at the level of involvement and engagement of stakeholders with a business. Both metrics are important for evaluating very different aspects and values of often very different businesses' performances.

That concept of return on involvement has stayed with me, although, of course, then I didn't articulate it in that way. At that time, it just felt like the right thing to do and to be. It brought about a happiness. "Es doe mer gelökkig bös." *As long as you are happy.* The principles apply to this day, in businesses and organisations for good, in partnerships for the right reasons, in social values, in corporate and social responsibilities, in those who are in it for the long run and the greater good and who believe that there is such a thing as society, and in those who want better for the rest.

In the context of more than a school, return on involvement is, of course, a heartbeat not to be missed.

There are many examples of the concept of return on involvement in the past and present, into which schools did and can invent themselves. In the United Kingdom, Cadbury's Bourneville, which was built because George Cadbury was appalled at the working-class living conditions and wanted to provide decent houses for Cadbury's workers; or Philips in the Netherlands and the development of its hometown, Eindhoven, the housing association "Thuis Best" ("No Place Like Home"), the Philips Stadium and PSV Eindhoven football club, the Frits Phillips Concert Hall; and of course, Tata, founded in India, where Tata Trusts contribute 66 per cent of the earnings made by the Tata firms under the holding company Tata Sons towards charitable causes. Manchester Airport and its "More Than an Airport" is another example and one I am so proud to have played a leading part in. The British shoe repair and dry-cleaning business Timpson offers a free service to anyone who is unemployed and has been invited for a job interview. Also, 10 per cent of the Timpson workforce is made up of people who have criminal convictions. These organisations, little and large, provide evidence that private sector partnerships can work and are not always entirely driven by profit and profiteering motives. Private sector involvement is not, by definition, wrong; it just needs redefining and, subsequently, being accountable in terms of values, principles, and who profits how. In this context, organisations like Cadbury, Philips, Tata, Manchester Airport, and Timpson have written different, better narratives of the possible.

When we think about more than a school, we need to embrace these examples, localise and contextualise them, and empower schools to scale them to their capacity. There are plenty of examples already, including more recent start-ups, and it feels that return on involvement could become a trend for good. As our schools are at the hearts of our communities, localisation and contextualisation are key in the aims of empowerment, enhancement, and (self-)improvement. No school and no community are the same. In Wythenshawe, the Manchester Airport was the catalyst and the lead organisation, with 29 schools in partnership. In the Arbourthorne community of Sheffield, it is the school. One size never fits all.

Partnerships are about shared values and visions. A child's education is an impact partnership. "Every child is everyone's responsibility."

Decision-making often needs to be by consensus, focusing on doing the right thing, by "polderen." "Polderen" is a Dutch verb meaning a "method of consensus decision-making." It gets its name from the Dutch word "polder," or tracts of land enclosed by dikes. Since the Middle Ages, when the process of land reclamation began, different societies living in the same polder had been forced to cooperate, because without unanimous agreement on shared responsibility for maintenance of the dikes and pumping stations, the polders would have flooded, and everyone would have suffered. Crucially, even when different communities in the same polder were at war, they still had to cooperate in this respect. This is thought to have taught the Dutch to set aside differences for a greater purpose. Partnerships are complex, often organic beings requiring constant adjustments within changing times and contexts. In our schooling and education, we need to place the child at the centre of our thinking and our polderen, and we need to keep reminding ourselves that, on the road to success, there can be no shortcuts.

With the benefit of hindsight, looking at all the schools I have worked in and with over many years, to me the recipe for the more-than-a-school concept contains a whole range of ingredients, but mainly the community aspect and its context, like Arbourthorne Community Primary School; scaffolding, safety nets, and partnerships, like Wythenshawe's full-service schools; that size matters, like Taverham High School; that learning is a satellite navigation system to better places in life and that not all classrooms have walls – like the Children's University; measuring what we value – like KidZania and, again, the Children's University – as well as, of course, courageous leadership, awe, and wonder learning, brilliant teachers and amazing support staff who, at all times, put the child first and in the centre of all things, with outcomes to match – like my *All-Time Teacher Eleven*. The recipe is also laced with aspiration and social mobility, aiming to make tomorrow better than today – like my grandad: "Promise me you will always do your best at school." "Why?" "Because I don't want you to have hands like mine." All this to enable us to know and serve our children and young people better.

The underlying questions related to the more-than-a-school concept are simple. Whom is the school for? Who are the children, and what are their contexts? What are the contexts of their families and the community within which the school finds itself? What do we need to get our children to succeed to the very best of their ability? Which conditions need addressing? Which barriers need removing?

Which expectations need raising? Which values need work? What are the key jigsaw pieces for this particular school and community? How does that affect our thinking about equity? And about resourcing? What does this village to raise a child look like? Who are our people? Our teachers? How can we all be our best? How and when will we know? Who and what do we want our children to be at the end of their schooling? And what does that mean for our learning, our teaching? To be more than a school means to know our children, to understand, to *visionise*, to give and expect accordingly, and to measure what we value. It means a focus on return on involvement. It means to educate as well as school, to take calculated risks, and to paint outside the frame. It means swimming against the tide of one-size-fits-all and centralised control. It means the highest achievable standards. It means disruption. It means, above all, trust and courageous leadership and self-governance. It means to be valued for what we do and who we are. It means, most of the time, at least, to be loved.

The *Up!* series of documentary films follows the lives of ten males and four females in England beginning in 1964, when they were 7 years old. The first film was titled *Seven Up!*, with later films adjusting the number in the title to match the age of the subjects at the time of filming. *Seven Up!*, first aired in May 1964, featured 14 very different 7-year-olds, all revealing their thoughts and aspirations to the camera. The prep schoolboys were already eyeing Charterhouse and Cambridge. East Ender Lynn Johnson wanted to work in Woolworths. The children, mainly boys, were at the sharp ends of the class divide – 5 of the 14 children were from elite private schools, and six from London's working-class primary schools and care homes, but only two from a middle-class Liverpool suburb and one from rural Yorkshire. In their interviews in *Seven Up!* these 7-year-olds unselfconsciously performed the hierarchies of class theatre. Who can forget the clip of Andrew Brackfield, Charles Furneaux, and John Brisby – the "three posh boys," obligingly recounting their reading material ("I read the *Financial Times*"), their plans ("I think I'm going to Cambridge University"), and their view that private schools were a very good thing, indeed, since otherwise, their schools would be "so nasty and crowded." Position that next to one of the working-class primary schools' children: "What is a university"? The documentary has had nine series so far – one every seven years, thus spanning 56 years. *Up 63!* was released in 2019. The series has been produced by Granada Television for ITV, which has broadcast all of them, except *42 Up!*, which in 1998, was broadcast on BBC One. Individual films and the series as a whole have received numerous accolades. Whether *70 Up!* will be broadcast in 2026, following the death of its creator, Michael Apted, in 2021, is not yet known. "People from Wythenshawe don't fly planes," said the children of Wythenshawe in the early 2000s. "The mind, once enlightened, cannot again become dark," stated political activist, philosopher, political theorist, and revolutionary Thomas Paine some 200 years before that, and "[t]he illiterate of the 21st century will not be those who cannot read and write, but those who cannot learn, unlearn and relearn" (offered American writer and futurist Alvin Toffler in the 1970s). The now, the what, and the how. So what happened to the 14 children from 1964? To Andrew, John, Charles, Bruce, Peter, Nicholas, Neil, Suzy, Sue, Symon, Paul, Lynn, Tony, Jackie? In social mobility terms, things turned out more or less true to form, via Oxford University in some cases, and children's homes in others. In terms of dreams come true, Bruce didn't teach in Africa, but he did so in Bangladesh instead. Tony, at the age of 14, raced against horse racing legend Lester Piggott. And Paul moved to Australia. As far as happiness is concerned, life deals cards differently, it seems, and it is not for sale. Some are happy where they are, others with who they have become, but little of this seems related to their socio-economic status. Lynn, who wanted to work in Woolworths and became a children's librarian instead, was the first of the 14 to die, passing away in 2013.

It is some years ago, when my son Tom was about 12, and we were on our way back from Rome to Bologna by train. I asked him which his favourite Italian city was, to which he replied, "Venice." When asked why, he replied:

> I love Rome, Florence, Bologna, and Venice. But you go to Rome and Florence to see sites – the Colosseum, the Pantheon, the Vatican, the Ponte Vecchio, the Cathedral of Santa Maria del Fiore, and to Bologna for the university and the food. You go to Venice to see Venice.

I have spent a lot of time in northern Italy since being adviser for modern foreign languages in Manchester in the early 1990s. I introduced Italian into many of the Manchester primary schools and established links with the city of Bologna. Bologna, home to the oldest university in Europe, and also known as *La Grassa* (the fat one, as the food capital of Italy), *La Dotta* (the learned one), and because of its politics, the red one, *La Rossa*, has become something of a second home. From their early ages, this has also been the case for my children. My love of Italy remains to this day, and especially for Bologna. I owe all that to Wythenshawe. So do my children.

Travel and exploration, in every sense of the words, are such important ingredients of education and schooling. Education equals journeying, and schooling provides the passport and visas. "Children can only aspire to what they know exists." This is the absolute truth when it comes to children's aspirations. It is equally true when it comes to children's understanding of the world around them and how they can help shape this world into a better place in the future. In educational travel terms, then, not every classroom has four walls. Empowering our children to broaden their horizons and their co-curricular menus means embracing thinking, feeling, experiences, curiosity, and exploration, leading to better self-confidence, deeper understanding, greater independence, and a clearer sense of purpose. The word "exploration" is key. Synonyms include analysis, examination, expedition, research, study, and of course, travel. So in our quest to widen children's horizons and enhance their experiences, to make them better learners and higher achievers, let us once more focus on exploration as education, on experience-based learning. Connect. Extend. Challenge. We must think of education as travelling on a journey during which children experience writing their own narrative of the possible. Learning is a satellite navigation system to better places in life. Travel is key to any child's learning and understanding of the world in which they live – any travel: metaphorical, virtual, real, travel in the mind and the heart. In teachers' for-examples, online, out there. Schooling, then, does become the passport and the visas. The benefits of what I call educational travel – how, by the way, can travel not be educational? – are beyond conventional measure. This travel invites curiosity, fosters teamwork, grows self-awareness and confidence, and invites us to be in charge of our own compass. This travel allows us, as educators, to better explain and exemplify through experience what we teach in school – in every lesson, every abstract should be followed by a for-example, because every for-example is a story and, thereby, a journey. There is not a single subject area that would not benefit from this educational travel. And not a single young person. I believe it imperative for us all to work in and with schools and other groups on how they can better develop their offers to cater for this children's real learning. Dovetailing into, extending current learning, and becoming the conduit through which theory is turned into practice all help transform the four-walled-classroom into a world of experiences – they help the children join their dots and make sense of the world around them, now and tomorrow. They turn a national curriculum into a real curriculum. The most important challenge we face, however, is making this travel accessible to all children – not just those whose socio-economic context affords them their passport and visas. Can we, together, consider this, be committed, creative, and fair, and to meaningfully bring our responsibilities into play? Is social mobility not travel? Answers on a postcard from a nice place, please.

Through this exploration and travel, KidZania and the Children's University enabled learning by doing, for all children, offering 4 or 5 to 14-year-olds fun, experiential learning opportunities to empower them to take charge of their own aspirations and learn from experience. There is not a subject area you cannot find; it is curricular, co-curricular, and cross-curricular. I worked closely with schools and listened to our children – the launch of KidZania London's pet welfare activity, for example, happened because 79 per cent of children told us that was what, how, and why they wanted most. KidZanias everywhere can also say that a very significant number of school visits are by children whose socio-cultural contexts are more challenging than most. Guiding us, I utilised private and public sector partnerships and established and chaired a think-tank which sat at the heart of everything educational – some of the world's leading educationalists steering and aiding such developments, including Professor Carla Rinaldi, president of the Fondazione Reggio Children, Italy; Organisation for Economic Co-operation and Development education and skills director, Andreas Schleicher; former UK schools minister and secretary of state for education Lord Jim Knight and Baroness Nicky Morgan, respectively; Ashoka founder USA-based Bill Drayton; president and CEO of Junior Achievement (JA) worldwide, Dr Asheesh Advani; Charles Fadel, co-author of the best-selling book *21st Century Skills*; Dr Ameena A. Hussain, the then director of programs and community development at the World Innovation Summit for Education (WISE), Qatar; Dr Swati Popat Vats, president of Podar Education Network and early childhood association in India; and of course, Thandeka Tutu-Gxashe, second child and eldest daughter of Archbishop Desmond and Nomalizo Leah Tutu, and chair of the Tutudesk Campaign. We journeyed off the map to be there for all children, and so our mission and responsibility needed to be clear: "The mind, once enlightened, cannot again become dark."

This experience of educational travel is everything. Purpose. Connect. Extend. Challenge. Learning as a satellite navigation system to better places in life. Cultural, local, regional, national, and international capital to build and extend our very own personal capital. The answer to why questions. Awe and wonder. One of my all-time favourite education and real travel stories is from the BBC television series *The Real Marigold Hotel*, set in India, when the actress Miriam Margolyes first sets eyes on the Taj Mahal in Agra: "There are no words for this." Awe and wonder, indeed. At all ages. And I was there, travelling with her, with my wife, and with my youngest daughter, from our sofa on our television in Sheffield, back in the United Kingdom.

All the work of the Children's University was, of course, connected into this educational travel concept. With its learning passport and learning destinations, its focus on experience, its internationalism, and its celebration of exploration, the Children's University sat at the heart of this journeying. The same, in many ways, can be said of the concept of "10 things to do before you are 7, 11, 14, and so on" – again, it travels beyond the four walls of the conventional classroom to new places, challenging our comfort zones, making us proud, and making us enjoy our continuous progress.

By the age of 11, I knew that Yerevan was the capital city of Armenia, and that Armenia was in the Soviet Union. I knew that Sofia was the capital of Bulgaria, and that Minsk was in Belarus. I knew that Berlin was split in half, and that there were two Frankfurts, one in West and the other in East Germany. I also knew what the Stasi was, the "Staatssicherheitsdienst," or Ministry for State Security in the German Democratic Republic. La Plata was in Argentina, Lisbon in Portugal, and Madrid was the capital of Spain, Milan was in Italy, Istanbul in Turkey, and Barcelona was the heart of Catalonia. I knew all this because of football, because Ajax Amsterdam played teams from these places at some point or another, because of Johan Cruijff, because of my atlas, and because Meneer Jutten, my teacher, knew me and encouraged me, cajoled me, and spent time with me. Ararat Yerevan, CSKA Sofia, Dinamo Minsk, Dynamo Berlin were affiliated with the Stasi, and FC Vorwärts Frankfurt/Oder with the East German army, Estudiantes de la Plata, Benfica, Real Madrid, Inter and AC Milan, Galatasaray, FC Barcelona, and many more. You have no idea how much I travelled, at least in my mind's eye and in my dreams.

Nowadays, of course, I would travel differently, further, better. I would travel virtually. I would know more about the clubs, their players, their origins, their towns, and their cities. The internet would be part of my mind's eye and of my dreams. This supreme learning tool that can only get better. Soon we will see the developments of hybrid 2.0, the system where, through artificial intelligence and global positioning systems, recommendations will be able to connect us between the virtual and real worlds, to take us from YouTube film clips about football to L. S. Lowry exhibitions and local parks in springtime. My 2024 version of Meneer Jutten, my teacher, who knows me and encourages me, cajoles me, and spends time with me, will, of course, still be there – nothing happens without him.

If we look at our schools as more than a school; as child-centred from birth and values-driven; as a community that is the village raising our children, as building longer tables, not higher walls, and we look at our children as better, wider, deeper-learned young citizens, experienced and with a self-discovered sense of purpose, we also need to look at our outcomes differently and at different outcomes. We need to stop merely valuing what we can measure and instead measure what we value. This, in turn, is about aspirations to personalised higher standards and a better quality of educational provision for all our children. Educationally, we seem to believe our own hype and are turning our so-called success stories into fake news. We test and publish our findings in league tables. We have come to believe that, to coin a phrase, "weighing the pig makes it fatter." And that is how we have grown to value that which we can measure, instead of measuring what we value. Our education world is Kafkaesque. What is it that we are trying to achieve? The questions remain: How well do we actually know our children, beyond, of course, their predicted grades, their attendance figures, their behaviour marks? And how well can we best cater for them, build scaffolding, have safety nets, all for their good and that of their families, our communities, and wider societies?

"Es doe mer gelökkig bös." *As long as you are happy.* On the back of the global KidZania research, in 2016, I was invited by the Crown Prince of Dubai Sheikh Hamdan bin Mohammed bin Rashid Al Maktoum to join the Dubai Future Council for Education, chaired by my now good friend Dr Abdulla Al Karam, then director general of Dubai Knowledge and Human Development Authority (KHDA). Dr Al Karam had been instrumental in developing Dubai's happiness agenda with the Minister of State for Happiness and Well-Being, Her Excellency Ohood bint Khalifa Al Roumi, with the aim to achieve a happier society. Schools had their part to play, with a specific focus on mindfulness and measuring happiness. KHDA, the educational assurance and regularity authority of the government of Dubai, released *Wellbeing Matters*,[7] a new guiding framework for Dubai schools. The framework creates a common point of reference of what well-being in schools should look like and how teachers, support staff, and parents can bring improvements. The framework is based on international research and policies and includes standards to help schools improve their well-being provision over time. International research is increasingly showing that improved well-being is important for children, their families, and their teachers and is a pre-requisite for the future success of humanity. As children's well-being becomes more important, schools are expected to consider and incorporate the government's *Wellbeing Matters* framework into their lives. Dubai has clearly decided to measure what it values. Not much happiness elsewhere, not as a concerted government effort, anyway.

We live, at least in schooling and accountability terms, in a world of averages. There is a particular obsession with reaching national averages in our assessment of success. If too many young people in a particular school perform at levels that are below national averages, that school is then judged not to be good enough, to be failing, or at least to require improvement. As if we all don't require improvement all the time as a fact of life, rather than a condemnation. These judgements are always at institutional levels, never against the expected performance of the individual learner as a minimum. I was told once that it is the aim of the government's target setting for everybody to be at least average, if not above average. I will just leave that there. Averages, of course, hide a variety of truths. Averages, at best, provide a simple summary of complex data, distort reality, and hide important variations and nuances. Averages hide a multitude of sins. By focusing too heavily on averages, we risk decision-making based on half-truths, leading to ineffective strategies and false expectations. When our target-setting is based on calculations of averages, we walk on quicksand, and we effectively enter the world of fake news. Yet in their own individual way, every child is above average at some point, somewhere. But we don't measure what we value.

Our obsession with targets, or so-called key performance indicators (KPIs), is institutional. It is a return-on-investment calculation, a value-for-money statement in the end, as opposed to a return-on-involvement judgement. Schools are judged, adjectives awarded, on crude figures without context. Ranking orders are arrived at and published based on formulas that lack insight and sophistication. In real terms, this type of performance management is a judgement of compliance – an "outstanding"[8] school with above-average attainment statistics is just outstandingly compliant as it excels at ticking someone else's boxes. It is no more than that. Individual children's attainment is not really analysed, not valued, not published, let alone contextualised. When we teach about climate change, it is classed as science, with test results as the outcome. Should we not measure levels of activism instead? See how many Greta Thunbergs[9] there are? The world of averages rules. More than a school seemingly does not matter.

Comparing apples and pears is just not a good idea. Even comparing apples with apples for the sake of it is dodgy. It leads nowhere, is a waste of time and energy, pays no dividends, and is actually grossly unfair on all concerned. Comparing the Taverham High School of 1985 and the Winifred Holtby School of 1989 is equally pointless. As would be a comparison in 2024. One was small, and one large. One's community was very poor, with all that entails, and the other's reasonably affluent, and all that follows from that. I could go on. One in inspection parlance would now probably be graded as "outstanding," the other as "inadequate."

Both judgements would be wrong. Both schools were much better than "outstanding," given the individual circumstances of each school and its community. Both schools were more than a school. In each, the children and their families had very different odds stacked against them, mostly because of their contexts, but some were "man-made," like Winifred Holtby's size and all the barriers that arose from that. In fact, the schools were beyond comparison in equity terms. What was clear, what I saw, was that both sets of children received the very best educational provision, given the context of each school. And if, in terms of standards of attainment, progress had been measured instead of crude examination outcomes, I suspect that the Winifred Holtby school may well have come close to outperforming Taverham High School – their children may have travelled further from start to finish in terms of context and progress over time set against expectations. Many years later, in Wythenshawe, contextual value added as part of an individual pupil-level database became an answer. Not liked by some of the powers that were, but an answer nevertheless.

There are, of course, lessons to be learned from comparisons, more often than not with the benefit of hindsight. Lessons about contexts, lessons about how to improve and how to do things differently, lessons about learning from each other, lessons about knowing our children better. But these lessons can only be learned if the agenda is different: an agenda to make things better for each individual child – scaffolding and safety nets. Not an agenda to name and shame. Wythenshawe once more became a test case to prove the point.

Contextual value added is a statistic that was used in England to differently assess the performance of schools. The statistic was intended to show the progress children have made whilst attending a particular school. Unlike statistics such as examinations or national test performance, contextual value added attempted to take into account the contexts of children attending the school that are beyond the school's control. It was, in essence, a progress measure evidencing the difference a school made to some of the children's achievements – it measured the value the school added within the context of the child. It measured the school's return on involvement. The aim to address fairness was clear, as was, subsequently, the opportunity to do better by individual children as we would know them better. Scaffolding and safety nets. It was never right and always unhelpful to compare the plight of children from Wythenshawe with that of children in, say, Westminster, to compare one of the poorest with one of the richest areas in England. Through no fault of their own, of course, the scaffolding and the safety nets required in Wythenshawe were, by and large, far higher and greater than those needed in Westminster. Westminster children were ready to be Usain Bolt and run the 100-meter sprint, whilst Wythenshawe children were running the 110-meter hurdles. Government expectation was, however, that both would and could end up with the same time. Bonkers!

The contextual value added statistic worked by comparing nationally a child's performance with that of children of the same age, with a similar prior performance and similar contexts. In England, typically, each year group in primary and secondary education consisted of some 600,000 young people. There were three levels: The first level measured performance of primary-age children. It measured the performance of children between the age of 7 and the age of 11. Level 2 measured performance of secondary schools, between the ages of 11 and 16. The third level measured the performance of post-16 learners from the end of secondary school to age 18. Contextual value added took into account nine factors that were known to affect the performance of children but outside of the school's control: gender, special educational needs and disability, eligibility for free school meals – a poverty measure, first language, whether children moved between schools, ethnicity, the month children were born in of different children within the year group, whether a child had been taken into care at any stage, the level of deprivation in the area the children lived using national indicators.[10]

Contextual value added was not without questions as to its accuracy and its use. For example, the measure still seemed phase-focused – primary, secondary, and post-secondary – as opposed to child centred from seven to 18. Care needed to be taken when making comparisons, as the degree of uncertainty in the score increased as the size of the cohort decreased. By the nature of things, different sets of children at the same school would almost certainly produce differing scores. Therefore, contextual value added being averaged across the country also meant that it was, of course, not possible to truly directly compare an individual school's score across a number of years. Some schools have also claimed that contextual value added disadvantaged schools with a traditional record of high performance.

The contextual-value-added approach enabled the identification of under- as well as overperformance. And of course, as always, in the wrong, self-serving hands, any statistic can be a damn lie. It is no doubt true to say that some schools manipulated the statistics in order to serve the system and for them to look good. It is also absolutely true to say that the vast, vast majority did not. They served their children. Of course, it made, at times, both surprising and uncomfortable reading when, in a school with high absolute performance outcomes, such as General Certificate of Secondary Education (GCSE) examinations, progress of individual children between the ages of 11 and 16, for example, could, at the same time, be seen to be below expectations. Similarly, of course, there were many schools with below-average absolute performance outcomes, such as Standard Assessment Test for children aged 11, where children's progress was still well above expectations. It wasn't so much that the bar had been lifted as that the goalposts had been moved. This was a new game. In this new world, it would be possible for my former hometown's Macclesfield FC's performance, in the third-tier non-professional English Northern Premier League, to be compared with that of Manchester City FC, the top-tier Premier League champions for the last four years and one of the richest clubs in the world. What is the starting point? What is the context? What are the results? What value is added? It would not be overly difficult to conclude that the citizens of Manchester City regularly perform as expected, and that the Silkmen of Macclesfield FC overperform almost all the time since 2021. Contextual value added.

Full-service schools, the re-allocation of resources targeted at individual children, the work-related programs for 14-, 15-, and 16-year-olds, which won both the national and global *Compass in the*

Community Awards,[11] the key and pre-key skills profiles, targeted literacy and numeracy support at primary and primary to secondary transition levels, focus on creativity and the arts (especially the expressive arts), targeted private sector support through Manchester Airport and beyond, targeted public sector partnerships with the local authority, and Wythenshawe regeneration organisations. What was clear to me from the start was that we would need different and additional ways of measuring impact. For example, could and should we measure contributory factors, such as the quality and value of collaboration? The national one-size-fits-all approach of examination, attendance, punctuality, and behaviour statistics, on its own, was really not it.

That it worked in the end was very largely due to the brilliant team of people I had been able to surround myself with at the Wythenshawe Education Action Zones, from quality development teachers to full-service schools managers, from my deputy director to our incomparable office-based "backstage" colleagues and our very own data geek. Collectively, we made the data meaningful, which, in turn, allowed us to work with individual schools and children and achieve, more often than not, the impact that was desirable. The data became live. I shall be forever grateful to Rick Wilson, our research information manager – it is one thing having the vision, seeing and being able to reason the bigger picture related to meaningful data, but it is another to translate this into a reality that is understood by all and is capable of serving the children. I am equally grateful for his patience and perseverance. I cannot recall how many times he had to explain the finer detail and its workings to me. Brilliant and visionary headteachers across the patch and their amazing colleagues also helped make this happen: John McKie, Dominic Mulcahy, Barry Morrison; the incomparable headteacher at Piper Hill Special School, Linda Jones; Brendan Treanor, the Peters Allonby and Eavers; Lynne Perry, Marcus Rashford's headteacher; "Father of the House" John Gretton; and many, many more. I shall be eternally grateful for their support and the lessons they allowed me to learn. Learning from your mistakes is wise, but learning from the things others do well is better. Many of those lessons learned would raise their head again much later on at the Children's University, at KidZania and beyond. The fact that we, collectively and transparently, amongst 29 schools, volunteered to have contextual value-added targets is testament to the culture that had grown. Twenty-nine schools individually and, from that, collectively set their own goals of minimum expectations plus the value they would each add for each child, their own goals of entitlement for each child over and beyond what was nationally required by government. What also happened and mattered was that our targets were no longer an abstract, no longer a number. Targets became names, the names of children. Achieving those targets became part of an ongoing dialogue, including the children and their families. Talking the talk sometimes matters too. And to think that before the formation of the Education Action Zones in 1999, that collective of 29 schools never met. The plus? Almost everything. The minus? We couldn't keep it going. In essence, the then Labour government applied the law of averages: There were 50 or so Education Action Zones in England, and the majority did not quite work in the way the government wanted them to. Short-termism, a lack of contextual thinking, and the law of averages prevailed. So they closed them down. End of project, despite all the successes. If I had a crystal ball, I might foresee a reinvention of this particular wheel before too long. In a 2.0 version, of course. But as the Dutch say, "Success komt te voet maar gaat met het paard". Or in English: Success arrives by foot but leaves on horseback.

Fischer Family Trust, or FFT, as it became in the vernacular, was founded in 2001 by the Fischer Family Foundation and by the late Mike Treadaway, a former science teacher and a local authority adviser. Mike established the Fischer Family Trust Data Analysis project in 2001. The Fisher Family Foundation, driven by the work of its founder, Mike Fischer, supports the implementation of innovative projects that aim to drive down social and health inequality in the United Kingdom and worldwide. Whatever anybody says, contextual value added was Mike Treadaway's baby, and Fischer Family Trust understood and did contextual value added better than anyone else, anywhere. Wythenshawe was in there like a shot. The conversations between us, Wythenshawe, and them, FFT, became part of leading the development nationally. Rick Wilson became, for us, the driver, and the quality development teachers translated this into the classrooms. It is a question I very often ask of any proposal and project: "So what does it look like at 12 minutes past two on a Wednesday afternoon?" Initially, in 2001 and 2002, the answer was, "Good, but . . ."

The "but" was about instant access to the data, there and then. These were the days before mass access to computers, laptops, iPads, or other, even mobile phones. Access to the internet was very limited and static, was expensive, and by and large, infrastructures were rudimentary in comparison to what we know now. On the other hand, it had become clear to us that, in an ideal world, teaching and non-teaching colleagues would have the easiest of access to the information on the children in front of them in order to constantly marry data and practice. At that time, this seemed both unachievable and unaffordable. Enter Manchester Airport; enter its partner, Shell UK, and Shell UK's truly incomparable education lead, Steve Smythe. Somehow, thanks to Steve, at some point in the early summer of 2003, in excess of 1,000 Shell UK desktop computers were delivered pro bono to and installed in 29 Wythenshawe schools. A computer on every teacher's desk in order for them to access the data on the children in front of them. A dream come true, the unachievable achieved, the unaffordable delivered. My most vivid memory is standing on the footbridge over the M56 in Wythenshawe, watching the lorries go past to deliver the goods. When I asked the question "So what does it look like at 12 minutes past two on a Wednesday afternoon?" in 2003, the answer was, "Good." No approach is, of course, perfect, but some approaches are more perfect than others. These are often also more real, more fair, and more transparent – a healthy dose of realpolitik.[12]

What Geoff Muirhead, the then chief executive at Manchester Airport, at that time was particularly good at was connecting me, at the most senior level, with all the other businesses and organisations within and associated with the airport. This was mostly done through an annual series of breakfasts with around 250 executives, during which I was able to report on our progress, our successes, our difficulties, and the barriers that had emerged. Subsequently, it also allowed me to lay out what was needed to remove those barriers.

A key issue for the airport and all associated businesses were skills for employability. Effectively, the mismatch between academic qualifications and readiness for their world of work. This, in turn, and over time, led, following a range of consultations, brainstorms, and other ways of communicating, and a lot of research, especially in partnership with the Manchester Metropolitan University, to the joint development of a key skills profile. What skills were actually needed to be employable in those places of work? There had been, at that time – and I am sad to say there still is – too much negative, cannot-do talk about the gap between academic qualifications and the readiness for work. It was time to stop sitting on the fence and moaning and instead come off the fence, roll up sleeves, and get on with the job at hand.

The question to some 250 executives at one of the breakfasts became this: "Tomorrow you are interviewing 16-year-olds for a job. What are the three things in particular you are looking for?" In other words, "What three things are non-negotiable in terms of an appointment as far as you are concerned?" The baseline for the key skills profile had been established. We collected 250 or so answers, which gave us the following, non-negotiable set of 11 headlines, in no particular order: effective oral and written communication, collaboration and networking, agility and adaptability, resilience and grit, empathy and global stewardship, vision, self-regulation, hope and optimism, curiosity and imagination and creativity, initiative and innovation and entrepreneurialism, critical thinking, and problem-solving.

Some 20 years later, in 2024, I found one of the original copies of our key skills profile. To me, it looked as relevant now as it did then. All the headlines still applied. The order of importance, if there was one, may have changed, and the details behind it all may certainly look differently. Effective oral and written communication, collaboration and networking, self-regulation, and innovation would now certainly include the online aspect, for example. But the essence remains. During a very recent series of keynote speeches in Qatar, the United Kingdom, Thailand, and India, I presented the whole story of how the Wythenshawe key skills profile was arrived at but set it not in 2003 and 2004 but in 2023 and 2024. Nobody batted an eyelid. In fact, the "new" concept was greeted most enthusiastically. There is an issue here of not throwing out babies with bathwaters and of not reinventing the wheel.

The key skills profile was designed for and with identified groups of young people, like those who participated in our Royal Bank of Scotland diploma. Young bright lights who were in danger of losing their spark, of losing their sense of purpose, who were disconnecting from schooling. A new and junior form of apprenticeship, or even internship, was born. Another case of babies and bathwaters and of not reinventing the wheel but of adaptation to our context and making it work, firstly for our young people, and also, of course, for all others involved, including the employers and the schools. The original apprenticeships and internships were brilliant for their audience, but not for our 14-, 15-, and 16-year-olds. We needed something more age- and context-appropriate.

In the end, our key skills profile was a mechanism to get to know our young people better and for them to do the same, in a clear way that made sense, and to a very significant degree managed by the young people themselves. Looking back now, in pre-internet times, our key skills profile feels like some kind of an early version of what we know now as the professional networking and recruitment platform

LinkedIn. It is somewhat ironic that, in 2024, in my role as adviser to the start-up My Global Bridge, its founder, Ben Mason, and I are looking to achieve exactly that: a junior version of LinkedIn in which 14-, 15-, and 16-year-olds can profile their key skills, amongst many other things.

The Wythenshawe Education Action Zones subsequently also developed a pre–key skills profile for children aged 9 to 14, because behaviours, attitudes, skills, and aptitudes do not all of a sudden appear as if by magic from the age of 14 but grow through their younger lives in many ways. This thinking and work are reminiscent of the KidZania approach and research which I led on globally some ten years later.

As we have seen, the Children's University was also conceived with a particular child in mind. Its mission was to inspire all children – but particularly those who needed it most, to love learning beyond the classroom and to engage their families and community in this learning, in and out of school, at home and online. It sought to remove barriers to the learning beyond the classroom so that no one would be left out. Its main target age range was 5- to 14-year-olds. In other words, the Children's University was there for all children aged 5 to 14, but particularly for those who needed extra scaffolding and, often, more safety nets. The learning journey was one of discovery, a Campaign for Real Learning (CAMRL) based on *Planning for Learning*,[13] a framework developed with the University of Cambridge, as opposed to the Campaign for Real Ale (CAMRA), which had, in principle and in practice, been its inspiration.

The learning journey was, in its evaluations, described by the University of Cambridge as a journey of "10 As"[14]: attendance, attainment, achievement, attitudes, adventure, awards, agency, aspiration, adaptability, and advocacy. What was remarkable about these learning journey descriptors was that they were almost immediately understood and owned by all, and that their appeal was international. Children and their families, teachers and their schools, learning destinations and universities all understood and valued their relevance, an understanding and appreciation which went as far as the Isle of Man, Northern Ireland, Scotland, Wales, and indeed, Cyprus, Germany, Italy, the Netherlands, Malaysia, and Australia. I have never since visited a school and not thought about the "10 As" – of course, they are applicable and most relevant to the learning there too. Just imagine. Connect. Extend. Challenge.

In the 2012 evaluation of the Children's University by the University of Cambridge, the organisational impact of the Children's University on the "10 As" was judged and summarised as follows:

- *Attendance.* Children who participate in Children's University activities have, as a consequence, better attendance records than children in the same schools who do not participate. This has been a consistent finding from 2007 to the present.
- *Attainment.* There is evidence that not only do Children's University–engaged children attain more highly than their non–Children's University counterparts, but that there is also a positive correlation between the length of time children are involved with Children's University and performance in tests and examinations.
- *Achievement.* Achievement also encompasses what has been realised by the Children's University trust itself, measured by its gross and outreach over five years.
- *Attitudes.* A change in attitudes for Children's University attendees has been a consistent finding over the last five years.
- *Adventure.* Mounting obstacles, testing yourself against more ambitious challenges, has been shown to encourage determination and perseverance.
- *Awards.* Children's University awards have their own special currency, as parents and children attest to the excitement of learning in new ways and in new contexts. The *Passports to Learning* play a vital role.
- *Agency.* Agency may also be applied to the Children's University itself, an agent of change in a systemic sense, in respect of changing local management, initiative, and innovation and, in a deeper sense, affecting the way in which we come to understand and evaluate learning.
- *Aspiration.* To be able to succeed in other contexts, to visit places beyond one's own immediate neighbourhood, to see the inside of university for the first time are demonstrated in the data as extending horizons of the possible.
- *Adaptability.* The value of Children's University is also measured by the adaptability of children and young people, of teachers and schools, and of the educational system itself.

- *Advocacy.* Perhaps the most significant measure of advocacy is the spontaneous adoption of the Children's University people and organisations in countries other than the United Kingdom, where it started. That it has such international appeal and relevance is hugely significant.

Over a period of seven years, the evaluations by the University of Cambridge researched and analysed organisational purpose; impact against its values, principles, aims, and objectives; impact on children, especially those who needed the Children's University most; impact on schools; impact on families and on communities; impact on universities; and of course, impact on the learning destinations – the museums, galleries, sports clubs, zoos, parks, book and film clubs, et al. Its findings, once and for all, proved the importance and impact of experience-based, out-of-school learning. The fact that, in 2010, the new United Kingdom government elected to ignore these findings was negligent and demonstrates a lack of responsibility towards its children, especially those from disadvantaged contexts. In other countries, including Australia, and notably Malaysia, out-of-school co-curricular learning experiences are now taken much more seriously – in the latter, a 10 per cent weighting is given to co-curricular achievements; 90 per cent remains academic.

Connect. Extend. Challenge. The 2010 evaluation of the Children's University by the University of Cambridge had provided equally important findings, albeit from a slightly different, more child-focused angle, concluding its findings thus:

- Being in the Children's University significantly improves school attendance.
- Achievement is significantly better for children aged 7 to 14 who participate in Children's University compared with non-attenders.
- The further children engage with Children's University, the better their attendance and achievement.
- Children's University provides an environment for self-driven, confident, and collegial learning.
- Children's University provides a safe haven and models positive relationships.
- Pupils and teachers testify to life-changing experiences.
- Opportunity costs are high for children in disadvantaged areas who do not attend Children's University.

- Certificates, credits, Passports to Learning, and graduations are valued incentives and rewards.
- University settings help inspire and raise aspirations for children and their parents/carers.
- Children's University has helped make learning a real reality beyond academic studies.

The purpose of evaluation needs to be to ascertain how well projects, programmes, and organisations work; how they have developed and performed against their values and principles, aims, and objectives; and what actions, if any, subsequently need thinking about. This involves a wide variety and range of aspects and could, of course, include, amongst others, attendance, attainment, achievement, attitudes, adventure, awards, agency, aspiration, adaptability, and advocacy, as well as, for example, contexts, actions, team, progress, resilience, innovation, drive, quality of provision and of assessment, and naturally, outcomes, organisationally and individually, and aspiration. School is about more than teaching and testing single subjects. A school is about preparation for the rest of children's lives in the best and widest possible sense. In order to achieve this, we need to also look at insights from beyond the test, and at information beyond curriculum subjects. As examples, evaluations like those of the Children's University and insights like those that arrived from KidZania data serve our thinking well in this respect. In our 5Ws and 1H, we need to look beyond the norm, and in unexpected places, in school and outwith. We need to think scaffolding and safety nets. The more we know our children, the better we can provide and serve them.

Both organisationally and from the viewpoint of the child, as well as, of course, their families and communities, there is so much in evaluations like those by the University of Cambridge that is and should be applicable to the assessments and judgements of schools. It would mean looking at the school multidimensionally, through a different lens, recognising its context and its wider ability to make a difference to its children's lives, leading as outcomes to both achievement and attainment at the broadest and highest levels. In it I recognise the importance of connecting, extending, and challenging. And of course, the importance of the 5Ws and 1 H, the what, when, where, for and by whom, the why, and the how. And perhaps that is the crux of things: If we assess the school as more than a school, we should make every effort to include better and more consistently the 5Ws and 1H and not mainly focus on the what. The for whom, the how, and of course the why are far, far too important for that, as of course, perhaps to a slightly lesser degree, are the by whom, the when, and the where. Schools are living organisms. Schools are not polaroid photographs, snapshots at a specific period in time. Schools are films, a continuum of moving and living images. Schools can be so beautiful. It is like in teaching and learning: The main focus is not the what at a set time and place. It is everything else; it is about creating the conditions for learning, and then the what begins to matter, better.

In the context of teaching and learning, one of my favourite, and the best, examples of the what being secondary to the other 4Ws and 1H but, as a result of this, mattering beautifully is a school inspection story attributed to the English author and educator, Yorkshireman, former teacher, and inspector Gervase Phinn. Gervase's path and mine crossed occasionally in Germany when, as part of the Children's University, I was working with the then Service Children's Education.[15] The story goes that a good number of years ago, there was an inner-city secondary school inspection in the north of England just before the Easter holidays. It was Friday afternoon and the last lesson of the week. The subject was religious education, and the class a "bottom set" group of 15- and 16-year-olds. The theme of the lesson was the story of the crucifixion of Jesus Christ. The Office for Standards in Education inspection grading for lessons and those days was: 1 = excellent, 2 = good, 3 = satisfactory, 4 = unsatisfactory, 5 = poor. "Imagine," started the teacher. "Imagine Jesus walking, stumbling slowly through the streets, beaten, bleeding, in pain, carrying the heavy, heavy cross. Imagine his mother standing by the roadside, and his friends. Imagine the mother's heartache, her unbearable pain." All the young people's faces showed their empathy. They were completely caught up in the story. Some of the girls could not hold back their tears, their mascara running down their cheeks. All of them were captivated. All, bar one. One tall, scruffy-looking boy at the back was looking out of the window, not flinching, not at all engaged. The inspector concluded quite early on that the lesson was heading for a grade 1 – it was already almost excellent. Almost all the boxes were being ticked: engagement and interest, participation, pace, variety; good learning was in evidence; progress was being made; behaviour was excellent; awe and wonder were in evidence; but involvement of all learners was not. There was still just this one boy not still showing any reaction, any involvement. "Then they crucified him. The hands and the feet." More tears, more horror. But not from this one boy. "And finally, when Jesus already seemed dead, one Roman centurion wanted to make sure. He grabbed a spear and rammed it into Jesus's side." Silence. And then: "The fucking bastard!" Grade 1 achieved.

"We must not, in trying to think about how we can make a big difference, ignore the small daily differences we can make which, over time, add up to big differences that we often cannot foresee."[16]

In whatever we try to achieve, the most important ingredient is people. Good people. The right people. There can be no meaningful change in education and schooling without our good and right teachers and without the non-teaching professions. Equally, all change for good will be better with the support of parents, carers, and families, the bedrocks of communities, and schools need to plan for this. The village that raises a child is full of people and full of partnerships that value returns on involvement. We collectively need to support our teachers, stand with them, value and respect them. As parents and carers, we need to see ourselves as co-educators alongside our teachers, for the benefit of our children. Teachers need to embrace parents and carers as partners in the education and schooling of our children. Our question needs to always be: Who are the teachers? The answer is, of course, all of us, in some shape or form! This includes our children – they are teachers too. We need to look globally for solutions that work, contextualise these, and make calculated but brave decisions. We need to invent and innovate, and we need to not throw out babies with bathwaters. We need to know our children, and we need to recognise that "[e]veryone deserves a chance to walk with everyone else."[17] Hand on heart, we also need to recognise that schools cannot be the answer to every societal question that arises. Nothing is perfect, and nothing ever will be, but these are choices we collectively and individually need to make. That aspect is in our hands alone. We already know that when we make the right choices, the momentum becomes unstoppable.

Governments need to support the education and schooling of our children through a long-term, ongoing societal dialogue, by valuing the child as a citizen of the now, by supporting parents, carers, families, and communities, by trusting our teachers and education leaders as the experts and professionals they are. Governments need to award education and schooling the highest priority of all. Only then will our societies be as successful as they might be, as healthy as they can be, and grow old as happily as they should be. And if governments fail to fulfil this duty as our elected representatives, the electorate needs to think again and exercise its democratic responsibility and duty.

Schools that are more than a school are the fourth emergency service. And the places that peddle hope better than most. Safety nets and scaffolding. Good schools will always be more than a school. But with our collective support, they could be so much better still.

If we truly personalise, empowering every young person to climb up their scaffolding as high as they can, we need to understand that there are no straight lines. Going to university is not a be-all and end-all; neither are apprenticeships. This is about tailored and appropriate pathways with destinations that, without barriers, suit the aspirations of the individual. To quote Mahatma Ghandi's phrase: "The future depends on what we do today." Our general view of social mobility is too simplistic. For example, the aspiration that every child should go to university, in fact, should do what the leading classes do, that every state school, however poor, should aspire to follow and emulate the top independent schools, is a nonsense and a fallacy. This is based on a class system and on inappropriate, unrealistic wishes, written mostly and, admittedly, stereotypically by "top" private school–educated special government advisers who are detached from any sense of reality, and not on the aspirations of the individual children and young people we know.

In the end, being more than a school is about aspirations and, in the longer run, social mobility, in the widest possible societal sense. When all is said and done – the community aspect and its context, scaffolding, safety nets, and partnerships, that size matters, that learning is a satellite navigation system to better places in life, and that not all classrooms have walls, measuring what we value, underpinned, of course, by that courageous leadership, awe and wonder learning, those brilliant teachers and amazing support staff who, at all times, put the child first and in the centre of all things – aspirations can flourish and social mobility can grow. Then, "Children can aspire to everything they know exists" means that children from Wythenshawe fly planes. Happily.

Notes

1 *Statutory instruments* (SIs) are a form of legislation which allows the provisions of an Act of Parliament to be subsequently brought into force or altered without Parliament having to pass a new Act. They are also referred to as secondary, delegated, or subordinate legislation.

2 Oasis were an English rock band formed in Manchester in 1991. Originally known as the Rain, the group initially consisted of Liam

Gallagher, Paul Arthurs, Paul McGuigan, and Tony McCarroll, with Liam's older brother, Noel Gallagher, joining as a fifth member a few months after their formation. The band is characterised as one of the defining groups of the Britpop genre. Their hits include "Wonderwall" (1995), "Don't Look Back in Anger" (1995), and "Champagne Supernova" (1995).

3 Education Policy Institute – *Report: School performance in multi-academy trusts and local authorities* (2016); *The Features of Effective School Groups* (2024).

4 Pink Floyd, *The Wall* (1979).

5 Barnardo's is a charity headquartered in Barkingside in the London borough of Redbridge. It was founded by Thomas John Barnardo in 1866 to care for vulnerable children in England, Wales, Northern Ireland, and Scotland. As of 2013, it raised and spent around £200 million each year, running around 900 local services, aimed at helping these same groups.

6 *Loadsamoney* was a comedy character created by British comedian Harry Enfield in the 1980s to spoof the attitudes of Thatcher-era Britain. He was a rich, loud, and obnoxious plasterer with a cockney accent and a wad of cash in his hand at all times. His catchphrases included "Loadsamoney."

7 *Wellbeing Matters: A guiding framework for the monitoring and improvement of wellbeing in Dubai private schools*, Knowledge and Human Development Authority (KHDA), Dubai, 2022.

8 Up to 2024, the inspection framework of the Office for Standards in Education (OfSTED) in England classifies schools as:
    - Outstanding
    - Good
    - Requires improvement
    - Inadequate

    From 2024, these one-word judgements will be replaced by a report card in a government move to achieve a better, fairer, and more meaningful way of judging and reporting performance.

9 Born in 2003, Greta Thunberg is a Swedish environmental activist known for challenging world leaders to take immediate action for climate change mitigation. Thunberg's climate activism began when, at a young age, she persuaded her parents to adopt lifestyle choices that reduced her family's carbon footprint.

10 In England, this is the *Income Deprivation Affecting Children Index* (IDACI). The index is calculated by the government and measures in a local area the proportion of children under the age of 16 who live in low-income households.

11 Compass Group PLC is a British multinational contract food service company headquartered in Chertsey, England. It is the largest contract food service company in Europe, employing over 500,000 people.

12 *Realpolitik*: from the German *real*, "realistic, practical, actual," and *Politik*, "politics." A system of politics or principles based on practical, rather than moral or ideological, considerations.

13 *Planning for Learning – A Framework for Validating Learning*, by Ger Graus and John MacBeath, 2008.

14 *Evaluation of the Children's University™ 2010 – Third Report to the CU Trust* and *Evaluation of the Children's University™ 2012 – Fourth Report to the CU Trust*, the University of Cambridge.

15 The British Service Children's Education (SCE) provided schools and educational support for the children of Her Majesty's Armed Forces, Ministry of Defence (MOD) personnel, and MOD-sponsored organisations stationed overseas.

16 Marian Wright Edelman, American activist for civil rights and children's rights.

17 From the song "Hero" by Family of the Year, 2012.

And finally

Education isn't something you can finish.

Isaac Asimov
Author and Professor

"You've got to write these things down!" And finally, here we are. Job done. Writing this book has been many things. A journey, memories and reflections, joy, sadness, fun, illuminating, a challenge, frustrating, hard work, happy and painful, an experience of hindsight and lessons learned, with reflections into the today and, occasionally, the tomorrow – the whole rainbow. I have been surprised how easy it has been to remember and to reattach, to reconnect. I have been even more surprised how easily the detail returned with what I am certain is pretty good accuracy. I have learned how contextualised hindsight is. What seemed insurmountable when I was in my late 20s now feels like just another bump in the road. What felt like an eternity when I was a child – waiting for a sleepover at my grandad's, for example – is now a blink-and-you-miss-it moment. Have you noticed, by the way, that when we are young, we long to be older? My youngest daughter has never been her own age; she has always been nearly the next one. This changes later in life – there is an app that recently told me that I look 11 years younger than I am. I welcomed that with open arms.

I have also learned that, whilst big things happen – from moon landings to Live Aid and the fall of the Berlin Wall – in many ways, not ever so much changes over a lifetime. Despite our dreams, aspirations, idealism, and hard graft. When, in 1997, the then government of Tony Blair announced its support for the most deprived parts of England, in education, in health, in crime prevention, and in other social aspects, it produced a list of initially the first 25, and subsequently a further 25, geographical areas. Some 25 years later, those 50 most disadvantaged parts of England of 1999 are still just that, the most disadvantaged parts of England. In fact, even the ranking order has barely changed at all. For a lifetime's political promises and bluster, for all the manifestos and elections, and for all the investment, after my very own nearly 68 years and counting, not much has changed. Certainly not as much as I would have wanted. The poor are still poor, and the rich are still rich. So with the benefit of hindsight, was it all worth it? Or has it all been in vain? A waste of time? "I don't think so" is my answer. I personally believe that it has been worth it, however difficult that sometimes is to see, particularly when looking at the bigger picture. I believe that, in our analysis, we should instead focus on the jigsaw pieces, on the children that were and are now better off than they were before because of the things I and so many, many others have thought, developed, and put into place. That is the difference we make. We turn up. And without the big dreams, the idealism, the aspirations, and the hard graft, I believe none of this would have been possible. We must always remember that social mobility is mostly about small steps over longer periods of time, whether we like it or not. And each step is made in its own present. From my illiterate Dutch grandfather, via my father and me, it took 128 years to my son's graduation from England's Oxford University. Time, in that sense, is not on our side. I still pinch myself when I think of that story. We must remind ourselves that "the future depends on what you do today."[1]

In recent years, I have often revisited the concept of hindsight and realise now that, through all the experiences, all the knowledge acquired, all the lessons learned, hindsight has become a kind of pick-and-mix. In my case, the pick-and-mix has resulted in focusing deliberately on the positive and as little as possible on the negative, intentionally sidelining some of the bad things and some of the not-so-nice people. Everything is relative. It is all about personal balance. From my experiences, both professional and personal, despite everything that was not so good, especially in my childhood, I realise that I am far more of an optimist than a pessimist. And a dreamer. But as Carla Rinaldi describes me, still with both feet firmly on the ground.

As we become more experienced, realities and our perceptions thereof tend to change. The relativity is different. The first time I, as a grown-up, came face-to-face with mortality was when a Taverham

High School pupil died suddenly and unexpectedly of heart failure. Gary was 14 years old. His death left a big mark, on the school and the community, on the children and the parents, on us as teachers, and on me personally. It felt like the unlikeliest, unfairest, and cruellest thing. What happened to that young boy stayed with me for a very long time. It made me nervous and suspicious of flukes and of the unexpected. As I got older, my perceptions changed. I realised at some point that you cannot control the unexpected, the fluke. That it will happen and that you learn to live with it, to equip yourself to cope with the unexpected items in the bagging area of life, good or bad. As I became a parent myself, I found myself thinking more about my former pupil's parents than I had done before. Becoming me. Now, I am beginning to learn from and live with the notion that people of my own age die, frequently. "He was only 70" is an utterance all too often heard in our house. "Seventy is the new 50," I keep thinking. It is an uncomfortable sensation, and I wonder whether, in time, I will get used to this too and look at it differently, contextually. I still struggle with people who are younger than me dying. The cruelty and unfairness remain. Curiosity gets me to think about how an 80-, 90-, or 100-year-old sees these things. Who knows, maybe I will find out one day. These things are difficult to talk about, I find. We live and we learn.

In an interview, I was recently asked what, looking back on my professional life, I would do differently. It is an interesting question. It is also interesting why we never ask what we would do the same. Hindsight as a negative versus hindsight as a positive. To answer the question, on both a professional and a personal level, of what I would do the same, I would answer, "Almost everything." One of the most positive sensations in life is to feel happy with who we are, who we have become. This applies to all ages, at all stages. I do worry and feel for children and young people, especially girls and young women, who too often find themselves in a constantly changing pursuit of perfection, always defined by others. Their mental and emotional well-being constantly under strain. And for what? This phenomenon has always existed, as long as I can remember, but I believe that now in the age of social media, this reaches unprecedented and potentially dangerous heights. Of course, this applies to all young people everywhere, but research, as well as my own personal experiences as a father of two girls, clearly shows that it is an issue for girls and young women in particular. We, as the responsible people around them, need to protect and love them more than we have ever done before.

I believe that for the vast majority of time, my three children feel happy and content with who they are and who they are becoming. There are not many things in the world that make me happier.

I am also asked with increasing frequency what, from all my experiences, one piece of advice I would give to younger people to put in their back pocket. For all the big thoughts and sentiments that enter my mind and my heart, my one piece of advice is very pragmatic but life-changing: to, if at all possible, follow Albert Einstein's guidance to "stay away from negative people. They have a problem for every solution."

I cannot end this book without Florence and Connie. Sisters, they have been my saviours in the last few years. Before 2020, my life was one of travel, aeroplanes, hotels, working globally, and meeting lots of interesting people. From 28th March 2020, this all changed. The globetrotter became a home-sitter, relying on technology and interacting via screens. In my book, there are few things so far removed from normality. As time went by, my family members returned to work and school and the excitement that goes with that. I, for a long time, remained a home-sitter – working from home had become my new normal. I did not find any of this easy. The whole technology thing took me well outside my comfort zone, and when not on calls, there would have been long silences, loneliness even. Florence was born on 1st September 2018, and Connie followed some 11 months later, on 18th August 2019. Both are miniature dachshunds; Connie is wire-haired, and Florence is the smooth one. They are the souls of our party, and when working from home came along, they became my saviours. Most of my colleagues and friends have met them, online, and know of their habits. Webinars, podcasts, and live streams are planned between 10:00 a.m. and 11:00 a.m., when the girls are on their walk with Auntie Sharon. We have lunch together, and later in the day, we wait together for mummy and Imogen to come home. We talk about what kind of day we are having – "Did you have a lovely walk?" – and they are familiar with the audio version of this book. You get my drift. I learned many things from Florence and Connie (full name: Constance), but most importantly, I learned what social creatures we all really are.

From the Dutch coal miner's grandson to Venice, the Taj Mahal in India, the Bolshoi Theatre in Moscow, Ground Zero in New York, the Pyramids in Giza, the Burj Khalifa in Dubai, the Great Wall of China, or wherever my life has taken me, I stand on top of my hill and see my grandfather over there, and in the other direction my children – my eldest daughter happy and very successful in her career; my youngest daughter happy and in her final A-level year, full of promise; and my son happy, having only recently completed his final year at Oxford University. Social mobility personified. The moral high ground is a beautiful vantage point. My grandad would have approved: "Promise me you will always do your best at school."

Life gives us many rewards, as well awards. I am not so sure that we are expert at recognising these and using them enough to make us better. Perhaps sometimes our busyness gets in the way, and perhaps a little too often there is a sense of, at times misplaced, humility. Genuine rewards and awards can be a light that shines even brighter when we feel good and that shows us the way to better places on darker days.

Somewhere I have a whole stash of emails, cards, Post-its, thank-you notes, online messages, as well as a few presents that I was generously given at some point, when people felt that I either had done a good job or had been kind and helpful. Sometimes, not often enough, I find a little time to look back and reminisce. Mostly, these memories, these rewards, make me smile, and sometimes they make me shed a tear; they almost always make me proud and happy. Rewards, I see as something resulting from what we have done well, also in the eyes of others, including making many new friends and acquaintances. Awards, I see as much more of a formal recognition, although they, in themselves, can, of course, be rewarding.

I remember fondly the engraved tankard and "good luck" cards I received in the library upstairs at Taverham High School from James Neill on behalf of the many children I had taught and accompanied on their German exchanges and Trimester Aufenthalte. The date was 31st March 1988. To this day, this fills me happiness. Every major professional event leaves its memories and sprinkles its magic, from *Shakespeare per i Ragazzi* in Bologna sharing in the successes of "my" schools, from teachers in many countries who feel that they have become better because of our collaboration and the many teachers who made me better, to Children's University graduations, to learning made visible at KidZanias all over the world, and to the impact of research and speeches as well as partnerships with all sorts of organisations who aim to make the world a better place.

It is rewarding to know that our efforts, individually and collectively, touch lives. I have always preferred the collective, in all my work, everywhere: from Taverham, Hull, Wythenshawe, Manchester, and Salford to the Children's University and KidZania; from all the corporates, start-ups, and charities to conferences, articles, and interviews; from the research paper into the contribution edutainment can make to children's learning at the National Research University – Higher School of Economics in Moscow,[2] where I hold a visiting professorship, to my work as a professor of practice with teacher training students at the University of Cumbria, to my membership of the Dubai Future Council of Education, and to my membership of the board of trustees of the Sharjah Education Academy; from chairing the advisory council at the Beaconhouse School System in Pakistan to advising the Organisation of Economic Co-operation and Development; from my membership of the Harry Volker Genootschap in the Netherlands to my column "Becoming Me" in the children's magazine *The Week Junior*; and from working with schools from Kuwait to Karachi and from Mexico to Mumbai to supporting Bianca Senna at the Instituto Ayrton Senna in São Paolo, Brazil, TutuDesk in South Africa, the Young Guru Academy in Turkey, and as Father Christmas, Arbourthorne Community Primary School back home in Sheffield. These rewards are part of all our journeys, part of our becoming me. Think of all the teachers, all the children, all the differences made over all the years.

Of all the awards – the formal recognition – I have received, my honorary OBE, my Order of the British Empire, stands out for me. Firstly, because I was awarded this as a result of commendations from my peers, colleagues, acquaintances, and friends. It feels close this way. Secondly, because I received my award at KidZania London. The then secretary of state for education, Nicky Morgan, now Baroness Morgan of Cotes, presented me with my honorary OBE on 30th June 2016. According to the rules, as a foreign, in my case Dutch, national, you can only receive an honorary OBE, which, in turn, means that it is highly unlikely that you can receive the award from a member of the British royal family in one of the royal palaces. KidZania London was perfect for me. Because educationally it was my baby and because I was surrounded by my family and friends. KidZania London kindly hosted the ceremony, and a sizeable crowd had gathered to celebrate the occasion with me. Of course, my wife and three children were with me. James Neil, my former pupil, was present, and my friend David Ngobeni, chief executive officer at KidZania Johannesburg, had flown nearly 6,000 miles to be there. Work colleagues had also travelled considerable distances, and many personal friends were in attendance. After the ceremony, my wife and children accompanied me for lunch in the Shard, overlooking the whole of London. It is not very often that we, as parents, experience at close range, directly, how proud our children are of us. It is, I would suggest, much more often the other way around. My lasting memory of that day is exactly that: how proud my children, and my wife, were of me. Such a contrast to the earlier years of my life. And another form of reward, measure of success, and long-term achievement: a tangible recognition that I am a loved parent. Pride, in the name of love.[3] Another contrast to the earlier years of my life. And such a very, very important and proud part of my becoming me.

It was the English writer, philosopher, and art critic of the Victorian era John Ruskin who said that "[i]n general, pride is at the bottom of all great mistakes." Only in general, though. There are many exceptions to every rule. I believe that pride, both in our achievements and in who we become, plays a vital role in our personal growth and fulfilment. Celebrating our accomplishments instils a sense of confidence and motivation, propelling us to strive for even greater success. When we take pride in our achievements, big or small, we acknowledge our commitment and dedication, reinforcing our belief in our abilities. It reminds us that we are capable of overcoming challenges and achieving the aims we set for ourselves. Moreover, pride in who we become as individuals is at least of equal importance. It signifies self-acceptance, embracing our true selves, and valuing our unique qualities and experiences. By taking pride in who we are, we cultivate a healthy sense of self-worth and self-esteem, enabling us to navigate life with authenticity and confidence. This pride extends not only to our achievements but also to the values we uphold, the relationships we nurture, and the positive impact we have on others. We share our pride in all sorts of ways. From the professional, including school reports, glowing references at parents' evenings, examination results, future destinations, sporting and artistic achievements, endurance, awards, work promotions, to the more personal, such as contributions we make to our families and communities, places we have visited, or even material goods we have acquired. Sharing pride is a version of show-and-tell that, thankfully, is there with us throughout life. This show-and-tell makes pride visible and throws a very significant sense of joy into the mix. Who is not guilty of sharing endless holiday photographs with friends, neighbours, and family? Or talk about their children and their achievements? Or even drive the new car around the estate several times for all to see? Sometimes, sharing pride can go a little too far, perhaps. For me, personally, experiencing pride through those closest to me, especially my children, is (1) something totally wonderful and (2) something I have been fortunate enough to experience on many occasions. It is, as a parent and as a teacher, much rarer to experience your children's pride in you and to see their pride in you be made visible. I have, thankfully, experienced that too.

For some, however, I believe that pride matters even more than for others. A sense of pride is particularly important for children from disadvantaged contexts and communities, for a number of reasons. First and foremost, there are self-worth and confidence. Children who come from disadvantaged contexts very often face numerous challenges and prejudices that can undermine their self-esteem. By cultivating a sense of pride, they can develop a more positive self-perception and gain the confidence to overcome obstacles. A sense of pride enhances motivation and resilience. Pride can serve as a powerful motivator for children. When they take pride in their achievements, they are more likely to continue to work hard, set themselves even higher targets, and persevere through difficult circumstances. It helps them find the strength to rise above their lid and strive for more success. Experiencing a sense of pride can contribute to breaking the cycle of generational disadvantage. By instilling pride in children from disadvantaged contexts, we empower them to challenge societal limitations and begin to, bit by bit, break the cycle of poverty or marginalisation. When they feel pride in their heritage and community, they are more likely to strive for a better future, ultimately positively impacting their families and communities. Pride can enable cultural heritage preservation: Children from disadvantaged communities often come from rich cultural backgrounds. By fostering pride in their cultural heritage, we encourage them to embrace and preserve their traditions, language, and history. This fosters a sense of belonging and increases their confidence in navigating the world while preserving their identity. Ultimately, pride can be a catalyst for empowerment and social change. When children from disadvantaged contexts are proud of who they are and have become and where they come from, they are more likely to challenge systemic inequalities, advocate for their rights, fight against discrimination and injustice, and jump higher than their lids.

This particular sense of pride in children and their families is also infectious. Anybody who experienced Children's University graduation ceremonies, from Essex, Manchester, Bradford, London, Aberdeen, Cardiff, Douglas, Belfast, to Adelaide, Singapore, and Kuala Lumpur, became hooked, especially when they understood the simplicity of it all and saw the impact for good they themselves could have on the lives and experiences of the young people. The pride was there, amongst the children, of course, but also their parents and carers, their teachers. The pride was made visible through the local Children's University centres, the learning passports, the learning destinations, the certificates, the presence at a university, the pomp and circumstance of the graduation itself. Pride, like social mobility, is often a family affair, and beyond. It takes a community to raise a child. To experience pride in children is infectious and draws people in. As an example, Jackie Cooper, Edelman's global chief brand officer and senior adviser; Joel Cadbury, founder and chair of Longshot Ltd and founder of KidZania London; and James Bradburne, architect, designer, and museologist, witnessed Children's University graduations, thus becoming founding members of the then Friends of the Children's University, and my friends for life. Overall, a sense of pride plays a crucial role in helping children from disadvantaged backgrounds overcome challenges, develop resilience, and build a positive sense of identity. It empowers them to take pride in their achievements, heritage, and community, leading to personal growth and the potential for positive societal change. Pride is there when lids come off, jars are smashed, and our metaphorical fleas jump as high as they want to. Pride is there when we become us.

When, sometimes, as a result of my column "Becoming Me" in *The Week Junior*, I am asked about my becoming me and what it has meant to me, with all that entails, I mostly proudly, and humbly, refer to the testimony of others, of those who know me well. The testimony of those who know us well, for better and for worse, acts like a mirror – it allows us to see ourselves as we are in their eyes, not ours. This is an outcome in itself. It sometimes also allows us – for a little while, at least – to sit back and be proud, happy, and content. We all need this mirror view from time to time. By posting the following about me on the business and employment-focused social media platform LinkedIn a few years ago, my friend and colleague Eric Abrams, former chief inclusion officer at Stanford University Graduate School of Education, USA, and fellow Bett Global Education Council member, allowed me to see a view of becoming me that filled me with that very contentment, happiness, and of course, pride:

> Ger is so many things: Yes, he is a committed educator; yes, he has a brilliant mind; yes, he knows how to ask questions that get to the heart of the matter . . . but none of these touch on the compassion, kindness, and generosity that he has shown me and so many others over the years.

We met while serving on the BETT Global Education Council [in 2020]. I will confess that I walked into our first meeting more than a little apprehensive; after all, I was just a mid-level staff member at a college in California, and here I was in London with some of the leading minds in education in the world! Sure, I have ideas, and thoughts, but I definitely did *not* feel like I would fit in.

Ger introduced himself to me shortly after I had arrived, and we shared a bit of small talk that immediately put me more at ease. That small kindness has stayed with me for years; I do not know if he recognised the imposter syndrome I was feeling or if he was just being his usual kind and considerate self, but I think this example illustrates his generosity of spirit.

All too often, those of us who have a modicum of success start to believe that we are special, and we sometimes lose a bit of humility along the way. That is NOT Ger – he is constantly focused on the needs of the kids he serves and those of the people he works with.

Though I have left the education world, I would be honoured to work with Ger again – on just about anything! If you have the opportunity to work with him, you will see why so many people have so many nice things to say. He is sui generis – a one of one.

That will do me!

And even more so today than it did those few years ago.

Becoming me, like life itself, has turned out to be an unfathomable thing. You think you are about to close the book slowly and gently and in control, and then it turns out that there is another chapter, unplanned for, of course. And that in turn, again, changes the lens through which you see things.

The place seems to be where the oesophagus meets the stomach. It almost sounds like a rendezvous: I'll see you on the corner of such-and-such an alleyway with such-and-such a street. The word seems to be cancer.

So, the next story starts, with the benefit of hindsight and the hope of foresight. Still a journey, still an adventure. And through a very different lens. But, with the same outlook, with the same conviction, the same values and principles, with the same hope and the same optimism. With the same friends. With the same two little dogs. And, most importantly, with the same love and with the same cast of loved ones.

Notes

1 Mohandas Karamchand "Mahatma" Gandhi, political ethicist, lawyer, and anti-colonialist, India.
2 *Edutainment Centres as an Educational Phenomenon: The Case of KidZania* – Ger Graus, Sergey Kosaretsky, Anzhelika Kudryavtseva, Katerina Polivanova, Elizaveta Sivak, Ivan Ivanov – National Research University – Higher School of Economics, Moscow, Russia.
3 "Pride (In the Name of Love)," U2, from the album *The Unforgettable Fire*, 1984.

Afterword

Globalisation and digitalisation have connected people, cities, countries, and continents in ways that vastly increase our individual and collective potential. But the same forces have also made the world more volatile, more complex, more uncertain, and more ambiguous. The world has seen a growing disconnect between the infinite growth imperative and the finite resources of our planet; between the financial economy and the real economy; between the wealthy and the poor; between the concept of our gross domestic product and the well-being of people; between what is technologically possible and the social needs of people; and between governance and the perceived voicelessness of people.

No one should hold education responsible for all this, but neither should we underestimate the role that the knowledge, skills, attitudes, and values of people play in social, economic, and cultural development. While digital technologies, globalisation, and climate change all have disruptive implications for our economic and social structure, those implications are not predetermined. It is the nature of our collective responses to these disruptions that determines their outcomes – the continuous interplay between the technological frontier and the cultural, social, and institutional agents that we mobilise in response.

In this world, education is no longer just about teaching students something but about helping them develop a reliable compass and the tools to navigate with confidence through an increasingly complex, volatile, and uncertain world. Success in education today is about building curiosity, opening minds; it is about compassion, opening hearts; and it is about courage, mobilising our cognitive, social, and emotional resources to take action. And those are also our best weapon against the biggest threats of our times – ignorance, the closed mind; hate, the closed heart; and fear, the enemy of agency.

This is where *Through a Different Lens. Lessons from a Life in Education* makes such a refreshing contribution. Looking at learning through the lens of storytelling that helps us make connections with other people through sharing common experiences and emotions, the book reminds us that education is not a transactional business but a deeply relational experience. In fact, our ancestors all learned through apprenticeship; they always learned from and with other people through the sharing of experience and stories. The institutionalisation of education, where the prevailing norms are standardisation and compliance, where curricula spell out what all students should learn, and where it is both effective and efficient to educate students in batches all at the same pace, is a fairly recent phenomenon in the history of education. And at a time where the kind of things that are easy to teach and test have also become easy to digitise and automate and where artificial intelligence is beginning to unbundle educational content, delivery, and accreditation, it may well remain a peculiar outlier in the big picture of the history of education.

In the past, learners were passive consumers of educational content. The future will need people with curiosity and agency who take ownership over what they learn, how they learn, where they learn, and when in their lives they learn. That will require role models and hinge on the sharing of experience. As Ger Graus puts it, "children can only aspire to what they know exists."

The conventional approach in school is often to break problems down into manageable bits and pieces and then to train students on how to solve these bits and pieces. But modern societies create value by integrating different fields of knowledge, making connections between ideas that previously seemed unrelated, connecting the dots where the next innovation will come from, not educating people for jobs, but helping them create tomorrow's jobs.

In the past, schools were technological islands, with technology often limited to supporting and conserving existing practices and students outpacing schools in their adoption of technology. Now, schools need to use the potential of technologies to liberate learning from past conventions and connect learners in new and powerful ways, with sources of knowledge, with innovative applications, and with one another.

The past was divided – with teachers and content divided by subjects and students separated by expectations of their future career prospects; with schools designed to keep students inside, and the rest of the world outside; with a lack of engagement with families and a reluctance to partner with other schools. The future needs to be integrated – with an emphasis on the interrelation of subjects and the integration of students.

In today's schools, students typically learn individually, and at the end of the school year, we certify their individual achievements. But the more interdependent the world becomes, the more we need great collaborators and orchestrators. Schools need to help students learn to be autonomous in their thinking and develop an identity that is aware of the pluralism of modern living. At work, at home, and in the community, people will need a broad understanding of how others live, in different cultures and traditions, and how others think, whether as scientists or as artists. The foundations for this don't all come naturally. We are all born with "bonding social capital," a sense of belonging to our family or other people with shared experiences, common purposes, or pursuits. But it requires deliberate and continuous efforts to create the kind of "bridging social capital" through which we can share experiences, ideas, and innovation with others and increase our radius of trust to others. Ger, through quoting his favourite headteacher, repeatedly makes the point that "every child is everyone's responsibility."

All easy to say, really hard to do. It's so much easier to educate students for our past than for their future. Schools are inherently conservative social systems; as parents, we get anxious when our children learn things we don't understand, and even more when they no longer study things that were important for us. Teachers are more comfortable to teach how they were taught than how they were taught to teach. And policymakers can lose elections over education issues but rarely win elections over education, because it takes so much more than an election cycle to translate good ideas into better results.

This is where *Through a Different Lens. Lessons from a Life in Education* is so refreshing. Rather than talking us through how to tinker with existing education systems to seek marginal improvements, it helps us reimagine education afresh, through the lens of imaginary students who are leaders for a better future, teachers who are learners and creative designers of innovative learning environments, and communities that do not conserve but transform learning opportunities.

It shows us how mastery can be developed not at the expense of student well-being but through student well-being, agency, awareness, and connectedness. It helps us cut through the educational laws, regulations, and structures that too often cloud our minds, to discover the heart of educational improvement: the capacity to listen and envision, broadening perspectives and co-creating what success means and how we can see it. The ability to learn and design, building curiosity and critical knowledge, valuing learner ownership, and expecting higher-order thinking. The disposition to love and connect, building relationships, fostering belonging, nurturing culture and humanity. The openness to reflect and grow, to learn, unlearn, and relearn at every level of the system.

But the greatest power of the book lies in making us realise that this need not be fiction, that universal high-quality education is an attainable goal if we step back and tackle institutional structures that too often are built around the interests and habits of adults rather than those of learners. If we become better aware of how organisational policies and practices can facilitate or inhibit educational transformation. If we recognise emerging trends and turn good ideas into practice and good practice into culture. And if we use our understanding of power and influence to build the alliances and coalitions that are needed to create a better world through education. Ger Graus makes us realise that it is within our means to deliver a future for millions of learners who currently do not have one, and that the task is not to make the impossible possible but to make the possible attainable.

Andreas Schleicher
Director for the Directorate of Education and Skills
Organisation of Economic Co-operation and Development (OECD)
Paris, France

Acknowledgements

Thank you to all of you who have taken time to read my book—a book which would not exist if it were not for the following very special people in my life. Thank you to:

Opa.

My wife, Vanessa, and my children, Anna, Imogen, and Tom, for giving me a home. I love you – always. My two little dogs, Connie and Florence, for the unconditional love that keeps me sane at the loneliest of times.

My mentor and best friend Carla Rinaldi, for all the lessons you have taught me. Desmond Tutu, for a shared vanilla ice cream served with unimaginable quantities of kindness and wisdom, and that laugh. All other friends: "True friends are those who shine a light when it's dark."

All the children I have had the privilege to teach. Thank you for your company, your kindness, and your patience.

Meester Beurkens, for the book that changed everything. My *All-Time Teacher Eleven* for the role you still play. Teachers and educators everywhere.

Arbourthorne Community Primary School, for making me believe in Father Christmas.

My cousin Jac Erkens, for, in August 2024, and after 52 years, becoming my very own version of the British television series *Long Lost Family*, for reminding me of what friendship we could have had, and for telling me how much he has missed me over all that time.

Johan Cruijff – "Playing football is very simple, but playing simple football is the hardest thing there is" – and for making me practice your turn all my life.

David Winner's book *Brilliant Orange*, for teaching me things about myself I never knew.

Antoine de Saint-Exupéry's "few."

Rebecca Durose-Croft, who gave me the confidence to write in the first place and helped me along the way.

Routledge and its publisher, Bruce Roberts, for the opportunity.

Matthew Guest for the cover photograph, and Ali Harmanci for the cover design.

Everyone I have met along the way, almost always good and only sometimes bad. You have made me better! Thank you.

Biography

Professor Dr Ger Graus OBE is a renowned figure in the field of education – once described as "Jean-Jacques Rousseau meets Willy Wonka." He was the first global director of education at KidZania and the founding CEO of the Children's University. In 2019, Ger became a visiting professor at the National Research University in Moscow, Russia. He is also a professor of practice at the University of Cumbria, United Kingdom, and a member of the PhD advisory council at the University of Modena and Reggio Emilia, Italy. Ger is a frequent keynote speaker at some of the world's leading education conferences. Driven by his famous mantra that "children can only aspire to what they know exists," Ger champions the causes of equity and social mobility, purpose and experience, creativity, and awe and wonder in children's learning, so that each child becomes empowered to write their own narrative of the possible.

Born in the Netherlands, Ger moved to the United Kingdom in 1983, where he began his teaching career, later becoming a senior inspector and education director.

Ger is a member of Bett's Global Education Council, DIDAC India's Advisory Board, and Junior Achievement's Worldwide Global Council. He chairs the Beaconhouse School System's Advisory Board, Pakistan; advises the Fondazione Reggio Children, Italy; supports a range of education start-ups globally; and was invited to help shape the future of education in Dubai as a member of the Dubai Future Councils. In 2023, he joined the Global Teacher Prize Judging and the World's Best School Prize Academies as a judge. In 2024, Ger was invited onto the board of trustees of the Sharjah Education Academy by Sheikh Dr Sultan bin Muhammad Al Qassimi, ruler of Sharjah.

In the 2014 Queen's Birthday Honours List, Ger was made an honorary Officer of the Most Excellent Order of the British Empire

(OBE) for services to children, and in 2018, he received the Global Education Leadership Award at the World Education Congress, India. In 2022, he was granted the award of Iconic Leader Creating a Better World for All by the Women Economic Forum (WEF), and the following year, Ger was made a companion of the Harry Volker Genootschap in the Netherlands.

Ger's professional autobiography, *Through a Different Lens. Lessons from a Life in Education*, was published by Routledge in 2025.

For further information, please visit www.gergraus.com.